A Brief History of Justice

Brief Histories of Philosophy

Brief Histories of Philosophy provide both academic and general readers with short, engaging narratives for those concepts that have had a profound effect on philosophical development and human understanding. The word "history" is thus meant in its broadest cultural and social sense. Moreover, although the books are meant to provide a rich sense of historical context, they are also grounded in contemporary issues, as contemporary concern with the subject at hand is what will draw most readers. These books are not merely a tour through the history of ideas, but essays of real intellectual range by scholars of vision and distinction.

Already Published

A Brief History of Happiness by Nicholas P. White
A Brief History of Liberty by David Schmidtz and Jason Brennan
A Brief History of the Soul by Stewart Goetz and Charles Taliaferro
A Brief History of Justice by David Johnston

A Brief History of Justice

David Johnston

A John Wiley & Sons, Ltd., Publication

This edition first published 2011

Blackwell Publishing was acquired by John Wiley & Sons in February 2007. Blackwell's publishing program has been merged with Wiley's global Scientific, Technical, and Medical business to form Wiley-Blackwell.

Registered Office
John Wiley & Sons Ltd, The Atrium, Southern Gate, Chichester, West Sussex, PO19 8SQ, United Kingdom

Editorial Offices
350 Main Street, Malden, MA 02148-5020, USA
9600 Garsington Road, Oxford, OX4 2DQ, UK
The Atrium, Southern Gate, Chichester, West Sussex, PO19 8SQ, UK

For details of our global editorial offices, for customer services, and for information about how to apply for permission to reuse the copyright material in this book please see our website at www.wiley.com/wiley-blackwell.

Library of Congress Cataloging-in-Publication Data
Johnston, David, 1951-
A brief history of justice / David Johnston.
p. cm. – (Brief histories of philosophy)
Includes bibliographical references and index.
ISBN 978-1-4051-5576-2 (hardback) – ISBN 978-1-4051-5577-9 (paperback)
1. Justice (Philosophy)–History. 2. Social justice–Philosophy. I. Title.
B105.J87J65 2011
172′.209–dc22 2010051056

A catalogue record for this book is available from the British Library.

This book is published in the following electronic formats: ePDFs 9781444397536; Wiley Online Library 9781444397550; ePub 9781444397543

Set in 10.5/14pt Minion by Thomson Digital, Noida, India

1 2011

For

Charles E. Lindblom
Scholar Mentor Friend

and for

the students and staff of
Introduction to Contemporary Civilization

Contents

Acknowledgments

This book grew out of a longstanding dissatisfaction with contemporary academic thinking about justice, and especially with the estrangement between that thinking and a sense of justice that has been, and remains, widely shared across many cultures since the earliest times of which we possess written records. In order to pierce the academic bubble within which scholarly conversation about justice has been contained for at least the past several decades, I have immersed myself over the past few years in texts, both celebrated and relatively obscure, in an effort to recapture the various sensibilities that have motivated people's ideas about justice over the centuries. I hope that the results of this effort will cast some light on the idea of justice itself, as well as unearthing evidence for a history of ideas, some of which have long been either forgotten or summarily and unjustifiably dismissed.

This is a concise book, but it covers considerable territory, especially of the chronological sort. In order to make the narrative and arguments as accurate, clear, and incisive as possible for this subject, I have freely sought advice from others, and have accordingly acquired many debts. Danielle Allen, Robert Goodin, Ira Katznelson, Jennifer Pitts, Thomas Pogge, Melissa Schwartzberg, Annie Stilz, Katja Vogt, Jeremy Waldron, Gareth Williams, Jim Zetzel, and the members of the Columbia Seminar on Studies in Political and Social Thought, especially Jerry Schneewind, all have read and made suggestions on at least one and as many as four of the book's chapters. This book is a much better product than it would have been without their help. Luke MacInnis made suggestions for Chapter 6, Liz Scharffenberger helped to refine my understanding of a passage in Chapter 2, and Isaac Nakhimovsky assisted me on the Epilogue. David Londow asked the students in his lecture course on Justice at the University of California at Berkeley in the fall of 2009 to read the chapters and gave me useful and encouraging feedback toward the end of that semester.

Wendy Johnston read each chapter as it was being completed. Her advice has contributed a great deal to the clarity of the final product. Bryan Garsten generously took time to read the entire script when it was near completion and offered valuable suggestions, which have contributed significantly to the quality of this book. I am also the grateful beneficiary of reports from two readers for Wiley-Blackwell who were not identified to me, but who provided both strong encouragement and thoughts that helped me sharpen the script. Katherine Johnston proofread the entire text with me.

I wish also to thank Nick Bellorini, the editor at Wiley-Blackwell who cajoled me into agreeing to write this book and worked with me in its earlier stages, and Jeff Dean, who has served thoughtfully and effectively to help shepherd the project to completion. Andreas Avgousti gave me valued research assistance, useful suggestions, and a great deal of help in the preparation of the source notes and glossary. Elisa Maria Lopez provided much appreciated help in assembling and organizing materials for the final editing and correcting of the script and source notes. Manuela Tecusan gave me a great deal of valuable assistance in fine tuning the final text; she offered substantive corrections and additions to the text, for which I am very grateful. I should like also to express appreciation to the Warner Fund at the University Seminars at Columbia University for its help in publication. Material in this work was presented to the University Seminar on Studies in Political and Social Thought.

I have had the privilege for the past eight years of serving as Director and Chair of the Governing Board of the Society of Fellows in the

Humanities at Columbia University. The Society, and the Heyman Center in which it is housed, provided an environment for conceiving and compose this book that has few peers in collegiality and intellectual stimulation. I wish also to thank the numerous students and teaching assistants who have been through the mill of my lecture course on justice since I began teaching it, in the spring of 2001. I would not have been able to write this book if I had not had the opportunity to work through many of the ideas there first, in a rough and tentative way.

My greatest debts are not specifically related to the subject of this book. From the early days of my career in teaching, Ed Lindblom has given me consistent encouragement and support, as well as a good deal of direct instruction. Most of all, he has offered me the example of one of the finest, most discriminating, most tenacious minds I have known. No one has taught me more than he has. I also owe a great deal to the students and teaching staff of Columbia College's Introduction to Contemporary Civilization. For nearly a century, this course has opened the eyes of innumerable teachers and students to questions about justice, and I have been the beneficiary of its intellectual largesse for a quarter of that time. I dedicate this book to these last two exemplars of excellence.

Introduction

For many years now scholars have consistently mapped virtually all ideas about justice onto one of two continents. According to this cartography, the utilitarian territory is populated by views that stipulate a goal and derive a conception of justice from that goal or objective, usually by specifying a set of principles, rules, and institutions that are expected to be instrumental to its achievement. The most talked about goal in modern times has been the maximization of happiness. This goal is formalized in the principle of utility (or greatest happiness principle), which is the central idea of the classical utilitarian tradition. The label "utilitarian" is applied to this continent in recognition of the recent dominance of this school of thought, but this land is also inhabited by a number of other schools, devoted to variations on this theme or to objectives that are altogether distinct from it.

The "deontological" continent (in the jargon of modern moral philosophy) is the only other recognized territory. The class of deontological views is united by the conviction that justice is a matter of strict duties that cannot be overridden by any other considerations, not even for the purpose of achieving highly desirable goals. The rudimentary thought out of which this set of views springs is that some things are *right* whether or not they are *good*.

A Brief History of Justice, First Edition. David Johnston.

Although the principal views recognized by this division have relatively long pedigrees, the notion that all significant ideas about justice can be represented as incarnations of one of these two types goes back no further than the late eighteenth century, when the two principal traditions of modern moral philosophy – the utilitarian and the Kantian schools – acquired the distinctive identities they have maintained with considerable continuity since that formative period.

This representation of the geography of ideas about justice is neglectful of, or even oblivious to, the preceding 4,000 years of thinking about the subject. It is in fact astonishingly ahistorical. What is even more troubling, this mapping withholds recognition from a set of ideas and intuitions about justice that have been shared widely by many people who are not professional intellectuals (as well as by some who are) throughout recorded history and across innumerable cultures. An entire continent is missing from the geography of ideas about justice that is commonly transmitted and received through the modern community of scholars.

My main aim in this work is to offer a concise and accurate map of the principal ideas about justice that have seized the imaginations of people in the "western" world over the course of its recorded history. The oldest and probably most widely endorsed understanding of justice focuses neither on an overarching goal from which the principles and rules of justice are allegedly to be derived, nor on a conception of the right and a set of unyielding duties that flow from it – but on the characteristics of relations among persons. This understanding is rooted in the concept of reciprocity, a concept which is malleable enough to have been shaped and embellished over the centuries into a considerable range of elaborated conceptions of justice, but which retains a core meaning that ties together all those conceptions as members of a single extended family of ideas.

I hope, further, to give the reader some reasons to believe that a conception of justice focused on the character of relations among persons rather than on a single pre-eminent goal or on a set of strict duties is worthy of being revived as an estimable alternative to the two approaches that, taken together, have dominated scholarly discussions about justice for the past several generations. I do not mean to suggest that the particular conceptions of justice as reciprocity that have played the most prominent role in the history of ideas before our era can, without alteration, serve as reliable guides to puzzles about justice in the world today. These conceptions must be revised if they are to make a constructive contribution to the thoughts and actions that will shape our futures. Yet, in order to reconstruct a conception of justice focused on the character of relations among persons that could play a significant role in shaping our ideas, we must first recover some of the intellectual materials out of which earlier conceptions were fashioned, scrutinizing their strengths and weaknesses in the hope that we will be able to fashion ideas about justice that will serve us well. In this sense, the present book is an essay in retrieval as well as a survey of the past.

In the course of this study we shall see that, for the first 1,500 years or more of recorded history, human beings' ideas about justice were based heavily on the concept of reciprocity – an understanding that Plato attacked and attempted to replace with a new, teleological (that is, goal-directed) conception of justice. From Plato's time onward, the history of ideas about justice has been marked by a persistent tension between reciprocity-based understandings and teleological theories that have been developed with the aim of overthrowing those understandings. We shall also see that two momentous innovations in thought that first appeared in ancient times, but became ascendant only in the modern era, have, over the last few centuries, transformed the landscape of ideas about justice decisively. These innovations are the notion that human beings are capable of reshaping their social worlds so as to make them accord with their intentional designs – a notion that seems first to have appeared among the sophists of Athens in the fifth century BCE – and the idea that all human beings are equal in worth, which originated in the Stoic tradition of ancient philosophy and was disseminated very gradually, primarily through the efforts of the Christian movement. We shall also have occasion to notice that these two innovations, taken together with the insight that virtually all the wealth generated in modern societies is a social product rather than merely an aggregation of the products of individuals taken singly (an insight that is identified most closely with Adam Smith), led to the formulation of the modern idea of social justice. This idea has played an outsized role in thinking about justice for some two centuries.

No one is more aware than I am of the limitations of this study. I say little here about strictly legal justice, which is the most obvious form in which people usually encounter something resembling justice in the everyday world. My reason for this neglect, aside from constraints of space, is that I am not convinced that a comparison between strictly legal justice and justice is any less unfavorable to the former than the common comparison between military music and music is. It may be that, in the very best conditions, legal justice leads with some consistency to relatively just outcomes, but it has not done so in most legal systems of which we know over the centuries. I also say little about the deep skepticism about justice that can be found in the philosophical tradition, from the voice of Thrasymachus (as represented by Plato in the *Republic*) to the writings of Nietzsche and beyond. While I conceive this study in part as a response to that skepticism, it has seemed to me that the best way to frame that response is to present the positive claims about justice that have been articulated throughout that tradition as perspicuously as I am able to do. The skeptical view is based on a corruption of understanding, which forgets that the idea of justice is a tool that has been invented and refined by human beings, but, like other tools, is not infinitely plastic and cannot be reinvented in any form one happens to like, at least not if we want it to do the kind of work that the idea of justice was brought into being to do. I bestow what some might see as an inordinate amount of space and attention on a handful of "canonical" or "great" thinkers and only a little on the context of their ideas and on the ideas of others, who are considered less eminent in standard recent treatments of the history of political philosophy. I have allocated my attention in this way without misgivings, because I believe the writers on whom I have chosen to focus articulate the principal modes of thought about justice with at least as much fullness and clarity as could be found in any other selection. I have made no attempt to be evenhanded toward periods in the history of political thought, because I believe that some eras have been far more fecund with regard to ideas about justice than others. Perhaps most problematically, I have confined my attention to "western" ideas (including, however, the thinking of the ancient Babylonians, who borrowed heavily from the Assyrians and Sumerians before them, and that of the ancient Israelites). For this shortcoming my only excuses are the limited word count to which I agreed when I undertook this study, the design of the series to which this book is a contribution, and, most importantly by far, the limitations of my competence.

I hope that, despite its limitations, this study will be considered to be of some interest and use. For, notwithstanding its many omissions, the story it tells will uncover a set of ideas about justice that is as significant as it is neglected – ideas the contemplation of which may enable us in the future to frame issues about justice more constructively than we have been able to do for at least the past two or three generations.

Prologue

From the Standard Model to a Sense of Justice

It is often assumed that people's actions are invariably intended to promote their own interests. This assumption tints our perceptions both of public figures and of our acquaintances in everyday life. When we notice conduct we find hard to explain, we frequently suppose that closer scrutiny would reveal the self-interested motives underpinning that conduct. We take for granted that politicians and celebrities are moved by desire for personal gain in the form of wealth or fame or both, and we regard with suspicion claims that these figures are motivated primarily by an interest in the public good, or by other selfless goals. Philosophers and social scientists have produced many striking statements of the self-interest assumption. In the most celebrated work of political philosophy ever written in English, Thomas Hobbes declared that, "of the voluntary acts of every man, the object is some *Good to himselfe*." A century and a quarter later, in the book that is widely considered the founding work of the entire tradition of economic science, Adam Smith proclaimed:

> It is not from the benevolence of the butcher, the brewer, or the baker, that we expect our dinner, but from their regard to their own interest. We address ourselves, not to their humanity but to their self-

A Brief History of Justice, First Edition. David Johnston.

> love, and never talk to them of our own necessities but of their advantages.

Recent writers have followed suit. For example, Richard Alexander, writing of evolutionary biology, asserts that we will not understand human conduct until we grasp that societies are "collections of individuals seeking their own self-interests" – a claim that echoes Richard Dawkins' earlier announcement, in the same field of study, that "we are born selfish."

In modern times the self-interest assumption has been refined significantly by writers who have observed that a person's interests may encompass aims beyond his or her own individual good. This observation is fundamental to the theory of rational choice – a broad body of thought that has in recent years assumed a central role in a range of social sciences. According to this theory, individual behavior can best be explained by appealing to three factors: the individual's subjectively determined aims, whatever these may be, including the way in which the individual weighs or ranks them in relation to one another; the set of alternatives available to the individual; and the causal structure of the situation the individual confronts. The rational action for a given individual in any particular situation is then defined as the action that would best attain the individual's objectives, whatever those objectives may be.

The self-interest assumption, as refined in the modern theory of rational choice, is the central feature of what has become the standard model of human behavior. Thoughtful proponents of the theory of rational choice acknowledge that human actions are not always rational. A number of factors are capable of fostering irrationality. Sometimes the individual's aims may not be clearly defined, or they may not be clearly and consistently ordered, so that the individual is unable to rank them or weigh them consistently in relation to one another. Or the individual's beliefs about the available alternatives or the causal structure of the situation may be distorted by irrational processes such as self-deception and wishful thinking. People may also behave irrationally as a result of bias in the way they gather evidence about facts that weigh in their decision-making. Even if people *intend* their actions to promote their aims, those actions may not be optimally designed to do so. If actions fall short of being optimally designed to promote a person's aims, then, according to the standard model, they are irrational.

It is a truth that might be considered mildly embarrassing for the standard model, then, that people sometimes act with the intent of benefitting others at some cost to their ability to achieve their own aims, and that they do so in a manner that seems rational from a commonsense point of view. Here is one example. In an experiment, human subjects were told that they had been paired with a partner (who was actually fictitious) and were then asked to perform a simple task in an industrial setting, while their "partners" were performing a similar task in a different location. After completing the assigned task, the subjects were told that their partners had been given the chance to allocate their joint pay of $3 (this experiment was conducted a number of years ago). They were also told that they and their partners had performed their tasks equally well. The subjects were then led to believe that their partners had allocated them either $1, $1.50, or $2 out of the total of $3, keeping the remaining cash for themselves.

After learning of this allocation, the subjects were asked to respond to a series of questions about how they felt (happy, pleased, guilty, etc.), how they felt about their partners, how fair the allocation was, and the like. The results displayed a clear pattern. The subjects were happiest and liked their partners most when they received $1.50, which they believed to be equitable pay in view of their performance. They were less happy when they received $2, which they perceived as excess compensation, and less happy still when they received only $1, which they perceived to be less than they deserved. It appears that the human subjects in this experiment were affected by two motives: a desire to do for themselves as well as they could *and* a desire for joint rewards to be allocated fairly between them and their partners. The subjects preferred receiving $2 over receiving $1 because they preferred to do as well for themselves as they could. Yet they preferred receiving $1.50 over receiving $2 because they considered the greater amount of compensation unfair, even if they were beneficiaries of the unfairness.

Here is another example. In a survey about tipping in restaurants, people were asked two questions, presented here with aggregate responses (note that this survey was conducted in the 1980s, when the cost of restaurant meals was lower than it is now):

Question 1.	If the service is satisfactory, how much of a tip do you think most people leave after ordering a meal costing $10 in a restaurant that they visit frequently?
Mean Response:	$1.28
Question 2.	If the service is satisfactory, how much of a tip do you think most people leave after ordering a meal costing $10 in a restaurant on a trip to another city that they do not expect to visit again?
Mean Response:	$1.27

The respondents to this pair of questions seem to believe that the prospects that tipping behavior might elicit sanctions in the form of either exceptionally solicitous service or embarrassing retaliation by an irate waiter have virtually no effect on people's tipping behavior. Their responses tend to support the commonsense view that tipping behavior is guided by a sense of fair compensation for good service, without regard to any benefit that might accrue in the future to the person leaving (or withholding) a tip.

These findings are reinforced by a host of more recent experiments based on game theory. One large cluster of games with many variants (one example from this cluster is called the "trust game") mimics real-life situations in which people transfer things to one another in sequential order and there is no effective enforcement mechanism to prevent "cheating" in the form of withholding a transfer that another player would have reason to anticipate. Despite the presence of incentives to cheat, the general pattern in these games is that most players make the expected transfers, which benefit other players at some cost to the player making the transfer. This pattern of behavior is sometimes called "altruistic rewarding." It is complemented by a pattern called "altruistic punishment," demonstrated in another cluster of games, of which the "ultimatum game" is the best known. The overall pattern of outcomes in these games shows that many people – in some instances a majority – are willing to punish other players for behavior they perceive as unfair, and that they do so even at some cost to themselves, and even when the perceived unfair activity was inflicted on a third party rather than on the player doing the punishing. These experiments make it clear that people sometimes act in ways that are not intended to promote their own interests. Indeed, at a relatively high rate, they go out of their way and display willingness to incur loss to themselves in order to act fairly or to punish others for acting unfairly.

These patterns are evident also in many ordinary and extraordinary non-experimental circumstances. It is well known that people will sometimes go to great lengths to retaliate, to their own detriment, in cases where individuals have inflicted harm or acted with egregious injustice against them or against others. Similarly, some people (though perhaps not many) have taken serious risks and made great sacrifices to help others, including strangers, in cases where the latter are endangered or have become victims of injustice.

Willingness to incur costs in order to act fairly or to punish others for acting unfairly is highly variable from one person to the next. Similarly, perceptions about what constitutes fairness seem to vary significantly across cultures. Yet sensitivity to considerations of fairness seems to be ubiquitous, despite variations in the understanding of fairness. The standard model of human behavior suffers from a systematic failure to account for behavior in situations in which fairness is a salient feature.

It is evident, then, that human beings engage in far more prosocial behavior (behavior that benefits others, sometimes at some cost to those who undertake it) than the standard model would lead us to predict. Prosocial behavior is not unique to humans. However, unlike nonhuman animals, human beings also form evaluations and make judgments about the justice or fairness of their own and others' behavior, judgments that presumably shape or channel their prosocial behavior in distinctive ways. These judgments appeal to standards which, from the point of view of those who form them, are distinct from and external to their individual aims and desires. The capacity to be motivated by evaluations and judgments about fairness that transcend, or seem to transcend, what individuals take to be their interests appears to lie outside the purview of the standard model of human behavior.

Evaluations and judgments about justice and fairness can be contrasted with prudential evaluations and judgments. If I consider that it would be sensible, for the purpose of maintaining my long-term well-being, that I stick to a nutritious diet and that I exercise regularly, this is a prudential judgment. Similarly, if I decide to support my daughter's aspirations for a career in music by paying for lessons, that decision is based on prudential reasoning. Conclusions and decisions of these sorts are prudential because they are based on objectives that are contingent. Our lives are filled with occasions that call for prudential evaluations of all sorts of matters. Many of these matters are mundane: Should I listen to some music now, and, if so, what music would I most likely enjoy? Others are momentous: Whom should I marry (if I wish to marry)? Despite their variety, prudential evaluations have in common the fact that the objectives in light of which we engage in them are contingent on aims and priorities we happen to have, aims and priorities that another person might not share with us.

In contrast, evaluations and judgments about fairness are based ultimately on standards that human beings construe quite differently from the way in which they think about contingent objectives. Typically, we believe that the fundamental standards underpinning judgments about fairness should be shared by everyone. We also believe that prescriptions for conduct based on those standards should, at least in some important instances, take precedence over, or "trump," prescriptions based on prudential judgments. Of course, people often disagree about the standards that underpin judgments about fairness. But the fact that they disagree about them is compatible with the fact that they consider those standards to be objectively valid (in the sense of not being contingent on the subjective aims of individuals). People disagree all the time about objective matters, including matters of fact. Indeed, disagreement itself is premised on the assumption that there exists some objective matter about which it is possible to disagree. In the absence of this assumption, people regard their differences not as disagreements, but as mere divergences of opinion or taste.

The capacity to engage in evaluations about matters of justice and fairness and to be moved by judgments about such matters is known as the capacity for a sense of justice. The capacity for a sense of justice has long been associated with the capacity for language, and both these capacities have often been regarded as distinctive to human beings. In his *Politics*, Aristotle argues as follows:

> Nature, as we are fond of asserting, creates nothing without a purpose and man is the only animal endowed with speech [. . .] The object of speech [. . .] is to indicate advantage and disadvantage and therefore also justice and injustice. For it is a special characteristic which distinguishes man from all other animals that he alone enjoys perception of good and evil, justice and injustice and the like.

The seventeenth-century philosopher Thomas Hobbes, too, believed that the capacity for a sense of justice is distinctive to humans, and he associated that capacity with language:

> It is true, that certain living creatures, as Bees, and Ants, live sociably with one another [. . .] and yet have no other direction, than their particular judgements and appetites; nor speech, whereby one of them can signifie to another, what he thinks expedient for the common benefit: and therefore some man may perhaps desire to know, why Man-kind cannot do the same. To which I answer [. . .] [among other things, that] irrational creatures cannot distinguish between injury, and damage; and therefore as long as they be at ease, they are not offended with their fellows [. . .]

Although in his work as a whole Aristotle emphasizes that the capacity for a sense of justice makes possible the substantial sharing of norms and standards, while Hobbes calls attention to the fact that disagreement about those standards creates occasions for conflict, they agree that the capacity for a sense of justice is distinctive to humans, that it is associated with the equally distinctive capacity for language, and that this capacity is among the most fundamental of all attributes of human societies.

Although questions about the origins of both language and the sense of justice have been fodder for speculation for centuries, we have no accepted account of these origins, mainly because the evidence to which we might appeal to prove or disprove any such account is prehistoric and highly fragmentary. One recent hypothesis suggests that, as hominid societies grew larger and more complex, the capacity for language may have evolved in response to the need for an economical means to convey estimations about the reliability of grooming partners and other matters of a similar kind. While this hypothesis is interesting and seems compatible with the smattering of relevant evidence we possess, it is far from compelling.

We therefore cannot explain how the twin capacities for language and for a sense of justice developed in humans. If ever we are able to obtain a persuasive account of these origins, that account will constitute the first chapter in some future history of ideas about justice. For it is with the acquisition of the capacity for a sense of justice that our story would ideally begin. In the absence of such an account, we must content ourselves with the observation that the history of ideas about justice begins with the capacity for a sense of justice firmly in place within the repertoire of human attributes. Fortunately, we do possess substantial records of ideas about justice that go back several thousand years, to times of pre-alphabetic writing. We can begin our story, then, by glancing at some of the earliest available written records in human history.

Chapter 1

The Terrain of Justice

From a twenty-first-century vantage point, ancient ideas about justice are striking for two major reasons. First, the extant ancient texts reveal a preoccupation with retribution, and in some cases unbridled vengeance, that is unsettling to modern readers. Second, the ancient sources uniformly embrace stark hierarchies of power, status, and wealth as embodiments of a just political and social order. The commitments to freedom and equality that are widely shared today in those parts of the world which have been strongly shaped by European ideas are nowhere to be seen, at least not in the earliest sources.

The record of ideas about justice extends back many centuries before the beginnings of philosophy, which was a Greek creation. Collections of laws dating from the late third and early second millennia BCE have been preserved from several kingdoms that once existed in ancient Mesopotamia, including Assyria, Accad, Sumer, and Babylonia itself (into which the territories of Accad and Sumer were combined). Similarities among these sources provide strong evidence for the existence of a common customary Mesopotamian law in the third millennium that bridged political divisions. The most extensive of these collections is the Babylonian law, sometimes known as the Code of Hammurabi, although it more nearly resembles a series of amendments to the common law of Babylon or a set of guidelines than a code or collection of statutes.

A Brief History of Justice, First Edition. David Johnston.

The legal guidelines collected in the Code of Hammurabi are preceded by a prologue, written in semi-poetic style, and followed by an epilogue in similar style, both of which celebrate Hammurabi's role as promulgator of the laws and exhort the reader to maintain them into posterity. Although Hammurabi says that he was designated by gods to be a lawgiver to Babylonia, he (or the writer who represents himself as Hammurabi) claims to have written the laws himself rather than receiving them from a god. The prologue asserts that the gods Anum (leader of the pantheon) and Illil (chief executive of the pantheon)

> Called me by name Hammu-rabi,
> the reverent God-fearing prince,
> to make justice to appear in the land,
> to destroy the evil and the wicked
> that the strong might not oppress the weak,
> to rise indeed like the sun over the dark-haired folk
> to give light to the land.

Here we see clearly themes that can be found in writings about justice during the third, second, and first millennia BCE throughout the lands that have been described as the Fertile Crescent. The word "justice" (*mi-ša-ra-am*) and its variants run throughout the prologue and epilogue. The central purpose of justice is to prevent the strong from oppressing the weak. And the central means of accomplishing this purpose is the threat of violent retribution, directed toward those who might take advantage of the weak.

This representation of the purpose of justice might seem at least to gesture in the direction of the egalitarian concerns that are familiar in modern conceptions of social justice. In fact it does nothing of the kind. The concept of social justice – the phrase is anachronistic in this setting, though it is not entirely out of place – that is incorporated into the extant writings from Babylonian and other societies of this era had nothing to do with equality, nor even with relief from poverty. Social justice was conceived of as protection of the weak from being unfairly deprived of their due, that is, of the legal status, property rights, and economic condition to which their position in an established hierarchy entitled them. There is no suggestion that the rights or condition of the weak should be equal or comparable to that of others of greater status in their society.

The hierarchical conception of justice that runs throughout this collection of laws can be observed, among other places, in its provisions for punishment. Here is an example:

> 196: If a man has put out the eye of a free man, they shall put out his eye.
> 197: If he breaks the bone of a [free] man, they shall break his bone.
> 198: If he puts out the eye of a serf or breaks the bone of a serf, he shall pay one mina of silver.

The aristocrat cannot act with impunity toward his inferior in status, for those who are inferior have rights. But the punishment for infringing those rights is far less serious than that for violating the rights of a peer.

The Babylonian law's endorsement of hierarchical distinctions extends along a scale that runs from the highest to the lowest, as can be seen from a second example:

> 8: If a [free] man has stolen an ox or a sheep or an ass or swine or a [g]oat, if [it is the property] of a god [or] if of a palace, he shall pay 30-fold; if [it is the property] of a serf, he shall replace [it] 10-fold. If the thief has not the means of payment, he shall be put to death.

As these two representative passages show, the penalties in Babylonian law for violating the rights of another person (or institution) vary enormously with the standing both of the victim of wrong-doing and of the violator. The punishments prescribed for crimes against persons of high standing are far more severe than for crimes against persons of low standing. When the violator is himself a person of high standing, punishment is less severe than it is for violators of low standing. Stark inequalities of status and power are assumed throughout and incorporated into the Babylonian laws.

The Babylonian legal guidelines are also notable for the harshness of the punishments they prescribe. Death is recommended as appropriate punishment for many infractions, especially those committed against the church or the state. For example,

> 6: If a man has stolen property belonging to a god or a palace, that man shall be put to death, and he who has received the stolen property from his hand shall be put to death.

Maiming is held forth as the suitable penalty for many lesser infractions. While in some cases penalties seem proportional to the offenses for which they are inflicted – loss of an eye for destroying another person's eye, a broken bone in retribution for breaking another's bone – in other cases penalties are highly disproportional, for instance death for the criminal who cannot afford to make restitution to the victim, or for the unhappy thief who has preyed on the church or state.

A starkly retributive conception of justice also underpins the epilogue to Hammurabi's Code. The early lines of the epilogue restate the prologue's characterization of Hammurabi as the defender of justice and of the weak:

> In my bosom I have carried the people of the land of Sumer and Accad,
> they have become abundantly rich under my guardian spirit,
> I bear their charge in peace;
> By my profound wisdom I protect them,
> That the strong may not oppress the weak
> So [as] to give justice to the orphan [and] the widow [. . .]

The epilogue then urges Hammurabi's successors to preserve his laws, suggesting in sixteen lines of verse that the ruler who does so will enjoy prosperity and will reign as long as Hammurabi himself – and then, in more than 280 additional lines, threatening dire consequences for the ruler who fails to uphold Hammurabi's laws: revolts, famine, sudden death, the destruction of his city, the dispersal of his people, and the ruin of his land among other consequences. This emphasis on retribution for any ruler who fails to preserve and enforce Hammurabi's laws echoes the emphasis, within the Code itself, on harsh punishments for offenders – especially those who violate the rights of persons of higher standing.

The association of justice with harsh retribution on the one hand, and, on the other, either positive endorsement or tacit acceptance of vigorous hierarchies of power and status is ubiquitous in ancient writings far beyond the Fertile Crescent. The Code of Hammurabi was promulgated in an ancient state with a highly centralized apparatus of power; Homer's *Iliad* was composed in a decentralized society organized by way of clans or tribes. Yet the conception of justice that can be discerned in the *Iliad*, which took shape more than a millennium after the rule of King Hammurabi, shares both these features.

Justice (*dike* in the *Iliad*; another, later and more abstract Greek term is *dikaiosune*) is not the principal virtue in the *Iliad*; that distinction goes to *arete*, which is generally translated either as "virtue" or as "excellence." In the Homeric poems, *arete* is associated closely with the qualities of a warrior: strength, cunning, and skill in the use of instruments of war. When justice does enter into the picture, it does so in a context that is colored by emphasis on these warrior-like qualities.

The work opens with a quarrel between Agamemnon and Achilles. When it is revealed that the plague, lately unleashed on the Greek armies besieging Troy, has resulted from King Agamemnon's refusal to release a young woman he had taken captive, he reluctantly agrees to the release, but insists that he must receive in compensation Briseis, a prize girl from Achilles, one of the other military leaders. The latter objects:

> And now my prize you threaten in person to strip from me,
> for whom I laboured much, the gift of the sons of the Achaians.
> Never, when the Achaians sack some well-founded citadel
> of the Trojans, do I have a prize that is equal to your prize.
> Always the greater part of the painful fighting is the work of
> my hands; but when the time comes to distribute the booty
> yours is far the greater reward, and I with some small thing
> yet dear to me go back to my ships when I am weary with fighting.

When Agamemnon responds to Achilles' complaint by seizing Briseis, Achilles exacts revenge by withdrawing his forces and his own outstanding talents as a warrior from Agamemnon's campaign against Troy. The disasters that ensue for the Greek army set the stage for the tragic story that occupies the remainder of the epic. For Achilles, Agamemnon's grasping for gain from the war is unjust; the hubris manifested by the great commander in depriving Achilles of his prized booty constitutes a deeply personal injustice, to which revenge is the appropriate response.

Justice is associated with revenge throughout the entire *Iliad.* In a battle scene depicted later in the work, one of the Trojan enemies is taken captive and appeals to Menelaos, Agamemnon's brother, to spare his life. Agamemnon, aware of these events, rushes to the scene to declare:

> "Dear brother, o Menelaos, are you concerned so tenderly
> with these people? Did you in your house get the best of treatment
> from the Trojans? No, let not one of them go free of sudden
> death and our hands; not the young man child that the mother carries
> still in her body, not even he, but let all of Ilion's
> people perish, utterly blotted out and unmourned for."
> The hero spoke like this, and bent the heart of his brother
> since he urged justice. Menelaos shoved with his hand Andrestos
> the warrior back from him, and powerful Agamemnon
> stabbed him in the side and, as he writhed over, Atreides,
> setting his heel upon the midriff, wrenched out the ash spear.

Achilles' appeal to justice as fairness in the distribution of rewards, in the first of these passages, seems as familiar as a quarrel overheard yesterday among a group of children. In contrast, the vengeful responses registered in these passages, especially Agamemnon's deadly act in the latter one, will seem archaic and repugnant to many readers.

The *Iliad* does not call attention to hierarchies of power, status, and wealth in the explicit way in which we find these distinctions recognized in Babylonian law. It would be superfluous for it to do so. It is obvious that the Greek societies represented by the encampments outside Troy are organized into elaborate hierarchies of the weak, the powerful, and the more powerful, which are taken for granted and appear to be accepted as both natural and just. The quarrel with which the work opens is a dispute on the margins of this accepted order, in which Agamemnon claims his right to a pre-eminent share of the booty of war on the basis of his status as the chief leader of the Achaians, and Achilles claims his right to a greater share than he has hitherto received on the basis of his recognized superior excellence as a warrior and greater contributions to battle. No question arises about the justice of the hierarchical order as a whole.

These key features – acceptance of the justice of hierarchies and a strong emphasis on retribution – are also found, with significant differences of emphasis, in the ancient laws and other texts of Hebrew scriptures. Some of the numerous acts of God's retribution against the people he created (and against the Israelites, after God's covenant with Abraham and his later covenant at Mount Sinai) are well known. In Genesis 6, God resolves to wipe the entire race of human beings off the face of the earth because of their consistently evil thoughts, inclinations, and actions; he spares only Noah and his family. In Genesis 18, God decides to destroy the cities of Sodom and Gomorrah for the sins of their inhabitants. Abraham bargains with him until God agrees to save the city of Sodom in order to preserve as few as ten good men, if they can be found. They cannot, and God sends angels to rescue Abraham's nephew Lot and his family from Sodom before the place is burned to the ground; Lot and his family survive, except for Lot's wife, who is transformed into a pillar of salt after she disobeys God by looking back at the city as they flee. In Exodus, when the Israelites are camped at Mount Sinai and Moses goes up the mountain to receive laws for the Israelites from God, the Israelites become impatient and, following instructions from Moses' brother Aaron, they pool their gold jewelry to make a golden calf as an impostor god. The true God threatens to destroy them all, leaving Moses to begin a new nation from his own offspring; Moses pleads with God to spare them, and God relents, but soon afterward he enlists one of the Israelite tribes, the Levites, to kill many of the others, and thousands die in retribution for their infidelity to God. After this episode, the Hebrew scriptures are filled with stories of a cycle of infidelities to God, demonstrated by the Israelites, and of retribution inflicted on them through captivity, enslavement, and other sufferings.

The Hebrew scriptures apply retributive ideas to relations beyond those between God and the human beings he created. Retribution is the fundamental rule of justice that prevails in relations among the Hebrews as well. Here is a sample of the laws God transmits to the Israelites through Moses at Mount Sinai:

> Whoever strikes another man and kills him shall be put to death. But if he did not act with intent, but they met by act of God, the slayer may flee to a place which I will appoint for you. But if a man has the presumption to kill another by treachery, you shall take him even from my altar to be put to death.
>
> Whoever strikes his father or mother shall be put to death.
>
> Whoever kidnaps a man shall be put to death, whether he has sold him, or the man is found in his possession.
>
> Whoever reviles his father or mother shall be put to death.

According to these writings, justice is done when retribution is inflicted upon transgressors. Retribution is typically harsh, and in some cases, such as that of death for reviling a parent, disproportionately so, at least to modern sensibilities.

In addition to retribution inflicted or allowed by God as punishment for offenses committed by his people directly against him, and to retribution inflicted by human beings for offenses against one another, the Hebrew scriptures envisage a third category: retribution by God against people or rulers who fail to uphold justice for the poor and the weak. This theme is prominent in the prophetic writings. Here are examples from two of the major prophets:

> The Lord saw, and in his eyes it was an evil thing,
> that there was no justice;
> he saw that there was no man to help
> and was outraged that no one intervened [. . .]
> he put on garments of vengeance
> and wrapped himself in a cloak of jealous anger.
> High God of retribution that he is,
> he pays in full measure,
> wreaking his anger on his foes, retribution on his enemies.

> Tell this to the people of Jacob [. . .]
> They grow rich and grand,
> bloated and rancorous;
> their thoughts are all of evil,
> and they refuse to do justice,
> the claims of the orphan they do not put right
> nor do they grant justice to the poor.
> Shall I not punish them for this?
> says the Lord;
> shall I not take vengeance
> on such a people?

In the Hebrew scriptures, as in earlier Mesopotamian writings, justice is realized through retribution or vengeance when the rights of the vulnerable – which are not necessarily equal to those of the powerful – are violated.

A casual reader might think here, as in the case of Babylonian law, that the prophets' emphasis on justice for the poor and the vulnerable is indicative of an egalitarian bent. We shall see in a moment that there are significant differences between the views about justice that can be found in the Hebrew scriptures (which, it is important to remember, consist of a collection of diverse texts composed over a span of several centuries during the first millennium BCE) and those which we have noted above, in the much older Babylonian law. Nevertheless, there is no evidence in these scriptures of the egalitarian sensibility that is evident in many modern conceptions of social justice. Fundamentally, the Hebrew texts, like the Babylonian law, conceive of social justice as protection of the weak from being unfairly deprived of the legal status, property rights, and economic condition to which they are entitled within the established hierarchy.

It is nonetheless important to note that the duties toward the poor and the weak articulated in the Hebrew scriptures are duties of *justice*, and not duties of charity, as some interpreters have supposed. Many of the passages that evoke these duties do so by deploying a Hebrew term for justice (*mishpat*). A number of the relevant passages make their arguments in explicitly judicial terms. In the book of Isaiah, God enjoins the rulers of Sodom and Gomorrah to "pursue justice and champion the oppressed; give the orphan his rights, plead the widow's cause." The prophet Malachi reports:

> I will appear before you in court, prompt to testify against sorcerers, adulterers, and perjurers, against those who wrong the hired labourer, the widow, and the orphan, who thrust the alien aside and have no fear of me, says the Lord of Hosts.

Like Babylonian law, the Hebrew scriptures articulate a vision of social order that is recognizable as a conception of a sort of social justice, albeit an archaic one. And, again like Babylonian law, that conception focuses on rights, including the rights of the weak and oppressed, rather than on equality. Widows, orphans, strangers, and others figure prominently in many passages about the protection of these rights, because these people are at greater risk than most others of having their rights violated. Their rights constitute claims of justice, not of charity. But they do not constitute claims to equality. The ancient Hebrew laws and other writings were composed within the context of an unequal social order, and there is no suggestion in those writings that the inequality of that order is unjust.

In addition to assuming without objection the existence of the poor, the weak, and the otherwise vulnerable, the Hebrew scriptures, like nearly all other writings of equal or greater antiquity that deal with legal and social relations, paint a sharply hierarchical picture of the relations between males and females. Patriarchal figures like Abraham and Isaac often take more than one wife, and the role of husbands in relation to their wives as limned in the scriptures often more nearly resembles that of a property owner than that of a partner. When Abram (later called Abraham, in recognition of God's promise that he will have many descendants) travels with his wife Sarai (later Sarah) to Egypt to escape famine in the Negeb, he instructs Sarai to tell the Egyptians that she is Abram's sister, not his wife. The Egyptian ruler Pharaoh takes Sarai into his household, apparently to have her as a concubine, and treats Abram well on Sarai's account, so that he prospers. God shows his displeasure at the virtual prostitution of Sarai, the woman whose descendants will constitute his chosen people, by striking Pharaoh's house with disease, and Pharaoh sends Abram and Sarai away together, but Abram profits handsomely from the arrangement. While it is true that female figures in the Hebrew scriptures often show strength and cunning, they do so within a context of accepted relations of domination by and subordination to men.

The Hebrew scriptures also acknowledge the institution of slavery, accept its legitimacy, and accord it prominent legal recognition. Hebrew fathers were entitled to sell their children, male and female, as slaves, and the laws assumed that some would do so. The laws God transmits to Moses at Sinai for promulgation to the Israelites contain provisions for the buying, selling, and manumission of slaves. It would be difficult to discover more striking evidence of the prevalence and acceptance of hierarchies of power and status than that provided by statutes regulating the practice of slavery.

Yet the inequalities countenanced in ancient Hebrew laws differ significantly from those codified in the much older Mesopotamian documents. Consider the following provisions of the laws God dictates to Moses:

> When you buy a Hebrew slave, he shall be your slave for six years, but in the seventh year he shall go free and pay nothing [...]
>
> When a man sells his daughter into slavery, she shall not go free as a male slave may. If her master has not had intercourse with her and she does not please him, he shall let her be ransomed. He has treated her unfairly and therefore has no right to sell her to strangers [...] If he takes another woman, he shall not deprive the first of meat, clothes, and conjugal rights. If he does not provide her with these three things, she shall go free without any payment [...]
>
> When a man strikes his slave or slave-girl in the eye and destroys it, he shall let the slave go free in compensation for the eye. When he knocks out the tooth of a slave or a slave-girl, he shall let the slave go free in compensation for the tooth.

The differential treatment of male and female slaves suggested in the first part of this passage is one of its most noteworthy features. It is also noteworthy, however, that the provisions mentioned here confer rights upon slaves that are quite robust in comparison with anything provided in Babylonian law, or most other ancient legal codes. If they were enforced effectively (admittedly a big "if"), then slavery among the ancient Israelites must have been significantly less vicious than the relatively modern form that was imposed for centuries on Africans.

Further, the Hebrew laws do not recognize an aristocratic class with legal privileges that soften for its members the consequences of their wrongdoing, as the Babylonian and other ancient Mesopotamian laws do. Here is the passage that is, with the exception of the famous Ten Commandments, the best known of the laws dictated at Mount Sinai:

> Wherever hurt is done, you shall give life for life, eye for eye, tooth for tooth, hand for hand, foot for foot, burn for burn, bruise for bruise, wound for wound.

This formula, which is echoed in Leviticus 24 and Deuteronomy 19, has been given the label *lex talionis*, which derives from the central place held by an equivalent version in early Roman law. One of the most noteworthy things about it is that it does not prescribe different punishments for different classes of victims or perpetrators. True, the penalty for destroying the eye of one's slave, as stipulated by a separate article of this legal code, is loss of the slave to freedom, not loss of the owner's eye. Clearly the rights and obligations that were allocated to slaves by Hebrew law differed from those allocated to others. Unlike the Babylonian law, however, the code dictated at Mount Sinai makes no further distinctions among adult males within the Israelite camp. If the ancient Hebrew laws do not envisage a regime of equality in the sense imagined by some modern proponents of social justice, they do take a significant step in the direction of equality before the law, at least for free adult males.

It is also noteworthy that, although retribution is a central theme in Hebrew scriptures, as a general rule the punishments prescribed in these texts are more nearly proportionate to the wrongs for which they are imposed than was the case in earlier Mesopotamian legal codes. Here is an example:

> When a man steals an ox or a sheep and slaughters or sells it, he shall repay five beasts for the ox and four sheep for the sheep. He shall pay in full; if he has no means, he shall be sold to pay for the theft. But if the animal is found alive in his possession, be it ox, ass, or sheep, he shall repay two.

The five-to-one or four-to-one restitution ratios suggested here (two to one, if the original animal can recovered) are a far cry from the thirty-to-one and ten-to-one ratios mentioned for the same kind of offense in the Babylonian text we saw above. Similarly, the provision that an offender who cannot afford to pay the required restitution should be sold into slavery – presumably on the expectation of release after six years of service, as we have seen above – seems more nearly in proportion to the offence of stealing a piece of livestock (or at least less disproportionate to that offence) than the death penalty prescribed by Babylonian law.

From a modern point of view, the death penalty prescribed by ancient Hebrew law for anyone who strikes or reviles his father or mother (stipulated in one of the passages from Exodus above) is an exception to this generalization. The reasons for this exception become more apparent when we consider that a parallel between two relationships – between God and his chosen people and between parents and children – runs throughout the Hebrew scriptures. The Ten Commandments are divided into two parts, the first one of which dictates the Israelites' fundamental duties toward God, while the second prescribes their duties toward one another. The central message of the first part is the demand that the Israelites worship and honor their God consistently and exclusively. The second part begins with the famous decree "Honour your father and your mother, that you may live long in the land which the Lord your God is giving you." Parents are accorded a status in relation to their children that resembles that of God in relation to his people as a whole. In view of this parallel, it is not surprising that the penalty prescribed for dishonoring one's parents is as severe as the punishments God inflicts on the Israelites for their transgressions against him.

The strong relation of command and obedience between God and his chosen people portrayed in these scriptures goes a long way toward accounting for the fact that ancient Hebrew laws accord less recognition to hierarchies of status and power than Babylonian laws do. Babylonian law, as we have seen, extends exceptional recognition to the state and the church, as signified by the harsh penalties for crimes committed against them; and it also distinguishes persons into aristocratic and common ranks. For the most part, Hebrew law imitates neither of these features, because the central hierarchical relation in this literature is that between the Israelites and God.

Generally, then, the provisions for retributive justice in ancient Hebrew law rest on a sense of proportionality between wrongs committed and penalties prescribed. The tendency of this law is toward a principle of reciprocity: life for life, eye for eye, tooth for tooth, and so forth.

Looking back, it is not difficult to discern a similar principle at work in other ancient sources as well. In Babylonian law, the penalty prescribed for an individual who has caused a personal injury to someone of the same status is to suffer the same injury: destruction of an eye for destruction of an eye, breakage of a bone for breakage of a bone, and so forth. In the *Iliad*, Achilles' initial complaint is that Agamemnon has taken a larger share of the spoils of war than he deserves in proportion to his contributions. Achilles argues that he, Achilles, always contributes more, whereas Agamemnon always seizes the greater rewards, so that there is an imbalance in the proportions between contribution and reward, and thus a failure to conform to norms of reciprocity. In the battle scene in which a Trojan enemy is taken captive and appeals for his life to be spared, Agamemnon upbraids Menelaos for wavering from a principle of reciprocity in retribution: the Trojans have done harm, not good, to the Greeks, so it would be an act of injustice to do the Trojan captive the good of sparing his life.

The notion of reciprocity seems therefore to play a central role in all these ancient conceptions of justice. In fact, cross-cultural studies suggest that all known societies place considerable weight on values pertaining to reciprocity, so that we should expect to find that notion incorporated into virtually any conception of justice that is closely anchored to practices in the real world. Many philosophers across the centuries have endorsed the claim that people have a generalized duty to reciprocate for benefits received. The Roman philosopher Cicero suggested that "[t]here is no duty more indispensable than that of returning a kindness [. . .] all men distrust one forgetful of a benefit." In *The Origin and Development of the Moral Ideas*, written around the beginning of the twentieth century, Edward Westermarck argued that "[t]o requite a benefit, or to be grateful to him who bestows it, is probably everywhere, at least under certain circumstances, regarded as a duty." No idea, in fact, is more consistently regarded as a part of justice, nor as widely esteemed as a universal provision of morality, than the notion of reciprocity.

Popularly, reciprocity is assumed to entail an exchange of like for like, or at least of equal value for equal value. As sociologists and anthropologists have long pointed out, however, in reality the notion of reciprocity applies to a range of exchanges from the equal to the decidedly unequal; at the extreme of a continuum, one party may give nothing in return for a benefit it has received. Let us call exchanges in which all participants receive benefits equivalent to those they bestow instances of *balanced reciprocity* (bearing in mind that exchanges may involve more than two parties and that the "things" exchanged may be either benefits or harms). We can adopt the phrase *imbalanced reciprocity* for all exchanges that do not satisfy this equivalence condition.

Both ancient and modern writings frequently suggest that justice for people who are equals requires that their exchanges with one another exhibit the characteristic of balanced reciprocity, at least over the long term. Achilles' argument in the quarrel with which the *Iliad* opens is that his contributions to battle are superior to those of all the other Greeks, including Agamemnon, so that, even though Agamemnon is the acknowledged leader of the Greek army, for the purpose of distributing the spoils of battle, he (Achilles) should be treated as Agamemnon's equal, or at least very nearly so, and should therefore receive a nearly equal share of the spoils. The Babylonian laws dictate that noblemen who cause personal injuries to other noblemen, in other words to their equals, should be made to suffer the equivalent harm, so that the exchange between them (in this case, of harm for harm) will satisfy the condition of balanced reciprocity. Ancient Hebrew laws similarly tend toward a principle of balanced reciprocity in cases involving personal injury, by dictating that wrongdoers should suffer the same kind of injury as the kind they have inflicted on their peers. Historically, the notion – it may be apt to call it a principle – of balanced reciprocity among equals has commanded considerable assent, whether the things being exchanged are benefits or harms.

However, the principle of balanced reciprocity has usually been considered a principle of justice *only* with respect to exchanges between people who are regarded as equals. For the bulk of human history, nearly all societies have divided their members into groups that are unequal in power, status, and wealth, and in many societies these groups have also been regarded as unequal in merit. Stark inequalities of these kinds prevailed in ancient Mesopotamian societies and among the ancient Greeks; nor were they absent among the ancient Israelites, even though they were not encoded into law in the same way as they were among the Babylonians. Similar inequalities arose and persisted in most societies thereafter as well.

Among people who are considered unequal, imbalanced reciprocity has generally been regarded as just. In Babylonian law, fully free men were recognized as the superiors of commoners, whose circumstances were in some ways akin to those of serfs, and the legal remedies prescribed for wrongs committed by the members of one of these groups against members of the other were accordingly disproportionate. In the literary representation of ancient heroic Greece in the *Iliad*, arguments for treatment on the basis of balanced reciprocity were based on the premise that the claimants were equals; no one in this literary landscape supposed that the relations between unequals should be anything but unequal. Ancient Hebrew laws were exceptional in this era by virtue of approximating to a notion of equality before the law among free adult males; but even these laws accorded recognition to differences of status that provide a rationale for imbalanced reciprocity in many significant cases, including those involving relations between men and women. Historically, norms of justice based on the idea of imbalanced reciprocity have been as powerful and as prevalent as those based on the idea of balanced reciprocity.

Neither of these ideas (of balanced and of imbalanced reciprocity) is capable of applying itself to real cases without further ado. For inescapable practical reasons, neither idea can serve as the basis of a conception of justice in the absence of additional tools.

The principle of balanced reciprocity can be applied to ascertain whether justice has been done, or to determine how it might be done, only insofar as a standard is available as a basis on which to compare benefits or harms exchanged. The simplest case occurs when the benefits or harms in question are of the same kind. In the *lex talionis*, for example, the punishments prescribed – loss of an eye, of a tooth, and so forth – are identical in kind to the harms for which they are imposed.

When the benefits or harms in question differ in kind, the idea of balanced reciprocity can be applied only if those benefits or harms can be evaluated by reference to a common scale. In many cases, the kinds of comparisons that can be made are, at best, approximate and rough. If I publish an article praising your dairy farm that enhances your reputation and helps you attract business, you may repay me by offering to supply me with milk at no cost. In this case it is difficult to say whether the benefits we have given each other are equivalent in value. Similarly, if I harm you by allowing my dogs to attack some of your livestock, you may retaliate by diverting a flow of water away from my land, thereby depriving me of a valuable water supply. Is your retaliatory action equivalent in value to the harm you have suffered? In the absence of a common standard of value, it is impossible to answer this question.

The most important response to this problem is the introduction of a common currency. Currencies, of course, have multiple purposes. As a means of filling the need for a common standard for the purposes of justice, the adoption of a currency suffers from two significant difficulties. First, to the extent to which the currency value of a good is determined by a market system, significant discrepancies may arise between the currency or market value of the good and its value to the person involved in a particular case. Second, it is often believed that some goods are, or should be deemed to be, incommensurable with one another, so that, as a matter of principle, their values are, or should be, irreducible to a common standard. For example, it is sometimes said that it should not be possible to buy love with money. Similarly, in political systems in which some collective decisions are made through voting procedures, the principle that votes should not be available for sale is widely accepted. Again, it is commonly thought that there are some offences, such as rape or assault, to which no monetary value can (or should) be assigned. These inherent or prescribed barriers to exchange limit the range over which a currency can serve as a basis for comparing the values of benefits and harms that differ in kind. Nevertheless, that range remains considerable; and, for those benefits and harms which lie outside it, assumptions can be adopted so as to extend that range for the purposes of doing justice, as happens (for example) when a money value is attached to the harm of making libelous statements.

For the most part, then, adoption of a currency, together with some conventional assumptions that allow for the assignment of monetary values to those benefits and harms which are not normally commercially valued, makes it possible to determine whether an exchange has satisfied the condition of balanced reciprocity.

The case of imbalanced reciprocity is more complex. In order to determine whether an exchange is fair in accordance with the principle of balanced reciprocity, we must ascertain the values of the goods or harms exchanged. In order to determine whether an exchange is fair in accordance with the notion of imbalanced reciprocity, we must ascertain the values of the goods or harms exchanged *and* identify the unequal proportion to which an exchange of those goods or harms must conform if that exchange is to be deemed just. The number of variables involved in determining whether an exchange is just in accordance with the notion of imbalanced reciprocity is greater than the number of variables whose values we must ascertain in order to learn whether an exchange is just according to the principle of balanced reciprocity. Societies that endorse the norm of imbalanced reciprocity among unequals must both solve the problem of devising a standard for comparing the values of diverse benefits and harms and fashion a standard for determining the (unequal) proportion in which goods or harms should be exchanged.

In societies that divide their members into groups that are unequal with respect to a variable considered relevant for justice, whatever that may be (usually, status or purported merit or both), this problem is solved by means of a set of role definitions that prescribe status entitlements and obligations for each of the major groups. These entitlements and obligations constitute a sort of map of the society's "terrain," a guide to the locations of privilege and deprivation that are scattered throughout its population and to the patterns through which those differences are reproduced or reconstituted over time. Without a map of this kind, the notion of imbalanced reciprocity cannot take on a definite shape, and questions about whether justice, conceived of as imbalanced reciprocity, has been done cannot be answered.

Significant evidence suggests that values pertaining to hierarchy and respect are as widespread throughout human cultures as values pertaining to reciprocity and fairness. Although the emphasis on hierarchy in ancient ideas about justice seems striking from a twenty-first-century point of view that has been shaped by modern European notions of social justice, that emphasis is not exceptional from a pan-historical and pan-cultural standpoint. It should never be forgotten, of course, that most of our sources of information about nearly all societies, especially ancient ones, originated in privileged strata of those societies. For nearly the entirety of human history over the more than four millennia for which written records have been preserved, most of the population in almost every society has been illiterate. Even if, occasionally, a member of a less privileged stratum were to succeed in learning to read and write, that person would be unlikely to have the resources to produce and preserve written documents, except under the direction of the more privileged. For this reason, we cannot assume that the ideas about justice we find in ancient sources are accurate guides to the views of those societies' weaker and more vulnerable members. Yet cross-cultural evidence suggests that, even though specific privileges have often been resented by those to whom they were denied, most members of societies that endorse marked hierarchies of power, status, wealth, and purported merit have accepted these distinctions as a basis for their thinking about issues of morality and justice.

It is worth emphasizing that, as a general rule, a society's terrain provides a basis for judgments about justice because that terrain is accepted as normal, not necessarily because it is itself just. Psychological studies of adaptation suggest that any stable state of affairs tends to become accepted over time, at least in the sense that alternatives to it do not readily occur to those who play out their lives within it. A terrain that may initially have been seen as unjust, perhaps because the entitlements and obligations that constitute it were imposed by conquest or similarly forcible means, will often, over time, acquire the status of hallowed tradition – as British political and legal institutions gradually did after the Norman conquerors of the eleventh century replaced the existing Anglo-Saxon political and social order with new political and legal rules, which favored the Normans' interests. Changes of terrain through conquest or other forms of imposition are often followed by sustained ideological campaigns, designed to make the new order seem "natural" and normal. The success or failure of these campaigns goes a long way toward determining the durability of the new order.

Typically, the most prominent feature of a highly hierarchical terrain is an overarching "bargain" between the powerful and the weak, in which the powerful offer protection to the weak, often supplementing it with the promise of additional goods, in return for the promise of obedience and respect. This, in substance, is the bargain that Hammurabi dictates to the Babylonians. It is also, in broad terms, the bargain that God offers the Israelites, to whom he promises protection, fertility, prosperity, and national independence in return for their submission, fidelity, and worship.

This kind of overarching bargain is itself a form of imbalanced reciprocity, although it is not always easy to say which party to the bargain gives more and which gives less. The ancient Babylonian and Hebrew texts that promise to uphold justice for the vulnerable and threaten those who fail to do so extend these promises in accordance with the principle of *noblesse oblige*. In these promises, protection of the rights of the poor is a gift from the strong to the weak; but this gift reinforces the hierarchical relationship and thereby helps to maintain the privileged position of the strong. In societies with strong centralized authorities that engage in redistribution, the flow of material goods generally benefits the poor and the weak, so that, in a strictly material sense, the relationship of reciprocity is imbalanced in favor of the poor. Yet the process of centralized redistribution itself operates as a ritual of communion and subordination to central authority that reinforces the importance and power of the rulers.

Nearly all, and in some respects literally all, human societies in recorded history have been organized hierarchically. Yet vast differences exist between the modes of organization that have prevailed in these societies. Each society exhibits a distinctive terrain, with high points and low points – the loci of privilege and deprivation – to be found in varying locations and at varying elevations. Moreover, even within societies that can claim a continuous history and a single identity, the topography of the terrain has usually changed considerably over time.

If the conception of justice that prevails within a society is based on the notion of imbalanced reciprocity among unequals, and if the inequalities among the members of that society are based on their standing or positions within the social order, then changes in that order, or terrain, will lead to changes in the ideas about justice that are accepted within that society. Similarly, if one society's terrain – or the conception of that terrain as shared by its members – differs sharply from the conception that prevails in another society, we should expect the ideas about justice in those two societies to differ as well.

The history of ideas about justice is in large part a history of changes in the way in which the terrain of societies has been conceived. We can begin to see how that history developed, from its beginnings in the first half of recorded history, by turning from the pre-philosophical ideas of the ancient Mesopotamians, Israelites, and Greeks toward the far more systematic ideas about justice that can be found in the works of the Greek philosophers.

Chapter 2

Teleology and Tutelage in Plato's *Republic*

I

Plato's *Republic* is the first synoptic work of political philosophy that we know of in any language. Written in Athens during the middle period of his productivity, the *Republic*, like Plato's other works, is a dialogue – albeit one dominated by Plato's teacher Socrates – set several decades earlier, when Plato (429–347 BCE) was still in his teenage years and Athens was in the midst of a protracted war with Sparta. It is an astonishing piece of writing, one which lays out a distinctive conception of justice based on a radically hierarchical view of the political order.

In archaic Greek thought, as we have seen, justice was considered less important, at least as a quality of persons, than *arete* ("virtue" or "excellence"), which in the Homeric poems is associated closely with the qualities of a warrior. The pre-eminence of *arete* in the Homeric scheme of values was rooted in the need for protection. In a society of scattered households without centralized political authority or the rule of law, the individual with the outstanding warrior-like qualities of strength, cunning, and skill in the use of weapons would best be able to provide security to the (extended) household, and these qualities

A Brief History of Justice, First Edition. David Johnston.

accordingly were the objects of greatest admiration. This association of *arete* with the qualities required for success in battle was loosened at a later stage of Greek culture. In the poet Hesiod's *Works and Days*, the principal subject of which is how to be a successful farmer, to avoid famine, and to be prosperous, the concept of *arete* takes on a decidedly less militaristic tone than it had assumed in the earlier heroic compositions. In neither case, however, is *arete* intrinsically connected to justice. And in neither case is justice as highly esteemed as a quality of human beings as *arete*.

An early sign of change in this order of valuation occurs in a couplet attributed to the poet Theognis around the end of the sixth century BCE:

> In justice [*dikaiosune*] is every virtue [*arete*] summed up;
> Every man is good, Cyrnus, if he is just [*dikaios*].

This statement, which Aristotle much later treats as a generally accepted and even anodyne proverb, expresses a view that was probably held by a minority at the time of its composition. The writer seems to be claiming that justice is not merely a necessary, but also a sufficient condition for virtue, a claim that is incompatible with Homeric values. The growth of cities had changed the character of Greek society. Cities are best able to flourish when their residents are inclined to cooperate by making and keeping agreements and by refraining from doing harm to one another, practices that cannot easily be reconciled with a scheme of values that exalts the virtues of outstanding warriors. This observation is especially applicable to Athens, which was developing into a major commercial power and a crucible for experimentation with democratic institutions. The writer appears to have grasped this problem, and accordingly suggests a striking revision of the values that dominated Greek culture at the time – one that places justice at the center of the Greek ethical universe and sets the stage for Plato's extended reflections on the nature of justice.

Ostensibly a dialogue, most of the *Republic* is in fact a virtual monologue in which Socrates lays out an elaborate vision of the characteristics of a just man and a just city, the kinds of education and training that are required for each, and the principal types of unjust (and inferior) souls and regimes. Before launching into this exposition, however, Socrates is presented with several preliminary conceptions of justice. Cephalus, an elderly and wealthy man, raises the topic and then passes on to his son Polemarchus, in whose home the conversation takes place, the task of developing his fragmentary ideas into a fuller account of what justice is. Thrasymachus, a sophist (an itinerant professional teacher of "wisdom," modes of argument, and general education), then proposes an alternative view, which can be read as a denial that any such thing as justice actually exists. Finally, at the beginning of Book II (traditionally the *Republic* is divided into ten books, although this division may have been introduced by a later Greek scholar, not by Plato himself) Glaucon and Adeimantus, who were in fact the brothers of Plato, sketch a more elaborated theory of justice and challenge Socrates to show that it is wrong. This sketch is the springboard from which Socrates launches into his account.

Scholars of the *Republic* have sometimes described these preliminary conceptions of justice as versions of "common morality," suggesting that they are merely explicit statements of commonsense views about justice to which ordinary people usually adhere. This description is not wrong, but it misses some of the artfulness of Plato's renditions of these views. Consider the account Plato offers through the mouthpiece of Polemarchus, who tells us in the dialogue that he is drawing on the authority of Simonides, a prominent Greek poet of the late sixth and early fifth century. According to this view, "justice [. . .] consists in restoring to every man what is his due" (331e). Pressed by Socrates to elaborate upon this statement, Polemarchus explains that "the obligation due from friends to friends is to confer a benefit upon them, and to do them no injury whatever" (332a), whereas "there is due [. . .] from an enemy to an enemy what is also appropriate, that is to say, evil" (332b). In short, justice, which Socrates here calls a "craft" (*techne*), amounts to giving benefits to friends and doing harm to enemies (332d). Some further probing by Socrates leads to the following exchange:

> For what need or acquisition would you say justice is useful in peace?
> For contracts, Socrates.
> And by contracts do you mean partnerships, or something else?
> Partnerships, certainly. (333a)

After Socrates subjects Polemarchus' view to some searching criticisms, Thrasymachus intervenes vigorously to declare that "justice is nothing else than the advantage of the stronger" (338c). He elaborates by explaining that he means that in each city the stronger and ruling element makes laws to its own advantage, declares those laws to be just, and punishes those who disobey them as lawless and unjust. Whereas Polemarchus' view seems to be based on at least a rudimentary notion of fairness, Thrasymachus' account suggests that there is nothing fair about justice at all. "Justice" is nothing more than a name human beings use in order to cloak and blur the hard edges of the power relations on which societies are founded.

Now consider the description of justice with which Glaucon challenges Socrates in Book II:

> They say that to commit injustice is naturally a good thing, and to suffer it a bad thing, but that suffering injustice is more of an evil than doing it is a good; so that, after men have wronged one another and have suffered wrong, and have had experience of both, to those who are unable to avoid the one and attain the other it seems advantageous to form an agreement neither to commit injustice, nor to suffer it. And this, they say, is the beginning of legislation and of agreements with one another, and men soon learned to call the enactment of law just, as well

> as lawful. Such, we are told, is the origin and true nature of justice; and it stands midway between the best, which is to commit injustice without paying the penalty, and the worst, which is to suffer injustice without the power of retaliation [. . .]. (358e–359a)

Glaucon goes on to suggest that it is a general attribute of human beings to want to outdo others by getting and having as much as one possibly can. Uncurbed, this attribute would undermine cooperation and lead to perpetual conflict. Justice, then, is a human invention designed to curb the natural inclinations of human beings, which would have radically unsociable consequences if left unchecked.

Glaucon's account synthesizes elements from both Polemarchus' and Thrasymachus' views. It portrays justice as a strictly human artifact, as Thrasymachus does, but as an artifact that is concocted through an agreement rather than imposed by the strong upon the weak. It retains the connection between justice and fairness that is found in Polemarchus' account. In fact three points about Glaucon's theory of justice are noteworthy. First, Glaucon's account presupposes that human beings are motivated primarily by a desire to promote their worldly interests. This observation is also true of the other preliminary conceptions of justice, in Books I and II, even though Cephalus introduces the topic of justice in the context of concern about the fate his soul will face after the death of his body. Second, it is explicitly an account of a relation among equals – in other words persons of equal standing. The laws and covenants it depicts as the foundations of justice are products of an agreement among those who possess small or middling amounts of power – those who are at least roughly equals in power – and it would be unreasonable to expect eminently powerful persons to adhere to that agreement. Third, the central theme of Glaucon's account (and of that offered by Polemarchus) is balanced reciprocity. Polemarchus' account emphasizes the requital of benefits for benefits and the return of harms for harms. Glaucon's account emphasizes the mutuality of the agreement to abstain from doing harm to one another. Glaucon's theory of justice develops and sharpens the intuitions found in Polemarchus's account, without departing from the underlying theme of balanced reciprocity.

The theory of justice Socrates presents in the bulk of the *Republic* departs dramatically from Glaucon's view on all these points. Socrates argues that the interests that are relevant to justice are our ultimate interests rather than the mundane interests by which people are most often motivated in their everyday lives. The primary aim of justice is the cultivation of an order within individual human beings in which reason and wisdom rule strictly over human impulses and emotions. Further, Socrates argues that people are, by nature, deeply unequal – perhaps not in power, but in the qualities that are important for self-rule and for ruling others. So, insofar as the idea of justice applies to relations among human beings, it has to do essentially with relations among people who are unequal. Finally, Socrates shows little interest in the idea of balanced reciprocity, except as a foil against which to develop his own ideas. In his view, relations of justice among human beings are relations of command and obedience between unequals. These relations must be beneficial to all the affected parties – beneficial in the sense of bringing the souls of those parties more closely into conformity with the ordering prescribed by justice than they would otherwise be – in order to be just. Yet they cannot meaningfully be called reciprocal except by stretching the ordinary meaning of that term considerably.

II

It has long been noticed that, in moving from the preliminary conceptions of justice he sketches in Books I and II of the *Republic* to the distinctive theory he develops at length through the mouthpiece of Socrates in the remainder of the work, Plato actually changes the subject. This observation has sometimes been used as a ground for criticism of Plato's argument. Yet Plato's implicit point is that these preliminary conceptions are so wrongheaded that changing the subject is the only possible way to ascertain true ideas about justice.

Socrates offers a hint at the character of his theory early in Book I, when he responds to Polemarchus' attempt to formulate an account of justice. Where Polemarchus had argued that justice entails doing things that are beneficial for friends and doing harm to enemies – a formula that reactivates an heroic code, which had long played an important role in Greek thought – Socrates insists that it cannot be the function of a just person to harm anyone; hence it is never just to inflict harm (335e). Since we normally think of justice as a good thing and of the doing of harm as a bad thing, Socrates' claim may seem either trivially obvious or innocuous. In reality, it is far from being either. For the idea of balanced reciprocity – an idea that had long been fundamental to thinking about justice and is endorsed, under various formulations, by Polemarchus and Glaucon – entails both the return of good for good *and* the requital of harm with harm. Socrates' claim is a repudiation of at least one half of this standard formula.

Plato emphasizes in various indirect ways the gulf between the preliminary conceptions of justice he sketches in the opening pages of the *Republic* on the one hand and the theory of justice he develops through the mouthpiece of Socrates on the other. For example, when Socrates concludes that it is never just to harm anyone, he then proposes that he and Polemarchus "fight together, both you and I, if any one shall maintain that Simonides, or Bias, or Pattacus or any other of the wise and cultured men" (335e) has ever maintained a contrary view. Notably, his focus is on the views that might be attributed to Simonides and other respected authorities rather than on the things these authorities actually said. The message of this proposal, which foreshadows his later proposals to censor and eventually to expel poets from the ideally just city he imagines, is that practical reasoning as shaped by literary sources and other respected authorities is corrupt and untruthful. The dialogue also makes it clear that, in their exchange with one another, Socrates and Thrasymachus speak at cross purposes. Just as Thrasymachus assumes that people are invariably interested in gaining advantages over others, he is also interested in winning the argument – in effect, in scoring enough points to be declared the victor at the end of the speech-making. In contrast, Socrates, who maintains that people are ultimately drawn to their highest order interests, is interested in discovering the reality of justice. As the argument progresses, Thrasymachus is depicted as being dragged along with great reluctance, virtually against his will, by the logic of Socrates' argument, in the end assenting only in words to claims he does not want to accept. The difference between their approaches to argument is emblematic of the differences between their conceptions of justice.

As the exposition of preliminary conceptions of justice draws to a close, Glaucon and Adeimantus present Socrates with a dual challenge. Glaucon has sketched a theory of the origin and nature of justice, which he asks Socrates to refute if he can. Adeimantus insists that Socrates explain why people should be motivated to be just. Socrates takes up both challenges by connecting them intimately with one another.

Socrates' first move is to distinguish between the justice of an individual person and the justice of an entire city and to search for the latter first. His premise is that there are similarities between the "smaller" individual and the "larger" city, so that his inquiry into the justice of the latter will go a long way toward answering questions about justice in the individual. His second move is to reconstruct the origins of a city hypothetically, on the premise that in this way it will be possible to observe justice and injustice coming into being (as one might "observe" in a thought experiment).

Socrates then proceeds to describe the constituent elements of a city designed to meet human needs. This rudimentary city contains farmers and builders, weavers and cobblers, merchants, retailers, and laborers. Glaucon points out that this city, though healthy, supplies only the bare necessities of life to its members. So Socrates expands his inquiry and enlarges his city to include such people as hunters, artists, poets, servants, and doctors (this is what is usually referred to as "the city of pigs"); and, since the enlarged city will require more land than the rudimentary city, this luxurious city will also require fighting men – "guardians" – whose function is to acquire and hold territory and to defend the city against aggressors. Finally, after extensive discussion of the training and education the guardians should receive – physical training for their bodies and music and poetry for their souls (376e) – Socrates concludes that a complete city would require yet another class of persons, to serve as rulers. These people, winnowed from the class of guardians on the basis of their devotion to the good of the city (412d–e), should receive additional education in mathematics and other subjects, an education culminating in philosophical training. Ultimately, then, Kallipolis – this ideal city we have watched come into being – will contain three major classes of people. The first class constitutes the ruling group, people who are exceptionally devoted to the interests of the city as well as responsive to the further training, especially training in philosophy, that Socrates believes is required for ruling in the fullest and most genuine sense, at least in the hypothetical project of Kallipolis. This class consists of guardians in the proper sense, or philosopher-rulers. The second class is that of soldiers, whose function is to fight on behalf of the city. After calling them "guardians," Socrates adopts the label "auxiliaries" (414b, 434c) to distinguish them from members of the first group. The third class consists of farmers, craftsmen, traders, and service workers who provide for the needs and wants of the members of the city. Socrates refers to these people as the commercial or money-making class (434c).

Early in this discussion Socrates observes that different human beings are born with different aptitudes, in a way that is relevant to his search for justice in the city:

> I am myself reminded, while you are in the very act of speaking that, in the first place, each one is not born in every respect like his fellow-being,

> but differing in natural endowments, that one man has an aptitude for one task, another for another. Don't you think so?
> I certainly do.
> Well then, will a man be more successful when he follows many occupations, or when he confines himself to one?
> When he confines himself to one, he [Glaucon] answered.
> And further, I suppose, this too is evident, that a work comes to nothing when we let slip the right time for doing it.
> Yes.
> For the enterprise, I think, will not wait for the leisure of him who undertakes it, but the workman must keep to his task, making it his chief concern.
> He must.
> Hence we conclude that the several commodities are produced in greater abundance, of better quality and with more ease when every man turns from other pursuits and, following his natural bent, does one thing at the proper time.
> Undoubtedly. (370a–c)

Doing "one thing at the proper time" is more replete with meaning than it first appears. Slightly later in his description of the origins of a city, Socrates observes:

> We did not allow the shoemaker to attempt to be at the same time a farmer or a weaver or a builder, in order that our shoemaking work might be well done; and to every other workman we in like manner assigned one task to which he was naturally adapted, and in which, if he turned from other pursuits, and worked at it all his life, not letting his opportunities slip, he was likely to work successfully. (374b–c)

Plato's conception of the allocation of functions in a city is different from the notion of a division of labor in Adam Smith. The assumption that a craftsman should work "all his life" at a single task and be prevented from attempting any other line of productive work is starkly incompatible with the "system of natural liberty" Smith championed and from the market principles most economists have favored from Smith's time onward. Unlike Smith and many other modern thinkers, Plato appears to have believed that people are born with dramatically and unalterably diverse capabilities. For him, it followed that a well-ordered city would compel its inhabitants to cultivate these distinctive capabilities and would prevent them from wasting their efforts by going in other directions.

It should come as no surprise that Plato's conception of justice in Kallipolis reflects this assumption. After completing his sketch of the city's main parts, Socrates returns to the task that led him to analyze its origins, which is to locate justice in the city. If the city he has described is completely good, he argues, then it will exhibit four virtues: wisdom, courage, moderation, and justice. Socrates suggests that, if we can discover the locations of the first three of these virtues, it should be possible to find the fourth through a process of elimination (427e). The guardians or philosopher-rulers of the city as he has sketched it possess wisdom; so, even though this class is likely to be the smallest in the city, if it rules wisely, then we can say that the city possesses good judgment and wisdom. Courage is a specific virtue of the auxiliary class (the soldiers); so, if that class is constituted and trained as it should be, the city possesses courage. Moderation, unlike wisdom and courage, spreads throughout the city as a whole, though it manifests itself in different ways in the city's various members. The rulers possess "simple and moderate desires which of course are in harmony with intellect and right opinion, and are under the leadership of reason," whereas "the desires of the vulgar crowd are held in check by the desires and wisdom of the noble few" (431c–d). Justice, Socrates argues, is then a remaining element, which makes it possible for the other three virtues in the city to flourish. And, since these virtues flourish when each person and each class devotes itself to its own work without meddling in the work of the other classes or having to endure meddling from the others, justice consists of each class (and, within the money-making class, of each craft) doing its own work and not meddling in the work of others. Platonic justice is assured when the imperative "to prevent any man from appropriating what belongs to another or from being deprived of what is his own" (433e) is followed – and when what "belongs" to a man (or a class of people) is interpreted to mean, above all, the function of that person or class in a division of labor that is rigidly assigned on the basis of each citizen's natural and unalterable capabilities, whether that function is that of farmer, craftsman, trader, warrior, or philosopher and ruler.

Having reached this conclusion about the nature of justice in the city, Socrates returns to the problem of justice in the individual person. Like the city, he argues, the soul of an individual is divided into three main parts. (The notion of a soul in Greek thinking at this time was broader than the later Christian notion, and the idea that the soul is immortal was not assumed, although Book X of the *Republic* depicts just this idea.) The first of these is the rational part, which is the basis for the human ability to acquire knowledge and wisdom. The second is the spirited part of the soul, which is the source of anger and the basis of courage as well as of the impulse to attain eminence, glory, and honor. The third is the locus of bodily appetites, both necessary appetites like hunger and thirst and unnecessary appetites for various indulgences and pleasures.

Socrates connects each of these parts of the soul with a corresponding class in the city. The people who belong to the class of farmers and craftsmen, traders, and service workers are driven primarily by their appetites. The souls of the auxiliaries are dominated by the spirited part. In the rulers or philosopher-kings, the rational part of the soul is pre-eminent. Moreover, the natural and rightful relation among these parts is similar to the rightful relation among the three major classes in the city. The rational part should, rightfully, moderate the appetites and impulses of the others and rule over the whole. Although these parts of the soul are often at odds with each other (at more than one point, Socrates speaks of "the civil war of the soul" [440e; cf. 444b]), in a well-ordered soul the spirited part will align itself far more with the rational part than with the other, so as to maintain the whole in a harmonious condition. This idea of a well-ordered soul is a culminating point in Socrates' inquiry:

> In reality justice is a principle of this kind, a principle, however, as it seems, not concerned with the outward performance of a man's actions, but with the inward performance, dealing in very truth with the man himself and his duties. Hence the just man will not permit any one of the parts of the soul to do its neighbor's work, or the several faculties within him to intermeddle with one another; but having really set his house in order, and having become his own master, he will be a law unto himself and will be at peace with himself, and will harmoniously combine the three elements, as if they were three terms of a musical scale, the lowest and highest and intermediate, or whatever others may intervene; and when he has bound all these elements together, and has in all respects become one out of many, a temperate and perfectly harmonized nature, thus equipped he will then proceed to act [. . .]. (443c–e)

III

In an argument that unfolds gradually from the first book of the *Republic* to its last, Socrates explains – hesitatingly at first, but unapologetically in the end – that his ideal of justice in the city and in the individual can be attained only if the rulers pursue a rigorous course of what I may call cultural purification, or indoctrination, and only if they are willing to apply the prescriptions of justice to the ruled, without any need to elicit the latter's consent. The case for indoctrination begins, as we have seen, with Socrates' assertion that it would be wrong to attribute to Simonides (or any other purportedly wise man) the view that justice entails inflicting harm on anyone, regardless of what Simonides or any of the others might actually have said (335e). Since justice, according to Socrates, cannot prescribe the doing of harm, it would be confusing and unhelpful to ascribe the view that it does so to thinkers who are held in high esteem.

Socrates develops the case for cultural purification by degrees. He claims that Homer, Hesiod, and other poets composed false tales that must be censored for the purpose of educating the guardians (377–403). He explains that some kinds of falsehoods – those which convey underlying truths through stories that are not the literal truth (352–353, 415) – are useful because of their salutary effects on the souls of those who hear them. These falsehoods should be encouraged, among them the famous "myth of the metals" through which Socrates proposes to persuade the inhabitants of a just city that they have all been nurtured inside the earth with a mix of different metals that corresponds to the classes to which they are assigned (414b–415d). He suggests that the writers of tragedies praise tyranny and democracy, the two worst kinds of political regime, and that writings of this kind must therefore be banished from a just city (568). Finally, he concludes that hymns to the gods and eulogies to good people are the only kinds of poetry that should be permitted in the just city, since all other kinds (including Homer's poems) appeal to and nourish the lower parts of the soul and undermine the higher, rational part (595a–608b). In short, the culture of a just city must be controlled through censorship so as to be truthful to ultimate realities. These realities, for Plato, are infused with value, so that to ascertain the truth is to grasp the correct valuation of things. Plato's conception of truth, then, is not to be confused with (what we might think of as) the accurate representation of facts.

Coercion is a necessary tool in the kit of the rulers, or at least of the founders, of a just city – alongside indoctrination. Of course, an element of coercive power is common to every form of political rule. In comparison with ideas about the rightful uses of coercion that are widely held in modern democratic societies, however – if not in comparison with the practices of his own time – the thoughts Plato entertains about the rightful use of coercion are stunning. In the course of his discussion of the founding of a just city, Socrates suggests:

> When the true philosophers, whether one or more, shall be placed in command of the city [. . .] regarding justice as the most important and

> most indispensable of all things, and devoting themselves to its service [...] they will relegate to the country all the inhabitants who are more than ten years of age, and they will segregate the children of these from the influence of the prevailing customs, which are also observed by their parents; the children thus taken in hand they will bring up in accordance with the manners and principles of the true philosophers [...] (540d–541a)

The expulsion of all adults from the city would leave Socrates (or his philosophical kin who have attained power) free to form those few persons who are capable of being so formed, male and female, into the internally harmonious, rigorously self-controlled individuals who embody justice in its most complete sense. It would also allow him or them to shape the city's culture, its habits of thought, and its practices, so as to make them accord with the idea of justice as a relation of command and obedience between unequals, which Plato envisages as the rightful relation among persons in a just city.

The contention that the ideally just city would consist of three classes in a harmoniously ordered whole, in which the desires of the many are kept in check, in accordance with the wisdom of the few (the philosophers), amounts to a sharp critique of the principal forms of political association familiar to Greeks in Plato's time. During the fifth century, Athens had become the dominant commercial power in the Greek world as well as a laboratory of sorts for experimentation with democratic institutions. No great leap of imagination is required to see that the *Republic*'s description of the third class (farmers, craftsmen, traders, and service workers) is rooted firmly in the reality of Athenian life during Plato's earlier years. Plato did not object to producing and trading, nor even (perhaps) to service occupations. But he did object to a regime in which the sorts of people whose lives are devoted to those activities, and whose souls are guided by the appetites that lead to their pursuit, are in command. Similarly, Plato's discussion of the class of soldiers or "auxiliaries" is replete with allusions to the militaristic regime in Sparta, with which Athens and its allies were at war at the time in which the dialogue of the *Republic* is set. Plato's assessment of the values and ethos of Sparta seems more favorable than his view of Athens' democratic values, but the *Republic* makes it clear that the Spartan regime, too, falls far short of the just regime he envisages. As he says in his acerbic portrait of the undiscriminating, fickle type of character he believes to be characteristic of democratic regimes,

> If at any time the charm of a military career attracts him, he straightway becomes a soldier; or if he admires the successful financier, he takes to money-making. In short, there is no order or law in his conduct, and he continues to lead this life which he calls agreeable, free, and fortunate. (561d)

The lack of a sense of direction and the misdirection that Plato depicts here stand in sharp contrast to the wisdom and purposefulness he attributes to his hypothetical philosopher–rulers.

Plato's tripartite theory of the soul is even more central to his purposes than his tripartite conception of a just city. In addition to linking each of the parts of the soul to a distinct class in the ideal city (the appetites to the money-making class, the spirited part to the class of soldiers, and the rational part to the class of philosopher–rulers), in Books VIII and IX Plato links the two lesser parts of the soul, the spirited and appetitive parts, to a series of inferior types of political regime. He bestows the label "aristocracy" (rule by the best) on his ideal city, reserving the label "kingship" for a similarly virtuous regime, which brings about a transition toward aristocracy. He then sketches four decreasingly virtuous types of regime (timarchy, oligarchy, democracy, and tyranny) and draws a portrait of a distinctive type of personality corresponding to each regime. A timarchy (or timocracy) is a city ruled by people whose souls are dominated by the spirited part and who are consequently motivated by the desire for honors and good reputation (*time*). Oligarchy is a type of regime ruled by people whose souls are ruled by their necessary appetites. In democracy and tyranny, the rulers' souls are dominated by their unnecessary appetites. Plato lampoons the fickle, directionless, or misdirected characters of these people at length, devoting much of Book VIII to a discussion of democracy and virtually the whole of Book IX to tyranny, the worst of all regimes.

IV

By stepping back from Plato's exposition and placing it in the context of the Greek culture to which he was an heir, it becomes possible to see that his theory of the soul constitutes a critique of the norms and ideals of character that had prevailed within that culture for many generations. It is impossible for a careful reader to overlook the politically charged quality of Plato's description of democracy, or for the informed reader to fail to connect that description with the Athenian democracy that had thrived in his youth. The feckless characters whom he casts as democratic men and who are driven, indeed enslaved, by their corrupting appetites are drawn from his perception of those people whose commercial interests dominated Athenian politics through much of the fifth and fourth centuries.

The object of Plato's most trenchant critique, however, reaches back much further and extends over a wider territory. That object is the heroic ideal that had been disseminated and celebrated by Homer and other poets and dramatists, an ideal drawn archetypically around the figure of Achilles, the character who is central to the story in the *Iliad.* Although scholars of Greek heroic literature are disinclined to attribute any conception of the soul to Homer, at the risk of some anachronism we may think of the souls of Achilles and his fellow heroes as consisting of two significant parts. Like all other men, the heroes have appetites that they feel driven to satisfy. When Achilles acquires Briseis as one of the spoils of battle, he does so primarily to satisfy his lust. Only afterward does she become the focal point of his momentous quarrel with Agamemnon, in which other motives come into play. In contrast to the souls of other men, however, the souls of the heroes are dominated by the desire to attain outstanding recognition from others – recognition, if possible, of a kind and degree that will cause their names to be remembered through the ages. This kind of desire is characteristic of the spirited part of the soul in Plato's division. Of course, heroic figures in Greek literature were also capable of calculation and ratiocination. The most notable example is Odysseus, whose ordeals as recounted in the *Odyssey* are at least as notable for their displays of Odysseus' cunning as of his strength and skill in battle. Yet in Greek heroic literature ratiocination is overwhelmingly the servant of the desire for eminence. It does not constitute the equivalent of a distinct part of the soul, with a distinctive motivational character. In effect, then, if one were to extend Plato's own terminology, one may wish to say that Greek heroic literature promoted a "bipartite" division of the soul (insofar as we can ascribe a conception of the soul to this literature): an appetitive part, which is shared by all and is dominant in ordinary men, and a spirited part, which rules the souls of the most admirable, most heroic figures.

This conception of the soul, or of the way in which soul was conceived before the concept of the "soul" (*psuche*) emerged, underpins the pre-eminence of *arete* in the Homeric system of values and is the central object of Plato's critique. In one sense, Plato's conception of justice is a reversion to an earlier type. *Arete* had been construed as an ideal fully realized in the characters of outstanding individuals. With the growth of cities, commercial activities, and orderly political institutions, that ideal began to give way, in the Greek order of valuation, to the idea of a set of rules designed to regulate the rights and transactions through which human beings coordinate the pursuit of their interests. These rules – the rules of justice, as formulated in Athens in the fifth and fourth century – provide much of the material out of which Plato constructed the preliminary conceptions of justice with which the *Republic* begins. Whereas the ideal of *arete* had focused on the outstanding individual, the idea of justice was equally applicable to all. Plato pointedly turns his focus away from rules intended to regulate the actions of all, equally, and toward an ideal of character, an agent-centered conception of values that places at center stage the outstanding few who are capable of attaining that ideal.

Yet, in so doing, Plato proposes a radical alteration in the content of those values. The *Republic* seeks to replace the ideal of the warrior–hero, whose principal features could be captured by a hypothetical bipartite theory of the soul where the spirited pursuit of glory dominates, with an ideal of the philosopher–hero, who is described by Plato's tripartite theory of a well-ordered soul, dominated and motivated by its rational part. This theory is the core of Plato's conception of justice, which is concerned far less with the actual conduct of worldly affairs than with the pursuit of ultimate truths by those few individuals whose characters possess the intrinsic capacity for it. As Socrates observes at the end of Book IX, "the man of understanding will devote all the energies of his life to this end [. . .] he will honor those studies that impress these virtues upon his soul, and despise others" (591b–c). Even if the kind of city that is designed to cultivate the philosophical character does not and will not exist anywhere on earth, a vision of that city can still stand as an effective ideal for those who are capable of the philosophical life:

> At least [. . .] in heaven there is perhaps laid up an exemplar of it which he who desires may observe, and contemplating it, found a city in himself. But it matters not whether this republic exists anywhere or ever will exist; for he will regulate his conduct after the manners of that city and of no other. (592b)

The contrasts between this Platonic conception of justice and ideas about justice that preceded it in both Greek and other cultures are sharp. In the first place, whereas the concept of retribution had played a central role in earlier ideas about justice, in Plato's theory that concept has no place. As we have seen, Plato does not shrink from suggesting that coercion be used in the cause of justice. But the uses of coercion he envisages are not intended for the purpose of punishment or retribution. Coercion is used to create and to maintain a just order, a terrain Plato conceives of both as a natural thing and as a product of human construction (because it cannot come into being without deliberate human effort). For Plato in the *Republic*, justice is the object of a craft (*techne*). He compares the state of justice with the state of health, and he compares ruling with various crafts, including that of the physician and that of the sculptor. The attainment of justice in the city and in the soul is like the attainment of health in the body, and the means by which justice is attained are a matter of secondary importance. The objective is to help construct a just terrain and ultimately to improve the characters of persons by whatever means are best suited to achieve this objective. Insofar as these means must be forcible, they may be compared more accurately with a statesman's use of force to settle issues and prevent violent conflict than with the use of force in retribution. Insofar as they involve cultural purification, they can best be thought of as the measures a teacher might use to improve the characters and virtues of his pupils. But Plato's philosopher–rulers can perhaps most aptly be compared with physicians who must sometimes employ painful measures for the purpose of preserving or restoring their patients' health. Plato's conception of justice is one of strict tutelage designed to improve its subject, not one of behavior control intended merely to enforce rules.

Plato's conception of justice is striking, too, for its lack of any sign of interest in social justice. As we have seen, while it is possible to discover a rudimentary precursor to the concept of social justice in ancient ideas, that precursor differs significantly from familiar modern notions of social justice. The aim of "social justice" in the ancient world was to protect the weak and the vulnerable, not to bring about social equality. Yet Plato takes no notice of the poor, the vulnerable, or the weak. It is true that he proposes the abolition of private families and the institution of private property for the portion of his city's population which is to receive training so as to yield the city's defenders, and from which the class of philosopher–rulers is to be drawn. These proposals have often been construed as harbingers of modern social democratic or socialist ideas; and in a narrow sense, focused on resemblances between Platonic and modern institutional ideas, this interpretation is not mistaken. But the purpose of Plato's proposals is almost diametrically opposed to that of these modern ideas.

The most consequential contrast between Plato's distinctive conception of justice and the more widely expressed ideas about justice that preceded (and followed) his theory is that, whereas the latter are based on the premise that the principal purpose of justice is to provide a framework for regulating the worldly interests of human beings, Plato's conception has rather a transcendent aim. For Plato, the aim of justice is the cultivation of an order in the city – and, most importantly, in the soul – that accords with the ideal form of justice. That form prescribes a hierarchy in which philosophical wisdom and judgment rule strictly over all other human impulses and capacities, both in the individual (for those who are capable of strict self-regulation) and in the city as a whole (for all). According to the ordinary conception – the conception Plato represents in several variants in the preliminary views he ascribes to Cephalus, Polemarchus, Thrasymachus, and Glaucon – the subject of justice is the regulation of rights, transactions, and more generally the mundane interests of human beings. That is why Cephalus suggests that justice is a matter of avoiding cheating or deception; why Polemarchus argues that justice is useful for forming and sustaining partnerships; why Thrasymachus claims that the idea of justice is merely a veil for the pursuit of otherwise naked self-interest; and why Glaucon associates justice with the making of laws and contractual agreements. Although these preliminary conceptions differ from one another significantly, they share the assumption that the primary subject of justice is the pursuit of worldly interests and that the primary purpose of a conception of justice is to articulate a framework for that pursuit. In contrast to this view, Plato proposes that the primary aim of justice is the pursuit of ultimate concerns.

"Justice" is the name he uses to designate the order, divine and natural, to which both the state and the gifted individual should aspire. His conception of *dikaiosune* dwelling in the state and in the philosophical individual is a close relation to the notion that the goddess *Dike* dwells in the city.

V

As we have seen, ancient ideas about justice prior to Plato are marked by two features that are noteworthy from a modern point of view: a preoccupation with retribution, and a readiness to confer the stamp of approval upon the hierarchies of power, status, and wealth that defined a society's terrain and were generally accepted as natural by inhabitants who were unfamiliar with alternative ways of life. These features are prominent in the heroic literature of ancient Greece as well as in a wide range of narrative and legal writings in other cultures of the ancient world.

The development of Athens into a commercial power and a laboratory for experimentation with democratic institutions in the fifth century BCE generated a set of ideas that eclipsed these long-standing features of thinking about justice. The idea that the society's terrain – its configuration of loci of privilege and deprivation and its norms regulating the relations among its various and differently situated members – is natural declined in favor of the alternative view that societal arrangements are overwhelmingly the products of human contrivance and convention. Thoughtful Athenians in the fifth century shared with more ancient writers the assumption that the principal purpose of thinking about justice is to help define a framework intended to regulate the pursuit of human beings' worldly interests. Yet they were far less inclined than those writers had been to accept inequalities and hierarchical relations as normal and natural. Although distinctions of power, status, and wealth persisted, they came to be seen more as products than as presuppositions of human societal arrangements. Thinking about justice gravitated toward the idea of balanced reciprocity, and the concept of justice came to be regarded as applicable primarily or solely to relations among equals. Contractual relations among (putatively) equal individuals came to occupy much of the ground of justice, displacing hierarchical relations among unequal individuals and groups. While imbalanced reciprocity could still be considered the proper form that justice should take in some instances, balanced reciprocity came to be deemed the paradigmatic form of justice, a baseline departures from which must be justified by specific reasons.

It is from this milieu that Plato extracted the preliminary conceptions of justice he uses as a springboard from which to launch his distinctive theory of justice, a theory that turns on their heads the views he received from his Athenian predecessors and contemporaries. In contrast to those thinkers, Plato takes only passing notice of worldly interests. For him, the primary aim of justice is to cultivate the rightly ordered soul, and its secondary objective is to construct and maintain a city that is ordered so as to cultivate the rightly ordered soul. Such a city is based, most importantly, not on contractual relations among equals, but on hierarchical relationships between persons who are unequal in capabilities and in virtues. Similarly, the concept of reciprocity, whether balanced or otherwise, has little if any place in his vision of a just city. The relations of justice between human beings that are central to Plato's conception are relations of command and obedience between unequals. These relations are just only if they are beneficial to the characters of all parties, but they are emphatically not relations of reciprocity.

Plato's re-imagining of justice entailed two momentous innovations, each of which would earn a significant role in the dynamics of later ideas about justice. First, Plato's theory effectively abandons the notion of reciprocity as a central point of reference for thinking about justice. Earlier thinkers had generally considered justice a matter of balanced reciprocity among equals and imbalanced reciprocity among unequals in power, status, and/or wealth. For Plato, the key form of justice is a hierarchical relation among the parts of a well-ordered soul and among the differently gifted classes of people in the city. This relation can be described, with some poetic license, as a highly exaggerated form of imbalanced reciprocity, in a way that may seem to preserve continuity with earlier ideas about justice. Yet in reality Plato's conception of this relation is not based on the concept of reciprocity at all. The relation he conceives of as an embodiment of justice is one of command and obedience, not one of reciprocal exchange, even if on unequal terms. Whereas earlier writings about justice invariably define some space within which the idea of balanced reciprocity among equals is applicable, Plato takes no interest in balanced reciprocity, and no real interest in reciprocity in any sense at all. The reason is that his theory of justice, unlike both ancient and contemporaneous views, focused relentlessly on putatively higher objectives. It is a teleological theory in the sense that it aims to bring the world, or least the city that is shaped in accordance with that theory and the individual who understands it, into harmony with their prescribed ends.

Second, Plato's theory helped to disseminate the idea that a society's terrain is itself subject to scrutiny and criticism rooted in a conception of justice. For the most part, ancient thinkers had assumed that a society's existing terrain provides an adequate basis for judgments about justice, because they believed or purported to believe that that terrain is natural and, above all, because they were unable or disinclined to envisage alternatives to it. The specific entitlements and obligations that were attached to persons and groups within that terrain served as an accepted basis for judgments about justice because no other basis was available nor, for the most part, was any such alternative basis even imagined. The sophists and others in fifth-century Athens had already rejected this traditional assumption long before Plato began to write as a philosopher. They held that the received institutions of Athens and other cities had been contrived by human beings for human convenience. Yet, in the long run, Plato's

Republic was a more influential vehicle than the work of the sophists for transmitting – especially in the Renaissance and beyond – the notion that a social terrain can be reshaped in accordance with ideas about justice.

Although the bulk of the text of Plato's *Republic* appears to have remained in circulation for some time after its composition in fourth-century Greece, most of that text eventually dropped out of circulation for close to a millennium, to be rediscovered and published in book form only during the Renaissance. We can only speculate about the course that ideas about justice might have taken had this work been available for wide study centuries earlier than it was. What we do know is that Plato's approach to justice, which entailed a re-imagining of the terrain of society as a whole, was eventually to re-emerge in a form that would have a significant impact on modern thinking about justice, including – despite Plato's intentions – the idea of social justice.

Chapter 3

Aristotle's Theory of Justice

I

Like Plato, Aristotle (384–322 BCE) believed that people are separated by dramatic differences in their natural capacities, so much so that, while some are qualified to rule or to participate in ruling, others – who comprise the bulk of humankind – are fit only to be ruled. For him as for Plato, the right relation between these two categories (the latter, according to Aristotle, consists of several diverse groups, including women, children, and people who are naturally suited to be slaves by virtue of their limited powers of reasoning) is one of command and obedience. For Aristotle, however, relations between those who are radically unequal are not the primary subject of justice. The concept of justice in Aristotle's theory applies primarily to a set of relations among men who are free and relatively equal to one another – relations that play a very slim role in the argument of the *Republic.*

The principal source for Aristotle's theory of justice is Book V of his *Nicomachean Ethics*, a book that is a companion to, and precedes, his *Politics* in expository order. The *Ethics* is essentially an inquiry into the nature of the good human life, and especially into the virtues that are integral to it. His theory of justice is couched within this (for him) much larger frame.

A Brief History of Justice, First Edition. David Johnston.

At the outset of his account, Aristotle takes pains to distinguish between "complete" (or "general") justice and "partial" (or "particular") justice. In one sense, he says, "we call things just which produce and secure happiness or the parts of happiness for the political community" (1129^{b}). Justice in this sense is "complete virtue or excellence [...] in relation to one's neighbour" (1129^{b}). Here Aristotle quotes the line "in justice is every virtue summed up" from the poet Theognis. Complete justice, then, is an attribute of character, the virtue that is exhibited by human beings in their relations with others insofar as these interactions promote a good life and lead to happiness for the members of the political community as a whole.

In contrast, partial justice has to do with the share of benefits individuals should receive and of burdens they should bear. Among the benefits with which partial justice is concerned, Aristotle specifically mentions honor, material goods, and security. Although he emphasizes burdens less than benefits, it is clear that partial justice is concerned also with the share of burdens and harms that individuals should bear. Injustice in the partial sense occurs when a person receives an unfair share of benefits or burdens.

Aristotle's decision to begin his discussion with this distinction between different types of justice is a typical example of his philosophical method and entails a departure from Plato's approach to philosophy. In the *Republic*, Plato insists that justice must be one thing only, being always the same in any and all of its manifestations. Plato's search for justice therefore proceeds by way of refutation and exclusion, that is, by showing what justice is *not* in order to arrive at a univocal view of what it *is*. Aristotle's approach, in contrast, accepts that justice may be several different things, and especially that it may be seen in a number of different ways, each of which may contain significant truth.

Aristotle's notion of complete justice is very broad. It corresponds roughly with the idea of rightness in modern English and denotes the quality or qualities of character that lead people to do the right thing, broadly speaking, whether that involves being fair or exercising good judgment in some other way. In contrast, his notion of partial justice is considerably narrower and corresponds roughly with the ordinary concept of justice or fairness in English. Although the notion of complete justice is important to his account of the virtues, the central subject of Book V of the *Nicomachean Ethics* is partial justice, which is a part of complete justice: the part that has to do with fairness. I shall follow Aristotle by focusing in this chapter on partial justice, namely on what we, today, would call "justice," as distinct from the broader subject of rightness – bearing in mind, however, that the larger context of his discussion is provided by the idea of complete justice and that Aristotle defined the idea of complete justice by reference to the idea of a good life for the members of the political community as a whole. For the sake of simplicity, I shall usually apply the label "justice" to this topic, dropping the more cumbersome "partial justice."

It is usual in discussions of Aristotle's views on justice to follow his own order of exposition. After drawing the distinction between complete and partial justice and declaring his intention to focus on the latter, Aristotle proceeds to distinguish two forms of it, namely distributive justice and corrective justice. He then goes on to discuss several additional topics: the relation between justice and reciprocity, justice in the political sense, and others. Most commentators have concentrated their attention on Aristotle's comments on distributive and corrective justice, treating the subsequent topics as appendages, despite the fact that these later discussions occupy about two thirds of his account overall. This approach has led to some curious difficulties, especially in treatment of Aristotle's discussion of justice and reciprocity. Many of his interpreters have concluded that this discussion is anomalous. Some have decided that it is distinctly out of place, a digression that might have been better located somewhere other than in the context of his discussion of justice.

In reality, Aristotle's discussion of the relation between justice and reciprocity is the anchor for his entire theory of justice in the sense of fairness in individuals' shares. The concept of reciprocity is the fixed point to which his ideas about (partial) justice, with all the ebb and flow and qualifications to which those ideas are subject, are tethered. Before considering his ideas about distributive and corrective justice, then, let us take a moment to understand the basic character of Aristotle's conception of reciprocity.

Aristotle opens his discussion of the relation between reciprocity and justice by noting that "some think [. . .] that reciprocity is without further qualification just, for the Pythagoreans defined justice unqualifiedly as reciprocity" (1132^{b}). He quickly goes on to suggest that this understanding of justice cannot be correct, since in many cases reciprocity and the just are not identical. For example, if an ordinary citizen strikes a police officer or other public official while the latter is on duty, justice is not served if the official merely returns the blow. Nor is justice done if a private citizen strikes back when struck by an official while the latter is acting to carry out his duties. Aristotle's point seems to be that, when the relations between parties are hierarchical or unequal in some way, justice does not take the form of reciprocity – or, more precisely, it does not take the form of (what I have called) balanced reciprocity, which entails the return of benefits or harms of equal value to those which one has received.

Many readers seem to have concluded that Aristotle's dismissal of the Pythagorean association between justice and reciprocity is the end of the matter, and that the sole conclusion to which he wants to lead his readers is that justice does *not* consist in reciprocity. Yet this conclusion is not consistent with the text. Immediately after the arguments discussed above, Aristotle offers the following observations, all within the context of his opening question about how we should conceive of justice "unqualifiedly":

> In associations based on mutual exchange the bond of union is this sort of justice, namely reciprocity in accordance with a proportion rather than with arithmetic equality. In fact it is by proportional requital that the city holds together. People seek either to return evil for evil – for

> otherwise they consider themselves reduced to slaves – or to repay good with good, for otherwise there is no mutual contribution, and it is by mutual contribution that men hold together. (1132^{b}–1133^{a})

Let us consider this crucial set of claims in some detail. What points is Aristotle trying to convey in this passage?

First, Aristotle associates justice with "reciprocity in accordance with a proportion" rather than with (what he alleges to be) the Pythagorean conception of reciprocity as an exchange of arithmetically equal values. In other words, an exchange will be just if the things exchanged are in proportion to the merits, desert, or contributions of the parties to the exchange. If the parties in question are strict equals and enter into a relation of exchange with one another, then justice is done when the benefits they exchange are of equal value. In this case the just relation between these two parties is one of balanced reciprocity. If, on the other hand, the parties are unequal in merit of the kind that is relevant to their transaction, then justice is served when the benefits exchanged differ in value in proportion to the different merits of the parties involved. In this case the just relation between these parties is one of imbalanced reciprocity, where the extent of the imbalance can be determined by comparing their respective merits. Justice is very much a matter of reciprocity, though that reciprocity is not necessarily of the "arithmetic" (as Aristotle calls it) or balanced sort.

Second, Aristotle's focus here is on collectivities in which people associate with one another for the purpose of exchange. Now a political community in the true sense, for Aristotle, is an association based on mutual exchanges that enable its members to flourish and to be self-sufficient as a collectivity. Such an association is made up of men who are free-born and stand in relations of relative equality with one another, at least in the sense that none has, by nature, the right to command any of the others to do his bidding. Human beings who are not at least relative equals of the members who make up a political community, such as women, children, and slaves, are not parties to

Aristotle's scheme of justice on the basis of proportional reciprocity. As we shall see, there is a qualified sense in which the relations between free adult men and those whom Aristotle believes to be their radical inferiors by nature can be said to be just or unjust, but the central and unqualified concept of justice applies only to the relations of proportional reciprocity among relative equals.

For Aristotle, then, ideas about justice – that is, about the kind of justice that deals with the fairness of individuals' shares - are concerned centrally with relations among men who are free and equal to one another in the sense that none is entitled by nature to command over any of the others. The focus of these ideas is upon the shares individuals receive – both shares of benefits, such as honors, material goods, and security, and shares of burdens or harms. And the concept to which any adequate theory of justice must be tethered is the concept of reciprocity.

II

Aristotle divides justice – understood as fairness in individuals' shares – into two forms, distributive and corrective. These forms are based on two distinct variations of the concept of reciprocity. Let's look first at justice in its distributive form.

Aristotle introduces the topic of distributive justice by saying that it is

> exhibited in distributions of honors, property, or anything else which is divided among the members of the community. For in such matters men may receive shares that are either equal or unequal to the shares of others. (1130^b)

This introduction is subject to two significant qualifications. First, although Aristotle is interested principally in analyzing justice in the context of the political community, the political community is not the only kind of association based on mutual exchange that is formed by men who are relative equals. The concept of distributive justice applies to any such association, and not merely to the political system. Second, the terms translated here as "equal" and "unequal" are *isos* and *anisos*, which are equally well translated in some contexts as "fair" and "unfair." So Aristotle seems really to be saying that it is possible for a man to have a share that is fair or unfair in comparison with his neighbor's share, where a "fair" share need not necessarily be an "equal" share.

Aristotle explicates the notion of distributive justice by sketching a simple illustration. The just, he points out, involves at least four terms, namely two persons and two shares. Distributive justice is achieved when "as the one person is to the other person, so is the one thing to the other thing" (1131^{a}) – in other words, when the ratio between the things in question is the same as the ratio between the persons. If two persons are equals, then their shares should be equal as a matter of distributive justice. If the persons are not equals, then their just shares will be unequal in proportion to the inequality between them. (Bear in mind that, for Aristotle, all the persons who come into play in anything to do with distributive justice are *relative* equals in the sense that none is entitled to command the others. Nevertheless, these relative equals may be, and often are, unequal in merit or desert.)

Aristotle offers only the most abstract account of the basis on which the equality or inequality of persons should be determined. He argues that

> all admit that in distributions justice should be determined on the basis of desert (or merit), though all do not acknowledge the same criterion of desert, democrats claiming that this criterion is free birth, oligarchs that it is wealth and sometimes birth, and aristocrats that it is virtue or excellence. (1131^{a})

In his discussion here, Aristotle makes no attempt to adjudicate among these alternative criteria of desert. That task is left to his

Politics, a work that appears to be the product of a significantly later stage in his thinking. In Book V of the *Nicomachean Ethics* he offers only a bare framework for thinking about questions of distributive justice.

Yet Aristotle is not wholly silent about the basis on which just distributions should be made. After declaring that "justice in the distribution of public possessions is always governed by the proportion described above," he goes on to observe that,

> if the distribution is made from public funds, it will be in proportion to the contributions the members have made, and the unjust opposed to this justice is that which violates the proportion. (1131^b)

Aristotle here suggests that, at least in the case of funds, the theory of distributive justice points to an unambiguous conclusion, namely that the participants in a common enterprise should reap benefits in proportion to their contributions to that enterprise.

Although Aristotle is clear that the idea of distributive justice can be applied to many types of common enterprise, the most important type of enterprise for him is the political association. A political association is constituted by human beings who share a common life in order to maintain self-sufficiency and to attain a good life. These ends are attainable only by way of contributions that are necessarily diverse in kind. The production of material goods is one kind of contribution. The provision of services is another. But, since human flourishing is constituted through participation in a range of activities – including, for example, the activities characteristic of friendship – the ends of a political association can be attained only if these economic contributions are complemented by a range of contributions of non-economic kinds.

It is plausible to infer, then, that, since the ends of a political community can be attained only through contributions that are diverse in kind, differences of opinion about the basis of desert in the community are, at bottom, differences about the comparative worth of diverse kinds of contributions to the common enterprise of the political community. As he demonstrates in his chapter on the relation between justice and reciprocity, Aristotle is aware that it is difficult to make quantitatively meaningful comparisons between the values of things that differ in kind (1133[b]). In relations of exchange between people who produce different kinds of goods, this difficulty can be addressed through the introduction of money, which makes it possible to measure the values of diverse goods by a single standard. This is the reason why it is possible to draw unambiguous conclusions from the theory of distributive justice in cases that involve the distribution of funds. In the case of contributions to a political community that are resistant to valuation in monetary terms, however, no such common standard is readily available. This may be one reason why "battles and complaints arise in consequence of equals having and possessing things which are not equal, or persons who are not equal having things which are equal" (1131[a]). In the absence of a common standard to which to appeal in adjudicating competing claims, such conflicts are probably inevitable.

Aristotle's theory of distributive justice appears to be underpinned by a version of what later came to be called the contribution principle, which states (roughly) that it is just for people to reap rewards from a common enterprise that are proportional in value to the contributions they have made to that enterprise. Some, but not all, of this principle's nineteenth-century champions (Herbert Spencer among them) seem to have thought that all contributions can be quantified in monetary terms and that the contribution principle can best be realized through an unrestrained free market system. The version of the contribution principle we may ascribe to Aristotle occupies a completely separate territory from this market-based conception. Indeed, it is a point of considerable importance in his theory that, in the absence of a common standard by which to compare the values of diverse contributions, this unambiguous principle will not lead to similarly unambiguous practical prescriptions and that it is only through political processes that such prescriptions can be devised fairly.

Nevertheless, the anchor point of the most plausible interpretation of Aristotle's theory of distributive justice is a version of the contribution principle in which the concept of a contribution is construed expansively rather than in narrow economic terms.

III

Let us turn to Aristotle's account of corrective justice. This concept, as he envisages it, applies to private transactions of two types. *Voluntary* transactions are those into which all parties enter voluntarily. Aristotle illustrates this category with examples that are financial in character: sale and purchase, lending funds with or without interest, renting, giving security, and depositing funds in trust. The second category is comprised of *involuntary* transactions. In modern English we normally apply the term "transactions" to voluntary exchanges, but for Aristotle any interaction between two or more persons that involves a transfer of benefits or harms is a transaction to which principles of justice apply.

Involuntary transactions are of two kinds. Some, by his account, involve clandestine activities, such as theft, adultery, poisoning, assassination, procuring, the enticement of slaves to escape their bondage, and bearing false witness. The other kind of involuntary transaction involves the use of force; examples include assault, imprisonment, murder, robbery, maiming, defamation, and libel.

Aristotle introduces his account of corrective justice by saying, immediately after he completes his discussion of distributive justice, that "the other kind of justice is the corrective kind" (1131^{b}). This claim, together with his earlier statement distinguishing justice into two (and only two) forms, distributive and corrective, seems to have misled some of his readers and is probably a principal reason why many have treated his subsequent discussions in this chapter – that is, the bulk of the text – as a series of appendages to his central arguments about justice. In fact Aristotle's account of corrective justice in transactions presupposes a conception of just transactions. For transactions are subject to correction only when something has gone awry. When Aristotle focuses on distributive and corrective justice, what he seems to have in mind is the kind of justice that is effected by the self-conscious actions of an agent: in the case of distributive justice, some person or persons who have responsibility for distributing honors, material goods, security, or the like; in the case of corrective justice, a judge or an arbitrator. In the latter case, the self-conscious actions of an agent are required as a matter of justice only when the transactions for which correction is sought have been unjust.

Let us first consider corrective justice in relation to voluntary transactions. In order to grasp Aristotle's conception of this kind of justice, we must first understand his ideas about just transactions, which are laid out in his chapter on the relation between justice and reciprocity. We must therefore probe a little more deeply into his claim (discussed in Section I above) that justice "without qualification" consists of proportional reciprocity.

Although the finer points of Aristotle's account are beyond the scope of this book, the broad outlines of his view are plain enough. Aristotle illustrates his notion of reciprocal exchange made on the basis of a proportion through a series of examples: a builder and a shoemaker exchanging a house for some shoes; a physician and a farmer; a shoemaker and a farmer. In order to be equal and fair, any exchange between any of these pairs will have to be proportional. Specifically, Aristotle argues that proportional reciprocity will have been achieved when "the product of the shoemaker is to the product of the farmer as the farmer is to the shoemaker" (1133[a]). Aristotle assumes that producers in different professions or trades are unequal in some respect that permits comparisons among them, for "it is not two physicians between whom a community is formed, but a physician and a farmer, and in general those who are different and unequal" (1133[a]). Similarly, he appears to assume that products possess inherent value and that the values of qualitatively different products can be compared meaningfully through the medium of a common currency.

Suppose the worth of the builder (as measured by whatever standard enables comparisons among producers in different professions) is twice as great as the worth of the shoemaker. (Bear in mind that, for Aristotle, the builder, the farmer, and the shoemaker are all relative equals – that is, they are free as well as equal in the sense that none is entitled by nature to command the others.) According to Aristotle's formula, then, an exchange between them of shoes for a house will be fair if the inherent value of the shoes the builder receives is twice as great as the inherent value of the house he relinquishes to the shoemaker. The relation between the builder and the shoemaker (2:1) will then correspond to the relation between the given number of shoes and that of the house (2:1).

Aristotle does not explain the basis on which the relative values of the builder and the shoemaker, or of any pair of professionals or tradesmen, is determined. Yet it is reasonable to suppose that he may have been thinking about the contributions these professionals or tradesmen make to the overall stock of goods and services available to the members of the political community. Suppose that the builder in the example above is twice as productive as the shoemaker. The builder's high productivity accounts for his higher value than the shoemaker. It also explains why, as a matter of justice, the builder is entitled to receive shoes from the shoemaker worth twice as much as the house he transfers to the shoemaker. The builder contributes twice as much value to the overall stock of goods, and is justly entitled to receive twice as much value as the shoemaker in return. This, I suggest, is what Aristotle means by "reciprocity in accordance with a proportion rather than with arithmetic equality." Proportional reciprocity, in this context, is a form of the contribution principle in which the concept of a contribution is construed expansively – the same principle that appears to underpin his theory of distributive justice.

Now we may return to Aristotle's account of corrective justice in transactions, a form of justice that is predicated on the assumption that some injustice in transactions – some departure from Aristotle's principle of proportional reciprocity in exchange – has occurred. The principal feature of corrective justice is that it is based on what Aristotle calls "arithmetic" equality, not proportional equality. Unlike in the kind of justice that underpins the mutual exchanges holding the political community together, and unlike in distributive justice, in corrective justice the relative values of the parties' contributions to the overall stock of the political community have no place in ascertaining what constitutes corrective justice. "It makes no difference whether a good man defrauds a bad man or a bad one a good one, nor whether it is a good man or a bad one who commits adultery" (1132[a]). When one person has defrauded another, it is as if a line were divided into two unequal parts, the perpetrator possessing the larger part and the victim possessing the shorter part. A judge who has been called upon to correct the injustice committed will take the excess away from the perpetrator and restore it to the victim, with no regard either for the characters of the parties or for the value of their contributions.

Aristotle's assumption is that the worth of the parties to a dispute (where worth is determined by the value of their contributions to the common enterprise) has already been taken into account in determining the shares of goods they possess prior to the unjust transaction. It would be a perversion of justice, then, to take this factor into account again, in the course of adjudicating their dispute. The premise of corrective justice is that each party possessed a fair share prior to an unjust transaction. The aim of the adjudicator or judge should be to restore the equilibrium that existed between the parties prior to the injustice. The judge does this by depriving of his unfair gain the party who has benefited and by restoring to the aggrieved party any unfair loss. In the terms I suggested in an early chapter of this book, the principle underlying Aristotle's theory of corrective justice in relation to voluntary transactions is based on the concept of balanced reciprocity.

Now we may turn to Aristotle's ideas about corrective justice in relation to involuntary transactions. Many scholars have suggested that, in his theory of justice, Aristotle has nothing to say about issues of punishment or retributive justice, a point that more than a few of these scholars regard as an oddity at best and as a serious omission at worst. In fact the oddity is that this view, which can be traced back at least as far as a widely used 1926 edition of the *Nicomachean Ethics*, would ever have spread as widely as it has. The error may stem from an inclination to impose the modern distinction between crimes and torts anachronistically onto the writings of Aristotle, who lived in a society that entertained no such distinction. It seems clear enough that, although he offers few examples to flesh out his ideas about retributive justice, Aristotle has retributive justice in mind in his discussions of both proportional reciprocity (the basis for his thinking about partial justice generally) and corrective justice. The term that is translated as "reciprocity," *to antipeponthos*, means literally "suffering in return for one's actions" and is close in meaning to the well-known rule of reciprocity in retributive justice, "an eye for an eye, a tooth for a tooth [...]." Toward the beginning of his discussion of justice as reciprocity, Aristotle cites the rule of Rhadamanthys (the mythical son of Zeus and Europa), "if a man suffers that which he did, right justice will be done" (1132^{b}), though he does not endorse the Pythagoreans' interpretation of this rule. When he argues that simple, balanced reciprocity is insufficient as a rule of justice in the case of an ordinary man who strikes a public official, he seems to be suggesting that some form of punishment for the man would be just. And in his discussion of corrective justice (about which we shall see more below) Aristotle states that,

> when one man strikes and the other is struck, when one man kills and the other is killed, the action and the suffering have been divided into unequal portions, and the judge endeavors to equalize the profit and the loss by a deduction from the former. (1132^{a})

Aristotle's reasoning here evokes the notion that the just response to crime is to restore the equilibrium that has been disturbed by its commission – a notion that, by his time, had long been the dominant way of thinking about the subject of retributive justice. It seems clear enough that he did not ignore the subject.

As in the case of voluntary actions that have gone awry and hence require correction, Aristotle assumes that, prior to an involuntary transaction, each party involved possessed his fair share of any goods that might be at issue. Likewise, his thinking about corrective justice in relation to involuntary transactions assumes that, prior to the relevant "transaction," the parties involved stood in a relation of justice toward one another. Aristotle assumes it to be self-evident that theft, assault, murder, and other acts in which a perpetrator inflicts harm on an unwilling or unknowing victim are unjust.

Corrective justice as applied to involuntary transactions "treats the parties as equals, considering whether one has inflicted an injustice and the other has suffered it" (1132[a]). In the case of an offender who has wounded or killed another person, this equalization – or restoration of equilibrium – is achieved by inflicting harm on the offender. Aristotle does not offer a formula for determining precisely the kind or magnitude of the harm that should be inflicted on offenders. For him, the key point is that the harm that perpetrators unjustly inflict on victims should be requited by a harm that is imposed on the perpetrators in return, "for otherwise they [the victims] consider themselves reduced to slaves" (quoted above). As a general rule of thumb, however, he suggests that the magnitude of the punishment or loss imposed on the perpetrator of an unjust harm should be in "arithmetic" proportion with (that is, equal in value to) the magnitude of the loss or harm inflicted by the perpetrator.

The most plausible interpretation of Aristotle's theory of corrective justice in regard to involuntary transactions – his theory of retributive justice – is that it calls for something like an eye for an eye or *lex talionis*, or, in a more generalized form, for balanced reciprocity. The fundamental principles underlying both parts of his theory of corrective justice appear to be rooted in the concept of balanced reciprocity.

IV

Although the idea of justice is applicable to any association of relative equals that is based on mutual exchange, the most important locus of justice is the political community:

> what we seek is not merely justice in the unqualified sense, but also political justice, i.e. the justice of free and (proportionally or arithmetically) equal citizens living together with a view to the satisfaction of wants. (1134[a])

Aristotle subdivides what is just in the political sense into two categories: what is just by nature and what is just by convention. This distinction has been a source of considerable puzzlement on the part of Aristotle's interpreters.

The most common interpretation of Aristotle's notion of what is just by nature (or "natural right") identifies that notion with Stoic, Christian, and rationalist conceptions of natural law, all of which treat natural law as an eternal, universal, and immutable standard of justice. According to this view, Aristotle's theory is an early – perhaps the earliest – formulation of a conception of justice independently of any particular legal system, one that can be invoked to evaluate, criticize, and in some instances condemn existing legal provisions as unjust.

We shall see below that Aristotle's theory of justice is indeed adorned by an aureole of ideas that purport to transcend the provisions of any particular existing system of positive law. However, his notion of what is just by nature is not the primary source of this light. That notion at best gives off only a faint glow, in comparison with the bright beams associated with the Stoic and later ideas of natural law. We can see why by considering two features of that notion.

First, unlike many other writers, including some of the Greek writers of his own time, Aristotle classifies what is just by nature as a subdivision of what is just in the political sense. If that notion were similar in status to the Stoic and later ideas with which it is often compared, then it would have made much better sense for Aristotle to characterize it as independent of, and in a sense prior to, what is just in the political sense. That he does not do so suggests strongly that his notion of what is just by nature is not intended to play the role the idea of natural law or natural right was to perform in many later systems of ideas.

Second, Aristotle insists that what is just by nature is subject to change – indeed, that what is just by nature is as much subject to change as what is just by convention (1134^b). This claim – which has been a stumbling block for interpreters, from Thomas Aquinas onward, who see Aristotle as a source or founder of the theory of natural law – is irreconcilable with the usual conception of natural law as eternal and immutable.

The best interpretation of Aristotle's distinction is relatively simple. What is just by convention refers to matters about which we would be indifferent in the absence of a set of rules that we can regard as matters of agreement or convention. Aristotle suggests the example of the choice of animal (goat or sheep) that should be deemed suitable for a sacrifice. We might add the example of a choice between driving on the right or on the left side of the road. Inherently, it makes no difference whether we select goats or sheep to be the subjects of sacrifice, no more than it does to select the left or the right side of the road for forward travel. Once an agreement is reached, however, that choice becomes a convention and its violation becomes an injustice. In this case, justice and injustice are constituted by the adoption of a convention.

Conversely, what is just by nature refers to matters about which we are not indifferent, even in the absence of a set of agreed rules. It seems obvious that we would not be indifferent to acts of assault or murder, even if no legal provisions were in existence to prohibit and punish those acts. More generally, actions that contribute to human flourishing – ac tions that produce and preserve happiness for the social and political community – are just by nature, whereas actions that detract from the preservation or happiness of the community are unjust by nature. Because the kinds of actions that contribute to the preservation and happiness of the political community vary from one time and one situation to another, what is just (and unjust) by nature is subject to change. Further, and perhaps more importantly for Aristotle, each particular political community differs from every other political community in some respects. The kinds of actions that contribute to the preservation of one kind of political community differ from the kinds that contribute to the preservation of another kind, so that actions that are just in one sort of community may be unjust in another. Yet, at any given time or in any given circumstance, the set of actions that contribute to human flourishing is relatively clear. As Aristotle says, it is not difficult, except perhaps at the margins, to distinguish between those things which are unjust by nature and those which are unjust by convention alone (1134^{b}).

If Aristotle's conception of natural law is not intended to constitute an eternal, universal, and immutable standard of justice, does anything in his theory yield a standard to which one might appeal in order to assess the justice or injustice of existing laws? Or is the concept of justice in Aristotle so parasitic on the concept of law that justice for him is virtually synonymous with law?

Some passages in the *Nicomachean Ethics* suggest the latter conclusion. For example, near the beginning of Book V Aristotle comments that the "'just' then includes what is lawful and fair, and 'unjust' is what is unlawful and unfair" (1129^{a-b}). A few lines later, he observes that "it is plain that all laws are in a sense just. For laws are the products of legislation, and we acknowledge that each of the products of legislation is just" (1129^{b}). There is a sense, then, in which what is lawful is just, according to Aristotle.

However, it is clear from other parts of his discussion that actual positive laws can be imperfect, and even, in some cases, straightforwardly unjust, in a sense of justice that does not identify the just strictly with the legal. (Recall that, for Aristotle, justice may be envisioned in a number of different ways, each of which may contain significant truth.) For example, Aristotle observes that "the laws pronounce upon all subjects [. . .] enjoining some things and forbidding others, the rightly established laws doing this rightly, and the extemporized law with less propriety" (1129[b]). Here he seems to acknowledge that actual laws are sometimes flawed, even in cases in which the lawmakers were well intentioned. Moreover, Aristotle points out that even the best-framed laws are sometimes imperfect when applied to specific cases. Laws by nature are general prescriptions or injunctions, but "there are some cases for which it is not possible to provide in a statement which is general" (1137[b]). That is why conclusions based strictly on law can justly be set aside in the interest of equity when a judge finds that the laws fail to make sense in a particular case. "Though the equitable is just, it is not legal justice, but a rectification of it" (1137[b]).

Further, Aristotle notes:

> People conceive that the power to act unjustly rests with themselves, and therefore that to be just is easy. But this is not the case [. . .] [similarly,] people assume [. . .] that it requires no special wisdom to discriminate between things which are just and those which are unjust, because it is not difficult to apprehend such matters as are provided for by the laws. But it is only by happenstance that actions prescribed by law are identical with those dictated by justice. To be just, actions must be done and distributions must be made in a particular manner, and the knowledge required to do these things is more difficult to attain than knowledge of what makes people healthy. (1137[a])

In this passage Aristotle makes it clear that, even at their best, laws are inherently imperfect expressions of justice. To understand the just and the unjust requires wisdom, not merely knowledge of the law, because laws are not inherently just, but are made so only by being crafted carefully and judiciously.

The most serious discrepancies between law and justice arise when the regime lacks the key attribute needed to support justice "without qualification," namely, a common life among men who are free and relatively equal to one another. In the absence of this basis for justice and law,

> political justice does not exist, but only a semblance of justice. For justice exists only among those who have law to govern their mutual dealings, and law exists only where injustice occurs. (1134^{a})

Aristotle here has tyranny in mind, as his immediately ensuing words make clear. Tyrannical regimes are capable of adopting laws and ruling through them. Yet these laws will not embody justice, since they are not the products of relations among free and relatively equal men. It is clear that, for Aristotle, although there is a narrow sense in which the legal is just, there is no strict synonymy between justice and law.

Aristotle's idea of the political community is integral to his theory of justice, and especially to his conception of the role of reciprocity, which lies at the heart of his theory of justice. Community (*koinonia*) is in fact the underlying principle of his discussion of reciprocity. He uses the term *koinonia* six times in his chapter on reciprocity alone, and he makes it clear that community is one of the main goals of reciprocal exchange. Recall a portion of what he says at the outset of his discussion of reciprocity:

> in associations based on mutual exchange [. . .] this sort of justice, namely reciprocity in accordance with a proportion rather than with arithmetic equality, [. . .] [is the thing by which] the city holds together [. . .] for [. . .] it is by mutual contribution that men hold together. (1132^{b}–1133^{a})

He touches on the same point in the *Politics*:

> The parts which are to constitute a single organic whole must be different in kind. And thus it is the principle of reciprocal equality which is the preservative of every *polis*, as I have already stated in the *Ethics*; for this principle necessarily obtains even in a society of free and equal persons. (*Politics*, II.ii, 1261^{a})

For Aristotle, each act of exchange that accords with justice in transactions reaffirms the values that the community sets on its various members and on their products and services. Reciprocity upholds the norms through which the community is bound together into one entity. Similarly, each act of corrective justice, whether it is applied to voluntary transactions that have gone awry or to involuntary transactions, helps to sustain the bonds that hold the association together by enforcing its underlying norms and understandings of just and unjust actions. Aristotle did not imagine that we can make judgments about the justice or injustice of existing laws on the basis of an eternal and immutable natural law, because he did not believe that such a law for political and legal matters exists; in fact he seems not even to have conceived this idea of natural law. But he did believe that the concept of reciprocity supplies a standard to which we should appeal in assessing the justice or injustice of laws, because the well-being of every *polis* depends on the maintenance of relations of reciprocity.

V

Aristotle's writings repeatedly confirm that, in his view, the concept of justice applies primarily to relations among men who are free and relatively equal to each other. He contrasts these relations sharply and consistently with those that obtain among categorical unequals. Recall one of the key statements in his discussion of justice in the unqualified sense: "People seek either to return evil for evil – for otherwise they consider themselves reduced to slaves – or to repay good with good, for otherwise there is no mutual contribution [. . .]" (1132^b–1133^a). Healthy relations among equals are rooted in the practice of reciprocity, a practice that fosters a sense of community among men who are relative equals, yet who differ in the ways in which they are capable of contributing to their common life. For Aristotle, the practice of reciprocity binds together the political community.

Aristotle's conceptions both of justice and of the kind of community through which a healthy political association is constituted stand in sharp contrast to Plato's ideas on these matters. Just as he implicitly criticizes Plato's insistence that justice must be *one* and only one thing by opening his own discussion of justice with an account of the different kinds of things that justice can be, he also criticizes Plato for arguing that the best kind of political community is the kind that attains the greatest possible unity. On the contrary, in his *Politics* Aristotle argues that "it is evident, however, that, as a *polis* advances and becomes more of a unit, it will cease to be a *polis* at all" (II.ii, 1261ᵃ). A political community must be composed of different kinds of men with different capacities. Because they are of different kinds, those men must be bound together through relationships of reciprocity that acknowledge and strengthen the norms on which the community is based.

We see that Aristotle make a related argument, accompanied by a similar criticism of Plato, in his discussion of political rule. Recapitulating Plato's view, Aristotle recites the following:

> As it is best that this should be the case, i.e. that a man who is a cobbler or carpenter should be so always, so too in the political association it is obviously best that the same persons should, if possible, be perpetual rulers. (II.ii, 1261ᵃ)

Turning to his own view, however, he observes:

> Where, however, this is impossible owing to the natural equality of all the citizens, and at the same time justice demands that rule, whether it be a privilege or a burden, should be shared by all alike, in these cases an attempt is made to imitate the condition of original dissimilarity by the alternate rule and submission of those who are equals. Here there are always some persons in a position of rule and others of subjection; *but* the rulers of one time are the subjects of another and vice versa, as though their actual personality had been changed. (II.ii, 1261ᵃ)

Reciprocity plays a key role in Aristotle's conception of ruling – in ruling and being ruled in turn by one's equals – as well as in his theory of justice in transactions. In both cases, reciprocity plays a central role in maintaining community among men who are relative equals, but who differ in kind. In Aristotle's view, a healthy political community – a true *polis* – is one that brings together different kinds of men in a communion of interests that is bound together by common norms.

Although Aristotle applies the concept of justice primarily to relations among men who are free and relatively equal to each other, he agrees with Plato that a healthy association among categorical unequals is based on relations of command and obedience. Reciprocity among relative equals on the one hand and hierarchy between categorical unequals on the other are the two fundamental types of human relations for Aristotle.

Despite the fact that relations among equals are at the focus of his theory of justice, Aristotle also applies the concept of justice, albeit in a qualified sense, to relations among categorical unequals, which in his view are by nature hierarchical. "There is no injustice in the strict sense of the word towards what is one's own," because "the slave and the child, until he reaches a certain age and becomes independent, are as it were parts of oneself [. . .] [and] no one deliberately chooses to harm oneself" (*Nicomachean Ethics*, 1134^{b}). Here Aristotle restates his central theme that justice in its core sense "depends upon law, and subsists only among those with whom law is a natural institution, that is to say [. . .] those who have equality in ruling and being ruled" (1134^{b}). Yet there is a significant sense in which the concept of justice also applies to the relations between a male head of household and the various members of that household. Within the household, in Aristotle's view, the relation between husband and wife most nearly resembles the reciprocal relations among free and equal citizens, since women, though not as well endowed with reason as men, are considerably better endowed than children or those who are deficient enough in rationality to be deemed slaves by nature. Still, Aristotle concludes that what is just for the master of a slave and for the father of a child is similar to, though not identical with, what is just in the relations among free and equal men.

Aristotle is more explicit about the way in which the relations between master and slave or father and child differ from those among free and equal men than he is about the similarities between these relations. Hence the content of the kind of justice he envisages among categorical unequals is largely a matter for conjecture. His main contention seems to be that there is a similitude of justice in the relations among categorical unequals because the superior party in that relation cannot rationally intend harm toward the inferior party.

In the closing argument of his book on justice (Book V of the *Nicomachean Ethics*), Aristotle extends this similitude to the relation between the rational and the irrational parts of a person. He notes that it is possible for one part of the soul to frustrate the desires of the other parts. Alluding to Plato, he observes that some people infer that "these parts [. . .] may have a sort of justice with one another like that between ruler and subject" (1138^b). While Aristotle is wholly in accord with Plato's view that it is right for the rational part of the soul to rule over the irrational part, the central point of his allusion to Plato's conception of justice is, once again, to dissociate his own theory from that of his teacher. Plato applies the concept of justice first and foremost to the hierarchical relation between the parts of the soul, and only secondarily (and by analogy) to the hierarchical relation between those who are qualified to rule and those who are fit to be ruled. He bestows only cursory notice on questions having to do with the relations among equals and takes little interest in the subject of worldly interests. Although for Plato the *objective* of justice is the attainment of wisdom, the core of his *conception* of justice is a description of right relations of command and obedience.

Aristotle's theory of justice inverts these emphases. For him, the concept of justice applies primarily to relations among men who are free and equal and who have diverse capabilities, which enable them to contribute to the political community in different ways. That concept can be applied also to relations among categorical unequals, but only in a qualified sense, and it can be applied to the relations among the parts of the self in an even more qualified or extended sense. Justice is anchored not to a conception of proper relations of command and obedience, but to the concept of reciprocity.

For Plato, as Aristotle intimates (*Politics* 1261[a]), the *polis* is a highly hierarchical affair, rather like a military body. Plato's conception of justice reflects this hierarchical understanding of the political community. For Aristotle, in contrast, the *polis* is a community of relative equals, none of whom is entitled by nature to command the others, and each of whom should participate in ruling and being ruled in turn. His conception of justice, which is based on the concept of proportional reciprocity in the cases of justice in transactions and distributive justice and on balanced reciprocity in the case of corrective justice for both voluntary and involuntary transactions, is a product of his sharply different understanding of a political community.

In a broad sense, teleology played a far larger role in Aristotle's thinking than it did in Plato's. Aristotle's philosophy was deeply affected by his early training in biology, and his familiarity with life processes that led individual specimens of a species to grow into pre-established forms shaped his approach to a host of other subjects, including politics. Nevertheless, within the framework of a broad contrast between conceptions of justice that are founded on the concept of reciprocity – the concept that is at the base of all significant ideas about justice prior to the advent of Greek philosophy – and conceptions like that of Plato, who construes justice in relation to the attainment of a goal or ideal, it is Plato who is the more evidently teleological thinker and Aristotle who is the advocate of reciprocity as the proper basis for thinking about justice. Aristotle articulated a new and immensely important theory of justice, but he did so by elaborating on the concept of reciprocity, which had played a central role in every major set of ideas about justice except Plato's (and had played the role of a central foil even in Plato's thought). Where Plato's theory constituted a broad attack on conventional understandings of justice,

Aristotle's theory was framed with considerable respect for intuitions about reciprocity that are integral to the sense of justice.

With the formulation of his theory, Aristotle had created places for many of the principal ideas that would prevail in the later history of western thinking about justice. He developed a systematic, albeit schematic, framework for thinking about issues of distributive justice, a subject that had received scant attention before him. He offered a lucid analysis of the terms on which corrections to voluntary transactions that had gone awry should be made, as well as of the fundamentals of retributive justice. He provided an insightful analysis of justice in transactions. At the base of all these ideas lies a conception of reciprocity that would eventually come to be known as the contribution principle (or the principle of desert). For many centuries, this principle maintained a powerful hold on the imagination of those people who would eventually come to be known as Europeans. Indeed it retains a strong grip on the imagination of many people today, despite the fact that its intellectual foundations have been shaken by modern insights – particularly Adam Smith's insight that virtually all the wealth generated in societies with complex divisions of labor is better understood as a social product than as the sum of the products of individual producers, taken singly. In Aristotle's theory we can discern many of the principal concepts, categories, and claims about justice that have shaped western ideas down to the present day. No single thinker has had a greater impact on our ideas about justice.

Chapter 4

From Nature to Artifice: Aristotle to Hobbes

While the remarkable achievement that is Aristotle's theory of justice played a formative role in the history of ideas about this subject and in some respects remains vital today, that theory is founded on three major assumptions that nowadays may seem to some people as archaic as the Greek vases that adorn many of the world's great museums. First, Aristotle assumed that the sole locus of justice is the specific form of political community known in Greece in his time as the *polis*. His work offers only the barest suggestion that the concept of justice can be applied to relations among persons outside the *polis* and no suggestion at all that it can or should be applied beyond the Greek world. Second, like Plato and many other thinkers who preceded him, Aristotle believed that the diversity of human beings' natural capacities is so great as to be categorical. It seemed to him to follow that people whose capacities differ categorically from those of others should be assigned to sharply different functional roles in society, roles to which distinctive responsibilities and entitlements should be attached and which entailed different and unequal standing in a social order. Finally, Aristotle assumed that the *polis* is natural in the sense that the *polis* and its constituent parts are endowed by nature with purposes that bestow upon them their distinctive contours and characteristics.

A Brief History of Justice, First Edition. David Johnston.

In a generalized form, all these assumptions were commonplace prior to and during Aristotle's lifetime. Babylonians applied the concept of justice only to relations among Babylonians; Greeks applied it only to relations among Greeks, and usually only to relations among the Greek citizens of a given *polis.* Ancient legal codes and literary sources alike accepted hierarchies of power, status, and wealth, usually without question. And, with the notable exception of the sophists, virtually all ancient thinkers considered the primary contours of their respective social worlds to be prescribed by nature or by a non-human agent.

In the centuries that followed Aristotle's immensely productive life, each of these assumptions was challenged and ultimately at least partially displaced from its central place in western political thought. The postulates that emerged in their place have reshaped western ideas about justice dramatically.

I

The inclination to consider only those relations with persons with whom one shares a political or cultural identity to be subject to norms based on justice was universal in the ancient world during and prior to Aristotle's lifetime. In the Hebrew scriptures, for example, the laws that allegedly formed the basis for thinking about justice were said to have been given to the ancient Israelites by their God, as part and parcel of a covenant that established a unique relationship between the two parties – one in which the Israelites agreed to obey God's laws and God promised to make his chosen people a kingdom of priests and a holy nation. It is an emphatic theme in these writings that the Israelites are a special people. Their relations with other peoples are characterized by deception, distrust, and violent conflicts that do not appear to be subject to standards of justice in any ordinary sense. The idea of justice is equally absent from the depictions of relations between Greeks and non-Greeks in ancient Greek literature: these relations, too, are typically marked by deception and conflicts that do not submit to standards of justice. In writings prior to the fourth century BCE, the idea of justice is limited in application to relations among persons who share a significant common bond.

It is true that the Book of Psalms offers some enticing hints of the notion that the justice of the Israelites' God is universal. For example, Psalm 103 includes the following couplet:

> The Lord is righteous in his acts;
> he brings justice to all who have been wronged.

However, the "all" to whom this couplet refers does not evidently apply to all persons in the world. It seems more likely that it is intended to convey the thought that justice applies with full force to those among the Israelites who are weak and oppressed, as well as to the powerful – a thought that is one of the main themes in Hebrew scriptural passages about justice.

Another fascinating passage can be found in Psalm 9:

> The Lord thunders, he sits enthroned for ever:
> he has set up his throne, his judgement-seat.
> He it is who will judge the world with justice
> and try the cause of the peoples fairly.

The suggestion in this passage that the God of the Israelites metes out justice to the peoples of the world universally is explicit. However, this suggestion is immediately preceded by the following lines:

> Thou hast rebuked the nations and overwhelmed the ungodly,
> thou hast blotted out their name for all time.
> The strongholds of the enemy are thrown down for evermore;
> thou hast laid their cities in ruins, all memory of them is lost.

The "justice" portrayed in these lines bears little resemblance to the standards for relations among persons envisaged in the Israelites' laws, which, as we have seen, are based on a norm of balanced reciprocity among equals and imbalanced reciprocity among unequals. God's justice as depicted here entails his obliteration of his enemies. The justice here described is in fact a relation of absolute submission to a God who claims to be all-powerful. It is, in any case, a notion of justice that applies to the relations between God and his created creatures, not to relations among persons.

In Aristotle's writings, too, we find on one occasion a suggestion that, at first glance, seems to contradict the claim that the idea of justice in and prior to his time was applied only to relations among persons who share a political or cultural bond. In his *Politics*, while considering whether the best constitution is one that promotes the life of politics and action or, alternatively, one that promotes the contemplative life, Aristotle observes that some states systematically aspire to exercise despotic authority over their neighbors. He offers Sparta and Crete as examples and points out that, in addition to these, "all the uncivilized peoples which are strong enough to conquer others pay the highest honours to military prowess." He goes on to criticize these views:

> Yet it cannot, perhaps, but appear very strange, to a mind which is ready to reflect, that a statesman should be expected to be able to lay his plans for ruling and dominating border states without any regard for their feelings [. . .] how can it ever be lawful to rule without regard to the right or wrong of what you are doing? [. . .] But when it comes to politics most people appear to believe that mastery is the true statesmanship; and men are not ashamed of behaving to others in ways which they would refuse to acknowledge as just, or even expedient, among themselves. For their own affairs, and among themselves, they want an authority based on justice; but when other men are in question, their interest in justice stops.

The implication of Aristotle's comments is that, if the citizens of states like Sparta and Crete expect just treatment from others, they should be prepared to extend just treatment to those others as well. By associating the practices of such states with those of "uncivilized" peoples, Aristotle means to suggest the backwardness and inadequacy of their views. Although he does not elaborate a theory of international justice, he does make it clear that the concept of justice can be invoked beyond the borders of the political community within which justice achieves its most perfect expression. Even so, we cannot infer from this passage that Aristotle intended to suggest that the idea of justice should be applied outside the Greek world, or to relations between Greeks and non-Greeks, all of whom were "barbarians" in Greek parlance; Aristotle considered them intellectually inferior to the Greeks to the point of being incapable of rational dealings with them. Indeed, by citing Sparta and Crete as his sole examples of cities with despotic ambitions, he creates the impression that he means his observation to apply only to relations among Greek states and persons. For Aristotle, it appears that justice is still a relatively local idea.

This assumption began to change in the hands of the Stoic philosophers – beginning with Zeno of Citium (335–263 BCE), the founder of this doctrine, who was probably entering adolescence around the time of Aristotle's death in 322 BCE. Zeno's *Republic*, the first work of Stoic political philosophy, has not survived, but we can plausibly reconstruct some of its content from scraps of doxography and from references to and quotations from Zeno's thinking in subsequent writings. This work, it appears, continued the tradition and style of political philosophy that Plato had established in his *Republic* and was most likely intended as a kind of answer, from a Spartan point of view, to Plato's claims about the proper constitution of a *polis*. Zeno conceived of the *polis*, in its most perfect form, as a republic of sages. Love was the distinctive element in this political system. But the kind of love that is characteristic of Zeno's republic aims to transcend itself. Zeno's reasoning seems to have gone as follows. The proper object of a wise man's love is someone who is endowed by nature with a capacity for virtue, but who has not yet become virtuous. If the lover (in the Spartan context, Zeno no doubt assumed that both the lover and the beloved would be males) succeeds in helping his beloved develop virtue, the appropriate relationship between the two is then no longer love, but friendship. Ultimately, then, Zeno's city of love transforms itself into a city bound together by friendship and by the virtuous character of its citizens.

Zeno formulated his political philosophy with the distinctive type of Greek political association known as the *polis* in mind, but there is nothing in the logic of his argument to tether his claims to that form, and his followers in the Stoic tradition quickly moved away from the particularistic assumptions within which he framed that argument. For many of these followers, the task was to retain the ideas of community and citizenship they had inherited from the tradition established by Zeno while removing all its contingencies, such as those based on physical proximity or mutual acquaintance. For these Stoics, it was right reason, not the state, that directed individual rational beings to what they should and should not do.

Cicero, a professed Platonist who along with the Roman ruling class generally endorsed Stoic ethical ideas, was a principal spokesperson for this view. Written in the waning days of the classical Roman Republic, his dialogue *De legibus* (*On the Laws*) is an intensely cosmopolitan work, one that anticipates the universalistic aspirations of the Roman Empire about to arise. In this dialogue, Cicero (through the voice of its principal interlocutor, Marcus, who represents Cicero himself) identifies his topic as "the whole subject of universal justice and law," making it clear that he means to transcend the civil law (that is, the particular law of Rome). Justice, he argues, is rooted in "that highest law, which was born eons before any law was written or indeed before any state was established"; it is rooted in nature and, specifically, in the nature of human beings.

Cicero emphasizes that "whatever definition of a human being one adopts is equally valid for all humans" and that, in fact, "there is no dissimilarity within the species." In particular, all human beings share a capacity for reason, through which they are able to draw inferences, make arguments, and conduct discussions. This observation applies to every human being, Roman or barbarian, and is, according to Cicero, the one attribute that distinguishes humans from beasts.

It is true that the fact that all humans share a capacity for reason does not guarantee that all will develop that capacity fully or to the same degree. The capacity for reason is developed through education, and vast discrepancies exist in the quality and extent of the education that different people receive. Those whose education is defective are deficient in acquired reason and, consequently, in virtue – since, for Cicero, virtue is developed through the cultivation of reason. Nevertheless, he insists that "[t]here is no person of any nation who cannot reach virtue with the aid of a guide." All humans have the potential to be equally virtuous, just as all possess the capacity to become fully rational creatures.

According to Cicero, it follows that human beings have been designed by nature to acquire an understanding of justice from one another and to share that understanding with all people. Human beings acquire an understanding of the precepts of justice through the use of their reason. All people share the capacity for reason. This capacity is given to us by nature. Hence, Cicero concludes, justice is natural. It is also universal among human beings. On the one hand, therefore, our relations with *all* human beings – and not merely with our compatriots – are subject to standards of justice. In other words, we are obliged by nature to be just in our dealings with others, regardless of whether we share a bond of political connection or nationality with them; and they, in turn, are similarly obliged to be just toward us. And, on the other hand, there is only *one* justice, one set of precepts or rules of justice that apply equally to all human beings, regardless of their particular institutions and laws. While particular laws may be products of opinion or convention, justice is, to the contrary, rooted in nature. Among human beings, therefore, justice is universal.

This conclusion implies a remarkable reversal in thought. For Aristotle and his predecessors, and indeed for Zeno himself, the idea of justice is applicable only where established and particular bonds between human beings exist. Paradigmatically, the bonds that give rise to obligations of justice for these thinkers are those which tie together the members of a city or a nation. When human beings interact with people with whom they have no pre-existing bonds, their relations with these others are not subject to standards of justice at all.

The revision of the Stoic doctrine of a republic of sages that we can find in Cicero's writings transformed this understanding. It is true that Cicero and even the later Stoics retained the idea of the city as a central trope. Writing long after Cicero's death, Dio Chrysostom produced an especially vivid vision of the "cosmic city," the late Stoic successor to Zeno's original idea of a city of love. But, whereas Zeno's city of love was apparently local, Dio's city was evidently cosmopolitan. At the outset of his 36th ("Borysthenitic") discourse, Dio tells us that he was on an expedition that took him beyond the limits of the Greek world, to the barbarians, when he stopped in Borysthenes – an ancient colony in the Crimea and the locus for his oration. His speech makes it abundantly clear that Borysthenes represents a point of contact between the Greek and the barbarian worlds, a hybrid of dramatically different cultures. The particular location and description of Borysthenes conveys in an ironic fashion the message that Dio wishes us to understand his "city" in a way that is freed of ties to any particular location or culture.

Cicero had in fact already emphasized the universality of the Stoic conception of the city. Toward the end of Book I of *De legibus*, he argues that,

> when he [the person who knows himself] has studied the heaven, lands, seas, and the nature of all things [. . .] and when he has (so to speak) got a grip on the god who guides and rules these things and has recognized that he is not bound by human walls as the citizen of one particular spot but a citizen of the whole world as if it were a single city – then in this perception and understanding of nature, by the immortal gods, how he will know himself [. . .]!

By the first century BCE at the latest, then, the notion that standards of justice apply only within a relatively local setting – that is, to relations among persons who are tied together by political, cultural, or some other kind of particular bond – had evolved within the Stoic tradition into the idea of a universal justice that applies to relations among all human beings (or, for some writers, among all rational creatures).

The assumption that the concept of justice can and should be applied to relations among all human beings acquired a central place in western thought through the impact of writings and movements that were developed within the Roman Empire. The most important of these writings were the works of later Roman law, especially the *Digest* compiled under the Byzantine Emperor Justinian in the sixth century CE. The *Digest* codified an overarching distinction between the particular laws of nations, especially the laws of Rome itself, which had been framed and adopted by human beings, and the natural law, which was conceived of much as Cicero had imagined it: as the laws that can be derived directly from reason and applied universally. After the collapse of the Roman Empire in the west a century before Justinian's time, the influence of Roman law on actual legal practices had declined, as it competed for centuries with several major versions of barbarian law. Yet as a source of western thought Roman law began to regain influence through the *Digest* and other collections of Roman legal materials in the first centuries of the second millennium.

One of the principal conduits of this influence was the Christian church, which had originated in a movement that began inside the Roman Empire during the first century after Caesar Augustus attained pre-eminence. Christianity was the first great evangelical religion, a religion that sought and continues to seek universal allegiance, much as the Roman Empire itself had done. A central message of the Christian scriptures, especially the Gospels, is that *anyone*, whether Jew or Gentile and no matter how lowly, is capable of receiving the Holy Spirit that had empowered Jesus of Nazareth. Over and over again, the Gospels relate how Jesus, "armed with the power of the Spirit," was able to accomplish heroic feats that astonished all those who witnessed them. The language in which these narratives are couched – in this passage, with the words "armed" and "power" – should not be taken lightly; these words are not intended to serve as flaccid metaphors. Nor should the genuine universalism of the Christian message be overlooked. Although the Christian movement eventually led to the creation of an enormously hierarchical church organization, that organization continued to carry the basic Christian message that all human beings, regardless of their origin or station in life, are equally able to receive the Holy Spirit and to acquire the power that results from that reception by following the admonitions and example of Jesus.

It is primarily from this source that the postulate that justice should be conceived in a universalistic rather than a particularistic way was transmitted to early modern and modern moral and political philosophy. This postulate played an enormous role in the natural law tradition as well as in its near relation, the tradition of natural rights theories. But its impact is not confined to those traditions. The idea that justice has a content that is given by nature is not identical with the idea of universal justice, however closely these two ideas have been intertwined in some lines of thinking. Many thinkers who have dispensed altogether with the ideas of natural law and natural rights, including the utilitarians of the eighteenth century and beyond, have nonetheless embraced the claim that the idea of justice must have a content that applies to all human beings, universally.

The widespread acceptance in modern moral and political philosophy of this claim did not result in a complete defeat of its earlier competitor. Influential modern philosophers have championed the notion that many, if not all, duties of justice are contingent on the existence of significant, non-universal bonds among persons. Even so, the advent of the idea of universal justice planted a seed that has the potential to transform western ideas about justice decisively. Whether this seed will be cultivated in the future more systematically and successfully than it has been in the past is the single most important question about justice we face today.

II

The assumption that human beings differ categorically in capabilities and that they should be assigned to different and unequal functional roles in a social order on the basis of those capabilities, while not universal, was widespread in early ancient thought. As we saw in Chapter 1, ancient sources uniformly endorse hierarchies of power, status, and wealth as embodiments of a just political order. Early ancient legal codes recognize these hierarchies by prescribing punishments for wrongdoing whose severity is directly proportional to the status of the victims and inversely proportional to that of the wrongdoers. Ancient non-legal writings likewise recognize and accept the idea that human beings differ from one another categorically in capabilities and standing. The most striking instance of this recognition in the ancient sources is the general acceptance of the assumption that the institution of slavery poses no quandaries as a matter of justice. Women were likewise accorded a position of radical inferiority to men in ancient customs and writings. The view that justice is embodied in some instances in relations of imbalanced reciprocity – a view that is implicit in virtually all ancient texts touching on legal, political, and social matters – was linked with the assumption that human beings are unequal in capabilities and status.

Aristotle endorsed this assumption wholeheartedly, even though he also held, as Cicero did later, that human beings share in common the capacity to communicate by way of language. In the early pages of his *Politics* he declares (in a passage quoted in part in the Prologue, above):

> That Man is a political animal in a higher sense than a bee or any other gregarious creature is evident from the fact that Nature, as we are fond of asserting, creates nothing without a purpose and man is the only animal endowed with speech [. . .]

> The object of speech [. . .] is to indicate advantage and disadvantage and therefore also justice and injustice. For it is a special characteristic which distinguishes man from all other animals that he alone enjoys perception of good and evil, justice and injustice and the like. These are the principles of that association which constitutes a household or a *polis*.

This passage suggests that the capacity to use and to understand language is distinctive of and common to humans. Yet, despite this common attribute, Aristotle argued forcefully that the differences in humans' other attributes, including the capacity for reason, are sharp. So marked, indeed, are these differences that some human beings are naturally destined to be slaves, while others possess the capacities that make it natural and appropriate for them to be masters.

It is clear in Aristotle's works, in contrast to many ancient legal codes and other writings, that his belief that some human beings are suited by nature to be slaves was not an unexamined assumption. At the outset of his discussion of slavery, he mentions the hypothesis that all slavery is contrary to nature. Aristotle rejects this hypothesis. In his view there is a kind of man who "is only so far a rational being as to understand reason without himself possessing it," and it is this kind of man who is intended by nature to be a slave. Just as "it is natural and expedient for the body to be ruled by the soul," so is it natural and just, as well as beneficial to slaves, that they be ruled by masters whose capacity for reason is greater than their own. Indeed, so wide is the chasm in capacities between masters and slaves that Aristotle compares it to the difference between humans and non-human animals:

> Hence wherever there are two classes of persons, and the one are as far inferior to the other as the body to the soul or a beast to a man – and this is the condition of all whose function is mere physical service and who are incapable of anything better – these persons are natural slaves and for them as truly as for the body or for beasts a life of slavish subjection is advantageous.

Aristotle concludes with the observation: "It is evident then that there is a class of persons, some of whom are naturally free and the others naturally slaves, persons for whom the condition of slavery is alike expedient and just."

The distinction between masters and slaves is not the only major natural inequality among human beings to be recognized in Aristotle's work. Breaking once again with his mentor Plato, Aristotle also argued that women are by nature and without exception inferior in rationality to (free) men. In a later era, one of the most iconic representations of justice would depict a woman holding a scale while blindfolded. This image is evocative both of the idea of balanced reciprocity and of a refusal to accept the notion that there exist categorical differences between human beings that are relevant to questions of justice. In Aristotle's time, that era had not yet appeared on the horizon.

The Stoic tradition of thought played a significant role in a process of ideological evolution that eventually undermined the assumptions that human beings differ from each other categorically in capabilities and that people should accordingly be assigned to different and unequal functional roles, much as it played a key part in developing the idea of universal justice. Both Aristotle and Cicero linked the capacity to reason tightly with the capacity to use language. However, while Aristotle maintained that there is a category of human beings who are *both* like other humans in their capacity for language *and* like, or very nearly like, non-human animals by virtue of their lack of a capacity to participate fully in reason, Cicero inferred, to the contrary, that all humans, by virtue of their common capacity for language, are equally endowed with a capacity for reason. In fact Cicero is emphatic that no categorical distinction exists between the degrees of rationality of which human beings are capable:

> Reason, the one thing by which we stand above the beasts, through which we are capable of drawing inferences, making arguments, refuting others, conducting discussions and demonstrations – reason

> is shared by all, and though it differs in the particulars of knowledge, it is the same in the capacity to learn. All the same things are grasped by the senses; and the things that are impressed upon the mind, the rudiments of understanding which I mentioned before, are impressed similarly on all humans, and language, the interpreter of the mind, may differ in words but is identical in ideas.

Despite this seemingly ringing endorsement of the idea that human beings share equally in the capacity for reason, Cicero does not renounce the institution of slavery. Although he appears to reject *categorical* distinctions in rationality among human beings, he affirms that human beings differ sharply in their attainments and, consequently, in their suitability for command. In a fragment preserved in the writings of St. Augustine, Cicero says:

> Do we not see that the best people are given the right to rule by nature herself, with the greatest benefit to the weak? Why then does god rule over man, the mind over the body, reason over desire, anger, and the other flawed portions of the mind?

For Cicero, the difference between the "best" and the "weak" is sufficient to justify the relation of command and obedience that is codified in the practice of slavery.

By invoking the same analogies Aristotle had deployed – god over man, mind (or soul) over body, reason over desire – Cicero endorses a line of reasoning that seems indistinguishable from that of his influential Greek predecessor. Yet a subtle difference divides these two ancient thinkers. For Aristotle, the institution of slavery is justified by a categorical distinction between human beings that is rooted in nature. For Cicero, it is justified by a non-categorical distinction between those who are stronger (in intellect or decision-making acumen) and those who are weak. While the set of ideas that appeared to Aristotle to offer a natural basis for the institution of slavery had not disappeared in the three centuries that separate these two thinkers, in Cicero's thinking those ideas had evolved in a way that left that justification on shakier ground, even if it did not undermine the practice of slavery itself.

By the time the *Digest* of Roman law was assembled in the sixth century CE, this evolution had reached a pivotal juncture. While that work questions neither the fact nor the legitimacy of the institution of slavery, in at least one place it squarely rejects the claim that slavery exists by nature. Quoting from Florentinus' *Institutes*, the *Digest* asserts: "Slavery is an institution of the *jus gentium* [the human-made 'law of nations,' as distinct from the law of nature], whereby someone is *against nature* made subject to the ownership of another."

In the west, the institution of slavery survived well into the modern era, as did the legally enforced subordination of women and, more generally, the assumption that people differ from one another categorically in natural capabilities and in consequent civil status. Yet the seeds of doubt, both about these practices and about the underlying assumption, had been sowed.

These seeds were watered through the same channels that transmitted the idea of universal justice from the Roman Empire to the early modern world, namely the *Digest* and other compilations of Roman legal thinking on the one hand, and the doctrines, practices, and institutions of the Christian church on the other. Although the Catholic church grew over the centuries into an immensely hierarchical institution, that institution was rooted in the message that all human beings, no matter how lowly, are capable of receiving the Holy Spirit and of being granted salvation through the grace of God. In fact, the Christian scriptures suggest that the poor and the weak may be more likely to receive God's grace than the wealthy and the powerful, who are far more likely to be corrupted by worldly temptations. According to the Gospel according to Matthew, Jesus said to his disciples that "it is easier for a camel to pass through the eye of a needle than for a rich man to enter the kingdom of God." The Christian message that anyone is capable of receiving the Holy Spirit by which

Jesus had been empowered was in an important sense an egalitarian message, as well as a universalistic one.

In the process of cultivating the seeds of new, egalitarian assumptions about human beings, the ideology of Christianity also contributed to a shift in the basis of the conversation about equality and inequality. Aristotle and many other ancient writers had based their conclusions about the different functional roles and unequal responsibilities and privileges that should be allotted to human beings on views about their diverse capabilities, and specifically on the different functions that human beings are suited to perform for one another. Christianity, by contrast, is an otherworldly religion that trains its focus tightly on the relationship of each human being with God. In this light, human capabilities of the sort that had interested the ancient philosophers seemed to be of little consequence. In effect, Christian thinkers insisted on changing the subject of conversation, from the diverse *capabilities* of human beings to their potentially equal *worth* in the sight of God.

In the early modern era, this shift in the subject of conversation had acquired enough strength and breadth to begin to cause the foundations of the assumption of natural inequality to crumble. Nowhere in early modern thought are the results of this process of disintegration more evident than in the work of Thomas Hobbes. Writing in the seventeenth century, Hobbes is best known for his claim, in *Leviathan*, that no state can enjoy longlasting internal peace unless it is ruled by an "absolute and arbitrary" sovereign power. This claim was not itself novel. Hobbes was living in an age of absolutism, and many other writers of his time concluded that strong or absolute rulers were needed to quell the disturbances and rebellions that arose regularly in their states. What was more distinctive was the argument Hobbes developed to support this claim. Unlike most defenders of absolutism, Hobbes based his argument on radically individualistic premises. In his view, each human being has a "right of nature" that gives him (or her) "the liberty [. . .] to use his own power, as he will himself, for the preservation of his own nature, that is to say, of his own life, and consequently of doing anything which in his own judgment and reason he shall conceive to be the aptest means thereunto." Since each person is entitled by nature to this extensive liberty, the only way to create and sustain an absolute ruler is for each member of a nascent state to agree to give up some of his or her natural rights through a contract with the other members that paves the way for the creation of an absolute sovereign.

Since each prospective member of a state (or commonwealth, as Hobbes calls it) begins with a right of nature that is equal to the right every other prospective member possesses, Hobbes maintains that the contractual agreement he envisages will be possible only if each of these persons is willing to acknowledge all the others as his or her equal by nature. In framing this argument, Hobbes takes aim directly at Aristotle:

> I know that Aristotle in the first book of his *Politics*, for a foundation of his doctrine, maketh men by nature, some more worthy to command, meaning the wiser sort (such as he thought himself to be for his philosophy), others to serve (meaning those that had strong bodies, but were not philosophers as he)[. . .]

But this Aristotelian argument, Hobbes asserts, is

> not only against reason, but also against experience. For there are very few so foolish, that had not rather govern themselves, than be governed by others [. . .]

Since the commonwealth or state must be founded on an agreement among all its members, it follows, according to Hobbes, that each of those members must acknowledge every other of them as his or her equal by nature. In the absence of such acknowledgement, it would be virtually impossible to obtain the agreement on which political order and lasting peace depend.

Hobbes was most decidedly *not* arguing here for political or social equality. His argument is rather that political and social inequalities are the products of human laws and institutions, not their presuppositions. Although each human being possesses a right of nature that is equal to every other humans being's right, so that the consent of all is required in order to found a commonwealth that is to govern all, the institutions and practices of that commonwealth, once founded, may be highly inegalitarian.

Nevertheless, Hobbes's claim was momentous in the context of the history of ideas about justice. For it transported us from a world in which human beings were assumed to be highly (and usually categorically) unequal in capabilities bestowed on them by nature – so that no further argument was required to justify the kinds of inequalities in standing and in rights that were codified in laws designed to mete out justice on a basis of imbalanced reciprocity – to one in which legal, political, and social inequalities require justification by virtue of the tension between these inequalities, on the one hand, and, on the other, the postulate that every human being by nature possesses rights that are equal to the rights with which every other human being is endowed, also by nature.

From Hobbes onward, the line of thinking that had eroded the inegalitarian assumptions prevalent in the writings of ancient philosophers led in two directions. Some writers, such as Adam Smith, maintained the ancients' focus on capabilities while insisting, as Hobbes had suggested, that virtually all the differences in character and ability we find between different classes of human beings are products of their societies, of the educational opportunities they make (or fail to make) available, and of their specific division of labor:

> The difference of natural talents in different men is, in reality, much less than we are aware of; and the very different genius which appears to distinguish men of different professions, when grown up to maturity, is not upon many occasions so much the cause, as the effect of the division of labor. The difference between the most dissimilar characters, between a philosopher and a common street porter, for example, seems to arise not so much from nature, as from habit, custom, and education.

With this assertion, Smith brought us to the cusp of a revolution in thought that was to have an enormous impact on modern ideas about justice. If the differences in ability, character, and talent we observe on a daily basis among the diverse members of a society are overwhelmingly the products of social arrangements rather than of natural endowments, how, then, can the differences in fortunes that are aligned with these artificial distinctions be justified? Although Hobbes and (with greater evident reluctance) Smith believed that they could answer this question, their answers were not uniformly accepted by later thinkers, and the questions to which their common view about the natural equality of human beings in capabilities led played a central role in the further evolution of ideas about justice.

This line of thinking was complemented by another, which essentially sets aside questions about human capabilities to assert that all human beings, whatever their capabilities, are entitled to equal consideration in matters of justice because each possesses equal worth. Like Christianity, this latter approach to questions about justice was grounded in otherworldly or, at least, non-empirical ideas. Perhaps the greatest spokesperson of this approach was Immanuel Kant. Before we begin to examine these two modern schools of thought about justice, however, let us turn to a third Aristotelian assumption that came under attack in early modern thought.

III

In the vast bulk of ancient writings that touch on questions of justice, the idea that the primary contours – the terrain – of the social world might be reshaped to conform to a human design never arises. In the *Iliad*, for example, hierarchies of power and status are taken for granted. The drama begins when the great warrior Achilles claims a right to a larger share than he has hitherto received of the spoils of war on the basis of his recognized excellence as a warrior and of his unparalleled contributions to battle. The overall order in which the most powerful and the strongest persons claim entitlement to the greatest shares of goods is accepted as natural and does not appear to be subject to alteration through human efforts. Similarly, in Hebrew scriptures, the terrain of the ancient Israelites' social world is dictated, literally, by the Israelites' God in the form of a highly detailed legal code. Taken as a whole, that code prescribes the attitudes and actions the Israelites may adopt toward their God; the intentions and actions they may adopt toward one another; punishments for wrongdoing; the foods and combinations of them that the Israelites will be permitted to consume – along with a number of other seemingly arcane matters. The thought that the terrain of the social world might be re-graded to accord with a design of strictly human origins seems to have been beyond the imagination or mental horizon of the ancient Israelites and of the archaic and preclassical Greeks.

With the advent of critical, philosophical thinking among the Greeks, slow and gradual as this process had been, this limitation began to fall away. In a text that probably represents one of the earliest recorded arguments about justice, the sophist Protagoras (490–420 BCE) sketches a myth of the origins of all living things, of human civilization, and of justice in human affairs. After explaining that Prometheus had stolen specialized knowledge and fire to give human beings the means of livelihood, he observes that at that point human beings still lacked political knowledge and consequently treated each other unjustly. Zeus then sent Hermes to bring respect and justice to men and order to their cities, and to enable them to establish bonds of friendship. According to Protagoras, Zeus also directed Hermes to distribute these attributes to everyone, in contrast to most forms of knowledge (such as medical knowledge), which typically are reserved to only a few men. In Protagoras' speech, Zeus argues that, unless respect and knowledge are shared by all, there will be no cities. Accordingly, Zeus decrees that "if anyone is incapable of acquiring his share of these two virtues he shall be put to death as a plague to the city."

Although the active characters in Protagoras' story are gods, the story nonetheless suggests that the terrain of the social world must be shaped deliberately if it is to enable human beings to live in justice with one another. A similar sensibility can be found in Herodotus' *Histories*, which come down from roughly the same period (probably the second half of the fifth century BCE) – namely in the anthropological accounts of exotic, non-Greek societies and in a set of imaginary speeches delivered at the court of the king of Persia about the relative merits of three forms of government: monarchy, oligarchy, and democracy. In Herodotus' work we can discern the signs of an historical and social imagination capacious enough to permit the author to stand at least partway outside his own world and to view it from the point of view of someone with a sharply different cultural and political background. The intellectual capacity to re-imagine the contours of the social world seems to have arrived.

In the commercial society that Athens had become in the fifth century, that capacity blossomed. Unquestioned acceptance of the existing contours of society gave way to a cauldron of challenges and criticism, the remnants of which are preserved in a wide range of dramatic, literary, philosophical, and political works. The sophists, in particular, developed the view that political institutions and social arrangements are products of human contrivance and convention rather than being rooted in, and justified through, nature. With this belief, a radical re-imagining of the social world became possible.

In the *Republic*, in fact, Plato engaged in just such a re-imagining. Yet Plato recoiled from the implication that human beings are free to re-conceive and reconstruct their social worlds as they see fit. While he depicts the city to which he devotes the bulk of his discussion as a product of an effort of massive reconstruction directed by philosopher–rulers, his arguments rest on the claim that the design of that city is imbedded in nature. He imagines his philosopher–guardians shaping the inhabitants' culture, habits of thought, and practices so as to make them accord with the idea of justice as a relation of command and obedience between unequals; but, according to Plato, that idea – of justice itself – is given in the nature of things.

These two views – that the basic contours of the social world are given by nature, on the one hand, and, on the other, that the social world is (potentially) an object of free human design – competed with each other long after Plato's death. But the former view seems to have secured the more prominent advocates and ultimately to have prevailed into the second millennium CE. Aristotle was perhaps the most influential of all defenders of this view. In his *Politics*, Aristotle argues as follows:

> If it be allowed that the simple associations, i.e. the family and the village, have a natural existence, so has the *polis* in all cases; for in the *polis* they attain complete development, and nature implies complete development, as the nature of anything, e.g. of a man, a family or a horse, may be defined to be its condition when the process of production is complete [. . .] Thus we see that the *polis* is a natural institution, that man is naturally a political animal.

For Aristotle, the basic contours of the terrain of a *polis* – the set of role definitions that prescribe status entitlements and obligations for each of its major groups and determine its loci of privilege and deprivation, as well as the norms that regulate the relations among its members – are given by nature, in the same sense in which the working parts of a fully mature horse develop by nature. It would be a deeply wrongful act and a violation of nature for human beings to attempt to implement some alternative that had sprung from their imaginations.

Three centuries later, Cicero embraced this view. We have seen above that Cicero departed sharply from Aristotle's views by asserting the concept of universal justice – thereby undermining the privileged position Aristotle accorded to the *polis* – and by moving away from Aristotle's claim that human beings are categorically unequal in capabilities. Despite these differences, Cicero wholeheartedly endorsed the view that we must look to nature to understand the character of justice. The "justice of which I speak is natural," he says, and, likewise, "there is nothing more worthwhile than clearly to understand that we are born for justice and that justice is established not by opinion but by nature."

The view that the basic contours of the social world are determined by nature competed for the next several centuries with the view that those contours can successfully be made to yield to human design. With the collapse of the Roman Empire in the west, however, the sense of confidence in human capabilities that is expressed in the latter idea eroded rapidly. Early medieval writings and practices reveal a sense of the impotence of human beings, taken individually and collectively, in a world whose order and workings appeared to be knowable only to God. This sense of impotence was exhibited, among other places, in the judicial practice of the ordeal, a practice that was a product of Germanic rather than Roman law. Under that law (actually a variegated set of laws, which were applied unevenly over a wide territory) an accused person was often reduced to proving his or her innocence by submitting to an "ordeal" (*ordalium*) such as being thrown into fire or water. While ordeals took various forms, the basic theory behind the ordeal was that it would reveal the will of God. Whether an accused person had knowingly engaged in wrongdoing was not the central issue: an ordeal was supposed to show that it was God's will that an accused person be condemned or not, and hence that person would stand condemned, regardless of his or her actual intentions, knowledge, or acts.

Yet, as early as the tenth century, we can detect signs of a gradual recovery of confidence in the capacities of humans to understand and to bring order to their world, largely through a recovery of Greek and Roman ideas. At the outset of the Middle Ages, Boethius (*c.* 480–524) had conceived the ambition to present Greek learning to a Latin world that had come under siege. Boethius achieved only a small part of his ambition, but he did succeed in making available in Latin the main outlines of Aristotle's system of logic. Some five centuries after Boethius' birth, the scholar Gerbert began lecturing systematically on Boethius' logical treatises, and from Gerbert's time until at least the early twelfth century Boethius was the primary conduit through which scholars became acquainted with logic. By the twelfth century, scholars and practitioners had begun to develop a uniform system of canon law, for which they turned repeatedly to Roman sources. Likewise, many of the texts of ancient Greek philosophy had been rediscovered, at first from Arabic translations that started to percolate through western centers of learning from Arabic Spain, then from original manuscripts hunted by the great humanists; and these texts were translated in quantity from the thirteenth century onward. The combined impacts of logic and law demonstrated that it was possible, through human devices, to discern and to impose order on a world that otherwise appeared chaotic to human eyes. The basis had been laid for a renewal of confidence in the capacities of humans to understand and to bring order to their world.

The effects of this renewal were apparent both in texts of philosophy and literature and in many changes in human practices, small and large, over the next several centuries. In 1215, for example, the Lateran Council forbade priests to take part in the administration of the ordeal, effectively undercutting that practice and forcing those involved in legal proceedings to turn from the apparent certainties of divine judgment to the probabilities that can be arrived at by human agency. The shift in values that resulted was crystallized three centuries later in the writings of Protestant reformers, especially Martin Luther. In contrast to the prevailing teachings and practices of the Catholic church, Luther rejected the most expansive claims of clerical authority and insisted that Christianity is primarily a matter of faith based on a direct relationship between the individual and God. Luther, of course, was a believer in the power of human faith, not of human reason. He had no greater interest in the niceties of Aristotelian logic or in the orderliness of Roman law than his antagonists had. Yet he inherited from these traditions of thought an expansive confidence in the capacities of ordinary individuals to glimpse the truth. Turned in a different direction from what Luther intended, this confidence helped spawn the idea that human beings might be capable of refashioning reality as well as of understanding it.

At least a faint glimmer of this idea is evident in Sir Thomas More's *Utopia*, a work written on the eve of the Protestant Reformation. Ostensibly a traveler's report about a distant island country with strange customs and social arrangements, *Utopia* is in fact an ironic critique of some of the principal institutions and values that permeated English life at the outset of the sixteenth century. Yet More fashions his critique by imagining a society whose institutions and values are designed intentionally by its members to discourage the worst features of human nature and to steer our better features in the most constructive direction possible.

The idea that the basic contours of the social world are a product of human actions and potentially an object of human design rather than being prescribed by nature stood forth center stage in early modern thought, in Hobbes's *Leviathan.* Once again taking aim at Aristotle, Hobbes ridiculed the assumption that political associations are endowed by nature with an end (or, in Aristotelian parlance, a "final cause"). On the contrary, Hobbes argues, a political association is a product of human artifice. That product may be unintended or deliberate, and, if deliberate, it may be ill or well designed. Insofar as political associations can be perfected, that perfection will be achieved through human efforts, human knowledge, and human contrivance, not by allowing the association to grow into some imagined "natural" form.

Hobbes argues that he, in fact, is the first to have discovered how to perfect the design of a political association:

> As I have heard some say that justice is but a word without substance, and that whatsoever a man can by force, or art, acquire to himself... is his own, which I have already shown to be false: so there be also that maintain that there are no grounds, nor principles of reason, to sustain those essential rights which make sovereignty absolute [...]

> Wherein they argue as ill as if the savage people of America should deny there were any grounds or principles of reason so to build a house as to last as long as the materials, because they never yet saw any so well built.

Where Aristotle had drawn an analogy between the *polis* and a horse, Hobbes likens a political association (a commonwealth) to a house and suggests that how well or poorly a house is constructed is a function of the knowledge of its designer and builder:

> Time and industry produce every day new knowledge. And as the art of well building is derived from principles of reason, observed by industrious men that had long studied the nature of materials and the diverse effects of figure and proportion, long after mankind began (though poorly) to build: so, long time after men have begun to constitute commonwealths, imperfect, and apt to relapse into disorder, there may, principles of reason be found out by industrious meditation to make their constitution [. . .] everlasting. And such are those which I have in this discourse set forth.

Not only did Hobbes breathe new life and vigor into the sophists' view that political institutions and social arrangements are products of human convention rather than nature. He added to that view the claim that, with adequate knowledge, those institutions and arrangements can be perfected through human efforts.

This claim became a pillar of western political and social thought from Hobbes's time through to the Enlightenment of the eighteenth century and beyond. Encouraged by the successes of modern science, especially modern mechanical science, from Kepler and Galileo to Isaac Newton, many of the great thinkers of the eighteenth century, from Montesquieu to Rousseau and from Beccaria to Bentham and Condorcet, adopted much the same view about the perfectibility of human institutions through human efforts that Hobbes had proclaimed. This rush of confidence in the capacity of human beings to understand and to bring order to the social world did not go unchallenged. Numerous voices urged a more cautious approach to human affairs, from the common lawyers Coke and Hale in the seventeenth century to the philosopher and political figure Edmund Burke in the late eighteenth century, as well as to many other and later thinkers. The struggle between the relatively cautious and conservative approach to reform of human institutions of these latter thinkers and the bold radicalism of their Enlightenment counterparts has persisted from their time to ours.

Yet the thinkers of the Enlightenment, from Hobbes to Condorcet and beyond (the term "Enlightenment" is usually reserved for a set of eighteenth-century thinkers, though I have stretched it back in time to include Hobbes), had fundamentally changed the constellation of ideas within which questions about justice are mooted. The most decisive impact of that mode of thinking on ideas about justice was to suggest a new question, namely: How can human beings redesign and rebuild the terrain of the social world so as to make that terrain itself just? This question began to emerge as a staple of reflections on justice in the eighteenth century, and it has remained so ever since. It is true that, long after this question was posed, it remained possible for writers to deny that the concept of justice can be applied to the terrain of the social world as a whole, or even to deny that human beings are capable of reshaping that terrain in accordance with any deliberate design. What was not possible for any writer who wished to be taken seriously was to ignore the question.

Chapter 5

The Emergence of Utility

During the half century that began with the appearance of David Hume's *Treatise of Human Nature* (1739) and culminated in the publication of Jeremy Bentham's *Introduction to the Principles of Morals and Legislation* (and in the outbreak of the French Revolution, both in 1789), a school of thought developed that was to leave a lasting impression on every part of the world in which European ideas took hold. Bentham is widely and rightly considered the first rigorous theoretician of the utilitarian school, but his work was built on foundations that had been laid by a long series of writers who adhered to two beliefs they regarded as self-evident: first, that human institutions should promote the well-being of the people who are affected by them; and, second, that the well-being of *all* those people, from the least and lowliest to the most eminent, should be taken into account in any evaluation of how well those institutions serve their prescribed purpose. Many of these thinkers were fervent reformers. Collectively they developed a way of thinking about human institutions and justice that broke not only with Aristotle's assumptions about the naturalness of the *polis* and of human inequality, as Hobbes had done, but also with convictions Aristotle shared with most thinkers before and after him about the importance of reciprocity to justice.

A Brief History of Justice, First Edition. David Johnston.

In addition to Hume and Bentham, I shall here touch upon the writings of Cesare Beccaria and Adam Smith. These writers differ from each other in significant ways. For example, Hume deploys the term "utility" in a way that is distinctive and cannot be assimilated to the usage of Bentham and later utilitarians. Smith's notion of sympathy departs substantially from Hume's; and Smith's entire system of ethics (including his theory of justice) is mediated through the hypothetical figure of an impartial spectator in a way that is unique to his moral philosophy. It is arguable that none of these thinkers except Bentham can be labeled "utilitarian" without major reservations. Nevertheless, as we shall see, these thinkers share several assumptions and objectives that distinguish them as a group from all the writers we have hitherto considered, and they are tied to one another by several lines of critical engagement.

I

Like Hobbes, these thinkers rejected the Aristotelian assumption that the contours or terrain of the social world – of what Hume, following common usage in his time, called "civil society" – are determined by a set of purposes inherent in nature. For Aristotle, as we have seen, these purposes guide the development of a nascent society into a mature one, in the same way in which the purpose inherent in a horse guides the growth of individuals of that species (at least individuals who develop normally) into a fully mature form. In contrast to this view, the progenitors of utilitarianism inherited from Hobbes the notion that the social world is a product of human actions that is subject to improvement by way of human design. For them, Hobbes's analogy between civil society and a house that is well or poorly constructed depending on the knowledge and skills of its designer and builder was far more congenial.

As Hume, who regarded the institution of private property as the foundation of civil society and the basis of the virtue of justice, explains:

> All birds of the same species in every age and country build their nests alike: in this we see the force of instinct. Men in different times and places frame their houses differently: here we perceive the influence of reason and custom. A like inference may be drawn from comparing the instinct of generation and the institution of property.

For Hume the family, which is a product of the (sexual) instinct of generation, is the locus of the most important natural – and essentially instinctive – human relationships, duties, and virtues. It is natural, according to this view, for people to be partial toward their spouses, children, parents, and other near relations, and these various family members stand in a set of natural roles in relation to one another. These roles define the most important of the natural moral duties, and perfect conduct in accordance with these duties would be the result of the perfection of natural moral virtues. Hume placed personal ties of friendship, together with the duties and virtues that accompany them, in the same category as familial bonds, though he believed that the latter are typically stronger than those of friendship. He also believed that human beings naturally develop a degree of sensitivity to the happiness or misery of their fellow beings, though this generalized sympathy was in his view weaker than our attachment to friends and a fortiori still weaker than our family bonds.

The duties and virtues on which civil society is founded stand in stark contrast to these natural attributes. Respect for private property is the principal and the characteristic virtue of civil society; but it is, Hume emphasizes, an "artificial" virtue, because, according to the standards of natural morality, we should seek goods for those whom we love without regard to the possessions or property rights of others. The artificial duties and virtues associated with respect for private property can come to govern human actions effectively – and consequently enable civil society to flourish – only insofar as we successfully confine to a circumscribed *personal* sphere our instinctive inclinations to be partial toward those with whom we have personal ties, thereby creating a distinct *social* sphere within which the artificial duties and virtues can reign supreme. It is within this social sphere that economic behavior and governing institutions, which together comprise civil society, arise.

Hume's discussions of justice are dominated by the subjects of private property, exchange of goods, and contractual agreements. The duties of justice are defined by these practices; and the virtue of justice consists in fidelity to them or in the learned inclination to be faithful to them. The institutions of property, exchange, and contract are all products of human conventions that run against the natural human inclination to favor those with whom one has close personal ties. Hume believed that these conventions are adopted and enforced because people consider them useful despite their artificiality.

Implicit in Hume's discussions of justice, especially in his discussions of the foundations of a right to private property, is the assumption that these institutions can be improved by careful human design. In principle, of course, these institutions are also subject to corruption, by reason of poor design or careless construction. But Hume's tone was optimistic – like that of the entire movement of thought on which the label of "Enlightenment" has been bestowed. In a rhetorical flight, Hume invokes the iconic scientist Isaac Newton, in order to draw a comparison between the role of justice in civil society and that of gravity in relation to the movement of bodies:

> The necessity of justice to the support of society is the sole foundation of that virtue [i.e. the virtue of justice]; and since no moral excellence is more highly esteemed, we may conclude that this circumstance of usefulness has, in general, the strongest energy and most entire command over our sentiments [. . .] It is entirely agreeable to the rules of philosophy and even of common reason, where any principle has been found to have a great force and energy in one instance, to ascribe

> to it a like energy in all similar instances. This indeed is Newton's chief rule of philosophizing.

We now grasp, Hume implies, the forces that drive human beings to behave as they do. From this knowledge we can develop a systematic understanding of the laws of motion that account for human behavior, as well as a set of prescriptions for the fundamental institutions that are capable of enhancing human well-being.

Like Hume, Cesare Beccaria insisted that the institutions and practices that comprise civil society are artificial or conventional, as distinct from natural. It is true that Beccaria opens his work *On Crimes and Punishments* (1764) by acknowledging three sources from which the principles of morals and politics are drawn, placing revelation and natural law alongside human conventions as the sources of, respectively, divine justice, natural justice, and political justice. Yet it is striking that, even though his work purports to be a comprehensive treatise on the subject of the rights and wrongs of crimes and punishments, he excludes both revelation and natural law from its scope, apparently on the ground that these sources are concerned with "that justice which flows from God and whose direct bearing is on the punishments and rewards of the after-life." Justice among human beings is based strictly on conventions to which they have agreed for their mutual benefit. Beccaria goes so far as to suggest that justice is not something "real." Rather, it "is simply a way whereby humans conceive of things, a way which influences beyond measure the happiness of all."

Smith, too, maintained that the social world is constituted by conventions that are products of human actions and of innumerable, expressed or tacit, human agreements; and he believed that that world is subject to improvement through carefully designed and executed reforms, undertaken for the sake of promoting human purposes. Smith differed from Hume about the source of the sentiments that help to uphold justice. Whereas Hume had considered these sentiments artificial, Smith argues as follows in his *Theory of Moral*

Sentiments (1759): "Nature has implanted in the human breast that consciousness of ill-desert, those terrors of merited punishment which attend upon its violation, as the great safe-guards of the association of mankind [...]." While the sentiment of justice is natural, however, the institutions through which it is promoted or enforced, as well as the many other institutions and practices through which human actions are coordinated, are not. The most celebrated example in Smith's corpus, drawn from his *Inquiry into the Nature and Causes of the Wealth of Nations* (1776), is the division of labor. Although the division of labor "is not originally the effect of any human wisdom, which foresees and intends that general opulence to which it gives occasion" – in other words, it is not originally a product of deliberate human design – it is in fact a consequence of countless human agreements concluded over a great many years, some of which have given rise to established customs and practices, some of which have in turn developed into institutions. All these institutions and practices, though not originally the products of deliberate design, are subject to reform and improvement through human intervention aimed at advancing human purposes.

Bentham, a tireless advocate of legal and political reforms, likewise endorsed the broadly Hobbesian claims that the terrain of the social world is a product of human conventions, not of natural purposes, and that this world is, and should be, subject to reconstruction with the aim of promoting human ends. Perhaps the most famous piece of evidence of this view is his claim, in *Anarchical Fallacies* (1823), that "[n]atural rights is simple nonsense: natural and imprescriptible rights, rhetorical nonsense – nonsense upon stilts." Bentham was not, as is sometimes believed, railing against all appeals to the concept of rights. He was simply denying the claim that some rights are inherent in nature. For Bentham, rights, like all the other significant features of the human world of institutions and practices, are products of human conventions.

Hume, Beccaria, Smith, and Bentham also endorsed the proposition that human beings generally are roughly equal in capabilities, as well as equally deserving of consideration from anyone engaged in administering or reforming human institutions or practices. In his essay "Of the original contract" (1748), Hume says:

> When we consider how nearly equal all men are in their bodily force, and even in their mental powers and faculties, till cultivated by education, we must necessarily allow that nothing but their own consent could at first associate them together and subject them to any authority.

In his *Enquiry Concerning the Principles of Morals* (1751), Hume suggests that relations of justice are necessarily relations among people who are at least relative equals to one another, so that, if a species of creatures who were rational, yet sharply inferior to humans in strength of body and mind, were to be intermingled with humans, our relations with the members of that species would be ones of command and obedience, not of justice. This premise is strictly traditional; it goes back at least as far as Thucydides and is central to Aristotle's theory of justice. But Hume draws a conclusion that is diametrically opposed to that reached by Aristotle and innumerable other thinkers. For Aristotle, the implication of this premise is that the proper relations between some categories of human beings are relations of command and obedience, not of justice, since some human beings are naturally inferior to others. For Hume, the implication is the opposite: since virtually all human beings are, approximately, each other's equals in bodily and mental powers, it is appropriate that relations among them should be conducted in a just manner. In his *Enquiry*, Hume immediately goes on to criticize Europeans for throwing off "all restraints of justice and even of humanity" in their treatment of "Indians," which is based on the vain presumption of their (the Europeans') categorical superiority. In like fashion and on similar grounds, he criticizes men in "many nations" for subjecting women to what amounts in practice to slavery. For Hume, these denials of basic human equality are simply unjust.

Similarly, Beccaria seems to endorse the proposition that all human beings are roughly equal in capabilities as well as equally deserving of consideration. For example, in an age when the privilege of being eligible to give testimony in a court of law was rigorously withheld from many people, he argued that any reasonable person, including women, should be accepted as a witness. Beccaria also argued in favor of supplementing judges with jurors selected by lot and endorsed the practice of having every accused person tried by peers. He argued vigorously that noblemen and commoners should be subject to the same forms of punishment, effectively criticizing the practice of imposing fines on the wealthy, who could easily afford to pay, while inflicting corporal punishment on the poor. While Beccaria, who was intensely engaged in efforts at legal reform, did not enunciate a general principle of equality, he seems to have assumed that no human being should be held worthy of greater consideration than any other, at least in matters of law.

As we saw in Chapter 4 above, Smith energetically voiced similar views about human equality. In *Wealth* he argues:

> The difference of natural talents in different men is, in reality, much less than we are aware of [...] The difference between the most dissimilar characters, between a philosopher and a common street porter, for example, seems to arise not so much from nature, as from habit, custom, and education.

Smith was in fact a major champion of the idea that the differences in natural talent among human beings are relatively trivial. Smith was well aware that men who earn their keep by manual labor usually appear to be markedly inferior in mental capacities to those who have benefitted from an extensive education and leisure time. But this appearance is a product of the fact that, in a complex division of labor, "the employment of the far greater part of those who live by labour [...] comes to be confined to a few very simple operations," and this confinement has a seriously degrading effect on the knowledge and intellectual capacities of the working poor. That effect, he observes, can be mitigated only by active governmental intervention geared to provide educational resources and the like – intervention that Smith championed in *The Wealth of Nations.*

Bentham, too, believed that talents are generally distributed in a roughly equal way across human beings and that all persons merit equal consideration:

> What seems very frequently not to occur in these zealous promoters of the public good in the ardour of their zeal is that as a faggot is comprised of sticks, so is the public of individuals: that one individual is as large a portion of the public as another individual: and the happiness of the one as much a portion of the happiness of the public as is the happiness of the other.

The substance of Bentham's claim here is essentially the same as that of John Stuart Mill's much later and more famous proclamation of what he calls Bentham's dictum (though we have no record of these words in Bentham's writings): "Everybody to count for one, nobody for more than one."

II

If the thinkers we are examining here agreed that the contours of the social world are products of human conventions rather than of inherent natural purposes and that those contours are subject to reform in light of human design, what did they think should be the aim of that design? How did justice relate to that design? We know that these proto- and early utilitarians postulated that human beings are roughly equal in capabilities as well as equally deserving of consideration. Taking this postulate as a premise, what ultimate objective should the architects and builders of a social world pursue?

Hume's argument about justice is emblematic of the answers to these questions that would be offered by this entire line of thought. Hume assumes that the proposition that justice is useful to society commands widespread agreement. He undertakes to demonstrate a more radical proposition, namely that "public utility is the *sole* origin of justice, and that reflections on the beneficial consequences of this virtue are the *sole* foundation of its merit." This claim provides a significant clue to Hume's conception of the objectives that should be at the center of the institutions of civil society.

I have noted above that, for Hume, the virtue of justice is defined essentially as respect for private property. For this reason, it is sometimes claimed that Hume's conception of justice is exceptionally narrow. This claim underestimates the centrality, in Hume's view, of the institution of private property to civil society. A brief elaboration of Hume's argument for private property will suggest why he considered that institution to be the foundation of civil society, and at the same time it will clarify his conceptions of utility and justice.

Hume argues as follows:

> We are naturally partial to ourselves and to our friends; but are capable of learning the advantages resulting from a more equitable conduct. Few enjoyments are given us from the open and liberal hand of nature; but by art, labour, and industry, we can extract them in great abundance. Hence the ideas of property become necessary in all civil society; hence justice derives its usefulness to the public; and hence alone arises its merit and moral obligation.

This excerpt, while brief, offers an accurate sketch of Hume's main line of reasoning. The fundamental purposes for which human beings associate with one another in civil society are to secure peace and to obtain the goods that enable them to enjoy life. Nature offers us few of these goods through her "open and liberal hand." Instead we must obtain them by purposeful work, through which we transform the raw materials nature offers into goods fit for human consumption.

However, most people will be reluctant to allocate time and effort to the production of goods, unless they can be assured that they will benefit from their own labors. The institution of private property offers that assurance. When people obtain rights to the goods they have produced or to the land they have occupied, and when a government has been instituted that effectively enforces those rights, people acquire an incentive to be industrious and productive. When enforceable rights to goods or land, obtained through transactions with others, have been added to these rights, then, along with the effective enforcement of promises regarding future transactions (contracts), the foundations for a commercial society – one whose members typically engage in the production of goods for consumption by others, in the reliable expectation that they will enjoy an increased quantity of goods in exchange – have been laid.

In short, in addition to securing peace, the fundamental aim for which people associate among themselves in civil society is to create conditions that are conducive to their enjoyment of life. The institution of private property, along with conventions regulating the practices of exchange and contract, are instrumental to that objective. The virtue of justice is defined by respect for the rights of private property, exchange, and contract; and the inclination to be just – an inclination that is contrary to nature – is inculcated in order to secure the advantages of a society that will generate ample wealth through commerce for the purpose of enhancing human beings' enjoyment of life. Governments are instituted primarily to enforce the rights of private property, which in turn make it possible for a society to create wealth. "The use and tendency of that virtue [justice] is to procure happiness and security," and Hume supposes that the production of goods is one of the principal means that tend to promote happiness.

Adam Smith placed even greater emphasis than Hume on the creation of wealth as a central objective of legislation. Smith disagreed with Hume about the ultimate foundations of civil society and justice. Where Hume offers a strictly naturalistic account of the origins of the institutions and sentiments that constitute civil society, according to which those institutions and sentiments are products of a civilizing process through which human beings gradually learn to adapt themselves in order to obtain the benefits of security and wealth, Smith identifies God as their ultimate source. At the pivot of this difference lies the fact that, while Hume, following Hobbes, dispensed with the idea of final causation, Smith revived the Aristotelian scheme according to which final causes have their appointed place alongside efficient causes in any complete explanation. In a passage that might almost have been penned by Darwin, he remarks:

> In every part of the universe we observe means adjusted with the nicest artifice to the ends which they are intended to produce; and in the mechanism of a plant, or animal body, admire how every thing is contrived for advancing the two great purposes of nature, the support of the individual, and the propagation of the species.

Yet, in a distinctly un-Darwinian move, he goes on to observe that

> in these, and in all such objects, we still distinguish the efficient from the final cause of their several motions and organizations. The digestion of the food, the circulation of the blood, and the secretion of the several juices which are drawn from it, are operations all of them necessary for the great purposes of animal life. Yet we never endeavour to account for them from those purposes as from their efficient causes, nor imagine that the blood circulates, or that the food digests of its own accord, and with a view or intention to the purposes of circulation or digestion.

Smith has no inclination to imagine, as Darwin did after him, that the intricate workings we observe all around us could have come into existence in the absence of some being's intention that they should be as they are. According to Smith's view, the being who intentionally sets these workings into motion is God, who, like a watchmaker, contrives to arrange the innumerable parts, both of nature and of society, to work toward an end that he has determined.

In an implicit criticism of Hume, Smith argues:

> When by natural principles we are led to advance those ends, which a refined and enlightened reason would recommend to us, we are very apt to impute to that reason, as to their efficient cause, the sentiments and actions by which we advance those ends, and to imagine that to be the wisdom of man, which in reality is the wisdom of God.

Smith's target here appears to be Hume's account of the origins of the inclination that enables us to live in accordance with the principles of justice. Like Hume, Smith distinguishes between beneficence and justice. Again like Hume, he believes that, while human beings commonly have strong feelings of beneficence toward their families and friends and weak ones toward others, a powerful inclination to requite the actions of others with justice is far more important for the subsistence of society than beneficence is. Yet Smith parts ways with Hume in his account both of the source and of the content of this inclination. Whereas Hume argued that the sense of justice is learned gradually, as human beings become increasingly aware of its usefulness, Smith insists (in a passage already quoted in part, above) that the sense of justice is implanted in human beings:

> Nature has implanted in the human breast that consciousness of ill-desert, those terrors of merited punishment which attend upon its violation, as the great safe-guards of the association of mankind, to protect the weak, to curb the violent, and to chastise the guilty.

By way of proof, he observes that this innate sense of justice sometimes conflicts with what is required by the public utility. Public utility may demand that a sentinel who falls asleep in wartime be put to death, even if no harm is caused by his negligence, in order to give a powerful disincentive to others to do the same. But an impartial spectator would likely regard the sentinel as an unfortunate victim of circumstances rather than as a vicious offender and would be far more comfortable permitting the sentinel to go unpunished than allowing a murderer to escape punishment. There is often a discrepancy between what the sense of justice demands and what the public utility requires, and in Smith's view this discrepancy counts as evidence in favor of his – and against Hume's – theory of the source and character of the sense of justice.

Yet the final cause that God intended when he implanted the sense of justice as well as other inclinations in human beings is to promote well-being, in large part by bestowing on us motivations that lead us to generate goods for our own enjoyment and that of others. Just as the parts of a watch and the circulatory system of an animal accomplish their purpose without intending to do so and without knowing what that purpose is, human beings are motivated both to punish injustice and to create wealth without understanding the objectives toward which their actions are aimed. In the case of wealth creation, the inclination that leads to this result is the famous "propensity to truck, barter, and exchange one thing for another," a propensity that, according to Smith, "is common to all men, and to be found in no other race of animals." Since people's active benevolence usually extends only far enough to encompass their families and friends, they must look to other motives to provide for the needs and wants that cannot be met within those circles. The motive on which they can rely is the self-interest of others. If people can produce things that are wanted by others and can exchange them for the goods they desire for themselves, they will be able to improve their well-being by doing so. If they can increase their productivity by specializing narrowly, they may be able to reap even greater benefits through exchanges with others. So arises that great division of labor, which Smith identifies as the principal source of wealth in commercial societies.

Even though God has implanted in human beings inclinations that generally work to promote their well-being without requiring their carriers to understand how or why those inclinations are designed to accomplish this end – inclinations that lead a person "by an invisible hand to promote an end which was not part of his intention" – once that design becomes accessible to human intelligence, it is incumbent on legislators and policy makers to promote it. Smith's *Wealth of Nations* is, from beginning to end, a plea for legislation that will support the "system of natural liberty," an early version of the idea of a relatively free market system, which Smith regarded as the best means humans can contrive to generate wealth and thereby enhance human well-being, along with additional legislation and governmental actions designed to correct the adverse effects of that system on the working poor. Smith believed that the principles of justice, which he construed, much as Hume had done, as a set of rules based on respect for the institution of private property, tend to this end. He held that the system of natural liberty does so as well. Hence, while Smith's break with the Aristotelian view that the basic terrain of the social world is a product of inherent natural purposes is far less clear and sharp than the break of the other three thinkers we are considering here, he allies himself with his contemporaries in emphasizing the role that human agency can and should play in re-grading that terrain. The aim of his second and more famous book was to show the renovators of the social world, the legislators (for God was the architect, and human beings, unaware of the designs toward which their actions tended, were the initial builders), how they might design legislation that would abet God's plans for the happiness of human beings by promoting the creation of wealth.

Beccaria, too, championed the claim that the central objective of civil society should be to promote happiness. Hume and Smith trained their sights on achieving this aim by increasing the stock of goods available for human enjoyment. Beccaria, in contrast, focused on minimizing the pains associated with crime and punishment – an area of law and policy to which Hume and Smith gave only cursory notice. Beccaria maintained that existing laws regarding crime and punishment were "the residue of the most barbarous centuries," drawing on the legal codes of the ancient Roman Empire, the customs of the Lombards, and "the rambling volumes of obscure academic interpreters." While laws should be based on contracts among free men, nearly all the laws that have actually existed have been "the tools of the passions of a few men or the offspring of a fleeting and haphazard necessity." To this disarray Beccaria aimed to bring a kind of order that would serve the interests of all members of society rather than merely those of a privileged few.

Beccaria's proposals for legal and penal reform seek to accomplish three aims: to reduce the severity of punishments generally; to equalize punishments across classes of people, from the most privileged to the most deprived; and to channel punishments in directions designed to enhance the happiness of society's members. In a fashion reminiscent of Hobbes, Locke, and other social contract theorists, he argues that society's right to punish its members derives from each member's transfer of a portion of his natural rights to the whole, in the act of creating a civil society. Any punishment that goes beyond the need to preserve the bonds of that society is therefore unjust by nature. Beccaria asserts, for example, that severe punishments can be justified only if they can be shown to contribute positively to the public good – which in his view they rarely do. He argues strongly against the use of torture, which he regards as a relic of the barbarian practice of trial by ordeal, on the ground that this method of obtaining evidence is ineffective as well as unjust. He launches a vigorous polemic against the death penalty, which he views as an act of war on the part of society against the citizen. In one area after another, Beccaria attempts to persuade his readers that many of the practices of punishment that existed in his day are unjustifiably severe, and that (as we saw earlier in this chapter) both privileged and ordinary people should be punished in the same ways, for example by inflicting corporal punishment on privileged offenders too, if such punishment is inflicted on the less fortunate.

Beccaria's basic rule of punishment is that "the harm of punishment should outweigh the good which the criminal can derive from the crime." The rationale for this rule is that the purpose of punishment should be to prevent the criminal from committing additional crimes and to deter others from doing the same. Even though Beccaria offers a contractarian, rights-based account of the right to punish, a view that is in principle backward-looking (since, according to this account, the *right* to punish at any given time is based on events that must have happened prior to that time), his explanation of the *purpose* of punishment is strictly forward-looking:

> It is evident from the simple considerations already set out that the purpose of punishment is not that of tormenting or afflicting any sentient creature, nor of undoing a crime already committed. How can a political body, which as the calm modifier of individual passions should not itself be swayed by passion, harbour this useless cruelty which is the instrument of rage, of fanaticism or of weak tyrants? Can the wailings of a wretch, perhaps, undo what has been done and turn back the clock?

The laws in general and penal laws in particular should be evaluated "from the point of view of whether or not they conduce to *the greatest happiness shared among the greater number.*" It is better, Beccaria observes, to prevent crimes than to punish them. "This is the principal goal of all good legislation, which is the art of guiding men to their greatest happiness."

Jeremy Bentham was the great systematizer of the entire utilitarian approach to legal and institutional reform. Drawing heavily on Hume and acknowledging Beccaria, whose book on penal jurisprudence he called "the first of any account that is uniformly censorial" (in other words, the first book about laws that is critical and evaluative rather than merely expository), Bentham developed a theory that is rigorous and comprehensive and takes as its founding assumption the proposition that the architects, builders, and reformers of a civilized social world should aim to create laws and institutions that will maximize the happiness of its members.

Bentham is famously associated with the principle of utility. In a relatively early work, *A Fragment on Government*, he asserted that "it is the greatest happiness of the greatest number that is the measure of right and wrong." In his later works, Bentham modified this formulation significantly, speaking only of the "greatest happiness principle." Bentham never explained in print the reasons for this change, but it is plausible to surmise that he came to realize that his original statement was ambiguous and therefore lacking in rigor. When told to maximize aggregate happiness as well as to maximize the number of people who are happy, we are left to wonder what to do in cases where these two commands point toward divergent policies. Suppose, for example, the best available way to maximize aggregate happiness is to adopt laws or policies that would make many people extremely happy while making a few miserable, while the best way to distribute happiness to the greatest number of people would not result in maximizing aggregate happiness (perhaps because the happiest people under the latter scheme would not be *as* happy as they would be under the former). Bentham's initial statement of the principle of utility is flawed because it does not tell us which of these courses of action it entails.

Whatever his reasons for this change, Bentham went on to develop a highly systematic utilitarian theory, which has a great deal to say both about the legal and institutional arrangements that are likely to increase the enjoyment of a society's members – the subject on which Hume and Smith focused – and about reforms of criminal and penal law that could minimize the pain societies inflict on their own.

Bentham's theory is widely caricatured and poorly understood. Before touching on its most essential points, I'd like to dispel a few misconceptions about the theory.

First, although he opens his *Introduction to the Principles of Morals and Legislation* by asserting:

> Nature has placed mankind under the governance of two sovereign masters, *pain* and *pleasure*. It is for them alone to point out what we ought to do, as well as to determine what we shall do. On the one hand the standard of right and wrong, on the other the chain of causes and effects, are fastened to their throne [. . .]

– Bentham does not claim that all human beings directly or consciously pursue pleasure as an objective. Like John Stuart Mill after him, Bentham believed that the *object* of a person's actions may be anything whatsoever. Ultimately, he believed, the *cause* of those actions is the pleasure they bring to the person (or the pain they enable him or her to avoid); but Bentham does not maintain that all people deliberately pursue pleasure in all their actions.

Second, Bentham does not hold that *individuals* are under an obligation to seek to maximize social well-being or the happiness of their societies as a whole – to say nothing of the happiness of every person in the world – all or any of the time. The impression that he did hold this view has been fostered both by recent critics of utilitarianism such as John Rawls and by recent global utilitarians like Peter Singer; but this impression is erroneous.

Third and perhaps most importantly, Bentham did not advocate that legislators should attempt to implement the greatest happiness principle directly, by adjusting or fine-tuning the outcomes of legislation and policy to that end. He avoided this direct approach to the maximization of utility for at least two reasons. For one, he did not think that legislators in general are in a position to make accurate calculations of aggregate utility. He recognized that many people have what he called "idiosyncratical values"; in effect, he recognized, at least in a general form, what writers much later would come to call the problem of interpersonal comparisons of utility (or welfare). He was not, in short, the advocate of a simplistic "political arithmetic" he has often been made out to be. Further, Bentham believed that, in general, public utility can best be advanced when legislators lay the legal foundations on which human beings can build a secure pattern of expectations. Like Hume and Smith before him, Bentham was strongly inclined to think that people can best enjoy their lives if they are able to act freely within a stable system of rules, which minimize the contingent surprises that sometimes upset even the best laid of human calculations.

Also like Hume and Smith, Bentham believed that a stable, legally ordered framework is a prerequisite for the development of expectations that are a direct source of a great deal of pleasure (think of the hours people often spend planning and fantasizing about a subtropical holiday, or the time they imagine spending with an intimate friend), as well as for any large scheme of social cooperation (including a complex division of labor) that can yield a great deal of additional pleasure through the creation of goods. Unlike Hume, he argued that such a framework should be informed by what he called a "security-providing principle," which imposes on legislators an obligation to guarantee means of subsistence – the material conditions of freedom – to all members of society who could not provide these for themselves. (Smith did not explicitly argue that legislators have an obligation to provide for people who are so disadvantaged, though it seems clear that he believed such provisions would be good policy). Ultimately, for Bentham as well as for Hume and Smith, a central pillar of any strategy to promote the public utility was to devise a set of rules of property that would lead to the creation of great wealth, though Bentham (contrary to some modern misconceptions) laid a good deal of emphasis on the distribution of wealth as well.

Bentham also endorsed principles of punishment that were strikingly similar to Beccaria's. Bentham's first rule of punishment was that the "*value of the punishment must not be less in any case than what is sufficient to outweigh that of the profit of the offence.*" Since the first purpose of penal legislation should be to deter people from committing crimes, the suffering imposed on a wrongdoer should outweigh the good he can expect to incur from his crime – but, Bentham adds, only by the minimum margin necessary to deter crimes effectively. Bentham's theory of punishment is cut from the same cloth as Beccaria's. While they differ on points of detail, they agree that the objective of any system of criminal and penal law should be to arrange incentives so as to reduce the rate of crime to the lowest possible level, while also inflicting on the perpetrators the smallest amount of pain that may be sufficient to accomplish this aim.

III

The proto-utilitarians and the early utilitarians whose ideas we have considered here agreed, then, that the architects, builders, and renovators of the social world should be guided by the objective of enhancing human well-being, conceived as happiness or enjoyment of life. Beccaria focused on the contributions to this objective that he believed to be attainable through reforms of the criminal and penal laws and practices. Hume and Smith devoted the lion's share of their attentions to the means that could be used to enhance the production of goods for consumption and enjoyment. Bentham picked up both lines of argument and welded them into a general utilitarian theory.

This conception of the objective that should be pursued by those who are in a position to reshape the terrain of the social world was very much in keeping with its times. During the mid- and late eighteenth century in the parts of the world with which these writers were most familiar poverty was commonplace. Periods of famine and starvation were not exceptional. So the importance of maintaining a productive, commercial society that could provide for the needs and some of the wants of its members seemed self-evident to these writers. At the same time, the knowledge required to shape social arrangements in a way that would enhance the production of goods for human enjoyment seemed for the first time in history to be at hand. Hume was not alone among these thinkers in finding inspiration in Newton's apparently definitive grasp of the laws of motion that account for the movements of celestial and terrestrial bodies alike. The idea that a similar grasp of the laws of motion that apply to human societies was within reach appeared to require no great leap of faith, and with those laws in hand there seemed to be no reason to doubt that human beings would be in a position to reconstruct their institutions and practices in a way that would best be suited to meet human needs and wants.

Hume, Beccaria, Smith, and Bentham essentially defined justice by reference to this objective. For Hume, the essence of justice consists of respect for the rights of private property. But private property itself is justified because its adoption enhances the productivity of human societies. Neither Smith nor Bentham wandered far from Hume's conception of justice, although Bentham broadened his definition considerably.

Moreover, Smith raised the stakes by asserting that the premier source of productivity and wealth is a highly developed division of labor, in which producers acquire extremely specialized skills and great efficiency. Like Hume, Smith argued that "[c]ommerce and manufactures can seldom flourish long in any state which does not enjoy a regular administration of justice," which he equated with enforcement of property rights and contracts. But, while Smith agreed with Hume that enforcement of property rights and promises is a necessary basis for any successful commercial society, he went beyond Hume in suggesting the opulence that can flow from a well-developed division of labor. In the opening sentence of his magnum opus, Smith argues as follows: "The greatest improvement in the productive powers of labour, and the greater part of the skill, dexterity, and judgment with which it is any where directed, or applied, seem to have been the effects of the division of labor." The improvement made possible in this way, which can be observed in the developed countries of Europe, is so great, Smith avows, that "the accommodation of an European prince does not always so much exceed that of an industrious and frugal peasant, as the accommodation of the latter exceeds that of many an African king [. . .]."

Smith's confidence in the power of the division of labor to increase productivity spread quickly among political economists and more gradually beyond those circles. His was an epoch-making discovery that recast basic assumptions about the aims of legislation and about the shape a flourishing civil society should take.

Yet, in focusing tightly on the objective of enhancing happiness, these thinkers displaced reciprocity from the center of thinking about justice. To be sure, the idea of justice had been associated with protection of property rights since long before Aristotle's time. But in these earlier incarnations the concept of reciprocity had virtually always been central to the way in which that idea was defined. Corrective justice was thought of as *corrective*, not *ameliorative*. Its aim was not to enhance happiness, nor even to improve well-being conceived in some other way. Rather, as imagined, the aim of corrective justice with reciprocity at its center was to restore an order that had been violated either by forcing an offender to return property that he had wrongly acquired or by inflicting harm on a perpetrator in some proportion to the harm he or she had inflicted on a victim. When Hume and his followers redefined justice as an instrument in the service of utility, they pushed reciprocity to the margins of the idea of justice. Instead of thinking of reciprocity as fundamental to that idea, they re-imagined justice as a tool, whose purpose was either to provide a framework that would encourage the production of goods for human enjoyment or to underpin a set of rules designed to minimize the pain some members of a society inflict on others, or both. This observation is true even of Smith, who argued that retributivist emotions are implanted in human beings by nature, but who ultimately accounted for these emotions by their tendency to promote the public utility and invoked a principle of deterrence much like those which Beccaria and Bentham sketched as the rightful basis for determining the severity of punishments. In the theory of punishment, the notion of retribution – which is one application of the concept of reciprocity – was essentially abandoned. As Beccaria says (in a passage quoted at greater length above), in this re-imagined view, "the purpose of punishment is not that of tormenting or afflicting any sentient creature, nor of undoing a crime already committed [. . .]." Of course, no defender of retributive justice had ever asserted that the purpose of punishment is to undo a crime in the literal sense. In an ethical or rightful sense, however, that is exactly how earlier writers had envisaged that purpose.

At first exposure, the utilitarian conception of justice strikes many people as more sensible and humane than the older view emphasizing reciprocity. Why should people suffer more than they must, or be deprived of goods that might bring them enjoyment? But the utilitarian approach is afflicted with problems of its own. One of the most celebrated alleged problems is that the utilitarian conception would in some circumstances provide a justification for punishing innocent persons. Suppose a vicious crime has been committed. The perpetrator cannot be found, but the crime has received widespread publicity and the public demands that the wrongdoer be identified and punished, to allay its fear that the perpetrator might strike again. This fear is so powerful that it has a paralyzing effect, far beyond any rational response: people refuse to venture from their houses, commerce has dwindled to a trickle, factories and other places of work shut their doors because many people are too frightened to come to work. Under these circumstances, the greater good may be served by falsely identifying someone as the perpetrator, arresting him and either convicting or merely detaining him until calm can be restored. Critics of utilitarianism have often alleged that the utilitarian approach to criminal justice would endorse this scenario and have pointed to this implication as a fatal flaw in the utilitarian approach to justice. Some writers have argued that the most plausible and most widely held versions of utilitarian theory are immune to this charge, but the moves that allegedly insulate that theory from this criticism raise difficult questions of their own, and it is not clear in any case that they succeed.

The pre- and early utilitarian writers we have considered above thought of human beings as free and responsible agents. This is true even of Bentham, who is often wrongly caricatured as someone who considered human beings to be automata, or animals who respond to stimuli in a Pavlovian manner. But these writers did not draw from this conception of persons the inference that Aristotle and many others have drawn, namely that relations of justice among free and responsible persons are relations of reciprocity. Their re-imagination of justice was fundamental. Justice for them took on a teleological cast, as it had done for Plato, whose theory is an outlier in the history of ideas about justice prior to the eighteenth century. The objective they imagined for justice has little in common with the *telos* (goal) Plato conceived. For Plato, justice has to do primarily with the cultivation of rightly ordered souls and secondarily with the construction and maintenance of a city that is oriented toward the cultivation of these souls. The early utilitarian thinkers rejected both Plato's conception of the role of nature in determining the character of justice and his assumptions about categorical human inequality. But they substituted an alternative *telos*, that of aggregate happiness, that was equally inhospitable to the concept of reciprocity. This re-imagining of the idea of justice left a powerful impression, which remains vigorously influential today.

Smith's realization that the division of labor accounts for the bulk of productivity in highly developed commercial societies left its own significant legacy on ideas about justice. For the notion that it is the division of labor itself, rather than the efforts of individual workers taken singly, that accounts for the great bulk of the wealth generated in complex economies seriously undermined the contribution principle, a broad form of which Aristotle had placed close to the heart of thinking about justice and which had remained there ever since his time. Of course, all the goods that are products of labor are ultimately produced by the actions of individual workers, even if those actions are parsed into undetectably small slices. But if the skills and efficiencies that individuals contribute to a production process, whether within a single enterprise or, more importantly, within a society's division of labor as a whole, are made possible only by the fact that innumerable other persons possess and deploy their own specialized skills and achieve their own efficiencies, the goods all these people produce are largely social products rather than merely the creations of individuals. How much sense, then, does it make to base judgments about justice on the contribution principle, when the largest contributions in a complex division of labor are actually made by the division of labor itself? Smith's discovery of the role that the division of labor plays in the creation of wealth set the stage for a series of puzzles about how this social product should be distributed. In essence, that discovery gave rise to the modern problem of social justice.

Chapter 6

Kant's Theory of Justice

I

In the waning years of the century during which the utilitarian tradition took shape, Immanuel Kant produced a vigorous and critical response to that tradition that has remained a fertile alternative source of ideas about justice for over two hundred years. Like the advocates of a utility-based conception of justice, Kant wholeheartedly embraced the assumption that all human beings are of equal worth. On other fundamental points, however, he parted ways with Hume and his successors. Most importantly, Kant emphatically rejected the assumption that the promotion of human enjoyment or happiness can ever serve as a foundation for sound ideas about justice. For Kant, the essential truth about human beings – the truth that is relevant to considerations of justice – is that they are free, rational, and responsible agents. The proto- and early utilitarians did not deny that human beings are (at least potentially) free and rational creatures. However, such attributes did not constitute the basis of these philosophers' ideas about justice. For Kant, in contrast, the postulate that human beings are (potentially) free, rational, and responsible is the foundation of all sound ideas about justice and about morality as a whole.

An example Kant offers in his well-known essay on "Theory and practice" is emblematic of his differences with those who base their

A Brief History of Justice, First Edition. David Johnston.

ideas about justice on the concept of utility. Imagine that a person has been made the trustee of a large estate, the owner of which is deceased and the heirs to which are both ignorant of its existence and independently wealthy in their own right, while also being immensely wasteful and uncharitable. Suppose the trustee and his family of a wife and children are in dire financial straits and that the wealth contained in the estate would be sufficient to relieve them of their distress. Finally, assume that the trustee would be able, if he chose to do so, to appropriate the estate for his family's use without the possibility of his appropriation ever being discovered by the heirs or anyone else. It is clear in this scenario that the trustee would be able to increase the aggregate happiness of the concerned parties, taking into account all the heirs as well as all the members of his own family, by withholding the estate from the heirs and appropriating it for the relief of his family. He would be able to enhance the happiness of his family's members greatly, without diminishing that of the heirs by even the slightest measure. Yet Kant suggests that this act of appropriation would be wrong. The trustee has a duty to distribute the estate in accordance with the will of its deceased owner and would violate that duty by directing the estate to anyone other than the intended heirs. (Notice that Kant's reasoning would lead to the same conclusion if the impoverished persons, whose misery might be relieved if they were to receive some share of the estate, were strangers to the trustee.) Despite the tug some might feel to divert the resources in question from their intended beneficiaries in order to relieve human misery, Kant argues that the trustee's duty to distribute those resources in the manner their owner intended should trump the temptation to divert them for the promotion of happiness. This view has been summarized pithily in the observation that, for Kant, the *right* is (ethically or morally) prior to the *good.*

Kant's fame as one of the great modern philosophers was established once and for all with the publication of his *Critique of Pure Reason* in 1781. His major writings in moral and political philosophy came later, beginning with the *Grounding for the Metaphysics of Morals* in 1785 and culminating in his *Metaphysics of Morals* of 1797. During the nearly two decades he devoted to these writings, Kant elaborated and sharpened his arguments. I shall base my discussion primarily on his writings from the 1790s, including his essays on "Theory and practice" (1793) and "Perpetual peace" (1795), as well as on the *Metaphysics of Morals.*

Kant repeatedly invokes two arguments in rebuttal of the notion that utility can serve as an appropriate basis for reasoning about morality and justice. The first is that any conclusions we might reach by reasoning from the ground of utility would be uncertain. This is the central point of his trusteeship example. Kant argues that the trustee who chooses to decide how to dispose of the estate on the basis of utilitarian consequences would be compelled to estimate the consequences of every possible disposition (for example seizing the estate all at once, using it up gradually, or distributing it to the heirs in the hope that by doing so he could enhance his reputation and ultimately benefit financially from that enhancement) – an exercise that is sure to be inconclusive, leaving the trustee without clear moral guidance. In contrast, he argues, the trustee who chooses to do what (Kant believes) duty requires need have no doubt about the rightful course of action. Even a child of eight or nine, he suggests, can understand how to act in accordance with duty.

Second, Kant also argues that a sound theory of morality cannot be based on happiness, because the causes of happiness vary from person to person, so that only the individual affected is well situated to decide how best to pursue his or her happiness (43 [215]). People must learn from experience what brings them joy, and each person's experience is distinctive to that person. Hence no general (or at least no universal) conclusions about morality can be reached on the basis of happiness – and, in Kant's view, the precepts of morality must by nature be universal, commanding every person in the same way and taking no account of inclinations that vary from person to person. Moreover, Kant argues that it is right for each human being to be allowed to pursue happiness in his own way and wrong to attempt to impose on human beings any particular conception of happiness. He appears to suppose that it is characteristic of the utilitarian approach to attempt to impose happiness in this way.

Neither argument is compelling. The first assumes that there can be no such thing as a genuine conflict of moral duties. For if such conflicts were possible, the precepts of duty (as Kant conceives it) would sometimes fail to yield unambiguous conclusions about a person's rightful course of action. In that case, the alleged advantage of Kant's doctrine of duty over utilitarian reasoning would evaporate, since the conclusions of the former might be as uncertain as those of the latter approach to moral reasoning. Yet Kant's assumption that no genuine conflict of moral duties can arise seems strained. To borrow one of his own examples: Suppose that a person who has been shipwrecked is clinging to a plank to keep from drowning. Another survivor, who, like the first, is exhausted and certain to drown unless he can find some support to keep himself afloat, grabs onto the plank. Unfortunately, the plank is capable of supporting only one of them. Kant argues that it would be wrong for the first survivor to push the second away from the plank in order to save his own life. His reasoning is that it is an "absolute duty" for me not to take the life of another person, who has done me no wrong, but only a "relative duty" for me to preserve my own life. In other words, I am obliged to preserve my own life only if I can do so without committing a crime (that is what makes this duty a relative duty), and (he seems to suppose) pushing the other victim away from the plank would be committing a crime. Yet it is not evident that Kant's conclusion about this example is correct. Why is my duty to save my own life not equal in force to my duty not to deprive another person of life, when only one of us can live? It seems more plausible to conclude that this case is one of a genuine conflict of moral duties. A central reason for Kant's conclusion to the contrary appears to be his determination that his doctrine of morality should foreclose all possibilities for moral ambiguity, even if the basis for that foreclosure in some cases is less than fully persuasive.

His second argument is problematic – in part because it conflates moral principles, which arguably (and certainly in Kant's view) should be unequivocal, with policy prescriptions, which by nature (and for reasons he discusses) often cannot be; and in part because it is based on a misunderstanding of utilitarianism. As we have seen, the advocates of a utility-based conception of justice recognized that the causes of happiness vary from person to person. That recognition is the point of Bentham's notion of "idiosyncratical" values and is fundamental to the policies that Hume, Bentham, and many like-minded thinkers advocated. It follows from this recognition that the policy prescriptions that flow from a utility-based conception of justice cannot be fine-tuned to a pitch at which we can be certain that they will maximize aggregate utility. Even if no other obstacles to this ideal were to arise, the amount of detailed information that would be required to achieve it would be far too great to be practicably obtainable. The utilitarians' response to this problem was to support laws and policies that would enhance the opportunities and resources available to individuals, so that they could use those advantages to pursue happiness in their own, often idiosyncratic ways. This response also effectively deflects the force of the second horn of Kant's argument, which appears to be based on the supposition that utilitarian theories of law and policy prescribe the imposition of happiness of a particular kind. The moral principles advocated by utilitarian thinkers (at least by Bentham, who for this reason is largely regarded as the first fully systematic representative of utilitarianism) were unequivocal, just as Kant believed they should be, even if the policy prescriptions that flowed from these principles were not always so. And these moral principles allowed a great deal of room for individuals to pursue happiness in their own ways.

II

Whatever the weaknesses of Kant's criticisms of utility-based ideas about justice, the real interest of his work lies in his alternative to those ideas. Kant argues that the proper basis of morality and justice is freedom rather than happiness. In order to understand his conception of freedom and the implications for justice that he believes flow from it, we must first peer briefly into the peculiar world of Kant's metaphysics.

In the *Critique of Pure Reason,* Kant had argued that the scope of human knowledge is inevitably limited as a result of the ways in which human beings are (and are not) capable of knowing. Although it is unnecessary and would be unwise to attempt to summarize the argument of this famously esoteric work here, it is important for our purposes to note that, in the course of that argument, Kant develops a distinction between two fundamentally different ways of knowing. The first is the kind of knowing we can have of objects, or possible objects, as they appear, or could appear, to us. We can call the kind of knowledge we gain from this way of knowing *phenomenal knowledge.* (Phenomenal knowledge is roughly the same thing as empirical knowledge: the kind of knowledge we acquire through observations and experience of the world.) Kant argues that all our phenomenal knowledge is shaped a priori by certain universal (and hence inescapable) attributes, which he calls "categories." For example, whenever we conceive of anything in the world (i.e. in the universe), we conceive of it as being situated in space and as having spatial properties. (Even a point that we imagine to occupy no space has the spatial properties of occupying no space and of being located at a particular position in space.) In his view, everything that appears to us does so necessarily in a spatial way. Similarly, everything that appears to us necessarily does so in some relation to time: it has some temporal property. Kant also argues that all phenomenal knowledge – all our knowledge of things as they appear to us – is informed by certain categories through which we associate and disassociate things with one another. For example, everything of which we conceive appears to us to be related to other things by way of causality. Even when we do not know what the causal connections between things are, as we often do not, we think of things as causally connected with other things and we cannot really conceive of them otherwise.

The second way of knowing proposed by Kant is the knowing of things as they are in themselves, that is, as they might be known if they could be shorn of their phenomenal attributes. Kant calls this way of knowing noumenal, after the Greek noun *nous*, which designated intelligence, intellect, or mind, and the related abstract name of action *noesis*, which Plato uses to label the highest and truest form of knowledge.

Plato gives his readers the clear impression that *noesis* is accessible to human beings, though only to those few who possess a philosophical nature and in whom this nature is cultivated to the highest point. For Kant, in contrast, knowledge of things as they are in themselves – *noumenal knowledge* – is inaccessible to humans. We can imagine that this kind of knowledge is possible for some kind of being, but we cannot obtain it and cannot even know (in any strict sense of knowing) that it is in principle accessible to any kind of intelligence at all. The notions of space and time, as well as categories like that of causality, are inherent in the way human beings are able to know. We are not capable of transcending the limitations imposed by those notions and categories; or, at least, we are not capable of obtaining knowledge that transcends them.

According to Kant, human beings have an intense practical interest in reasoning about three things about which we are incapable of obtaining phenomenal (or empirical) knowledge. Those objects are freedom of the will, immortality of the soul, and the existence of God. The first of these objects is central to Kant's theory of justice.

In Kant's view, we can neither prove nor have certain knowledge that human beings possess free will. However, we can show that morality makes sense only if human beings are free. On this basis, we can reasonably *postulate* that human beings are free. And, on the basis of this postulate, we can reason extensively about the content of morality and justice. Through this route we can use reason to discover *laws of freedom*, as Kant calls them, laws that prescribe to us what ought to happen and what our duties are, as contrasted with *laws of nature*, which merely help us to explain what actually does happen in the world. This line of reasoning leads to the "doctrine of duties," in which

> Man can and should be represented in terms of the property of his capacity for freedom, which is wholly supersensible, and so too merely in terms of his *humanity*, his personality independent of physical attributes (*homo noumenon*), as distinguished from the same subject represented as affected by physical attributes, *man* (*homo phaenomenon*). (65 [239])

In other words, we must reason as if we knew that human beings, as they are in themselves, beyond the reach of our phenomenal knowledge, are free agents. And, although I shall not reproduce his line of argument here, for Kant it also follows that we must reason on the assumption that human beings are rational agents. Freedom and rationality are the attributes that form the basis of all moral reasoning; for, in the absence of these attributes, moral reasoning makes no sense.

Kant's theory of justice, then, is based on the same dualism that underpins his entire metaphysics. It is worth noting that this dualism between *homo phaenomenon* and *homo noumenon* is very much like the dualism between body and soul that has played a central role in Christian thinking since its earliest years. The body is the visible self; the soul is the invisible self in which the true personhood of men and women resides. In Christian thought, the soul is by far the more important partner in this pair. Similarly, in Kant's thought, *homo noumenon* plays by far the larger role. The non-physical ("supersensible") attributes of *homo noumenon* are the basis of Kant's theory of justice. Kant was a Protestant Christian, so it should be no surprise that some of the assumptions, concepts, and distinctions that underpin his theory of justice can be found within the large family of Christian thought.

As we have seen, the key postulate on which Kant bases his theory of morality, of which his theory of justice is a part, is that man, viewed as *homo noumenon*, is free. Because the subject of this statement is man viewed as *homo noumenon*, the statement is not an empirical one. In other words, it is not a statement about some attribute of man that we can discover, prove, or disprove through observation. It is rather a statement about the (postulated) essential nature of man. It is also a normative statement, a statement about what ought to be. To say that man viewed as *homo noumenon* is free is, in part, to say that man ought to be free, that man is entitled, or has a right, to be free.

Kant's conception of freedom lies at the heart of his theory of justice. In order to understand that theory, therefore, it is important to grasp that Kant does not endorse the commonplace notion of freedom as lack of constraints on one's actions. Instead, he defines freedom as subjection to no other laws than those which a person gives to himself, either alone or along with others (50 [223]). For him, to be free is not to lack constraints on one's actions, but to be independent of the constraints imposed by the arbitrary wills of others (63 [237–38]).

Moreover, because this idea of freedom is based on man viewed as *homo noumenon* – on the postulated, but not strictly knowable, essential nature of man – the empirical differences that distinguish one person from another have no bearing on the implications of this idea for justice or for the rights of persons. Aristotle seems to have based his assumption that human beings are categorically unequal to one another by nature on the observation that, as an empirical matter, people differ dramatically in capabilities. Hobbes, Hume, and Adam Smith based their claims about the equality of human beings on the assertion that people in fact are roughly equal in capabilities, at least if we set aside the impact of society and differences in education. From a Kantian point of view, observations about people's capabilities or other empirical attributes are irrelevant to matters of rights and justice. From this point of view, each person possesses absolute worth, and does so in equal measure with all other human beings.

III

Kant builds his entire moral theory, including his theory of justice, on the foundation provided by the postulate that man viewed as *homo noumenon* is free. He argues that, by reasoning from that postulate, we can arrive at a single supreme principle of morality, which he calls the "categorical imperative" (CI). The categorical imperative is an *imperative* in the sense that it is a command, in effect an order that describes for people what they can and cannot (should and should not) do. It is *categorical* in the sense that it applies to every person (indeed, to every creature who is free and rational), whatever aspirations, intentions, or objectives that person might have.

We can contrast the categorical imperative with (what Kant calls) "hypothetical imperatives." An imperative, or command, is hypothetical if its applicability to persons is contingent on the particular aspirations, intentions, or objectives they happen to adopt. (A more apt name might be "conditional imperative.") If I acquire the aspiration to become a virtuoso violinist, then it is a hypothetical imperative for me to pursue the means necessary to achieve this aspiration by taking lessons, practicing, and the like. I am under no moral obligation to adopt or to realize this aspiration and many other people do not share it. So this particular hypothetical imperative does not apply to them and applies to me only insofar as I maintain my aspiration. In contrast, categorical imperatives apply with equal force to every person. And they apply with greater force than hypothetical imperatives. Should any conflict arise that would make it impossible for me to obey both a hypothetical imperative and the categorical imperative in a given instance, the categorical imperative takes priority.

Although Kant formulated the categorical imperative in several different ways, he argues that, in reality, one and only one categorical imperative exists. That imperative (in one of its formulations) is: "Act only according to that maxim whereby you can at the same time will that it should become a universal law." According to Kant, the whole theory of justice is derived from this single command.

It has often been asserted that Kant's categorical imperative is a version of the "Golden Rule," which is commonly formulated in the statement: "Do unto others as you would have them do unto you." Certainly the similarities between the two are considerable. Both statements are categorical, in other words unconditional, commands. Both are reflexive, in the sense that both demand that the person to whom they are addressed put himself or herself in the place of another and consider whether a contemplated action would be acceptable to him- or herself in that hypothetical circumstance. Both statements are intended to apply universally to all human beings.

Nevertheless, Kant's statement differs from the Golden Rule as we find it in the Gospel according to Matthew. The Golden Rule is intended to apply to discrete actions. It demands from its addressee to consider how he or she would want others to act toward him or her. Although the categorical imperative also applies to discrete actions, it does so through the intermediary of maxims (maxims are principles or rules of action individuals adopt in pursuit of the objectives, purposes, and projects they happen to choose), and it asks us to judge maxims not on the basis of what we would want to happen to us, but by considering whether we could will that our maxims should become universal laws. The process of reflection Kant demands that we undergo resembles the process commanded in the Golden Rule, but it is more complex, more abstract, and more generalized.

The differences between Kant's formulation of the categorical imperative and the statement of the Golden Rule in the Gospel according to Matthew are significant in the context of Kant's theory of justice. We can gain an inkling of these differences by considering another well-known passage from the Sermon on the Mount – the same speech in which Jesus offers his statement of the Golden Rule. Shortly before he articulates that rule, Jesus observes:

> You have learned that they were told, "An eye for an eye, and a tooth for a tooth." But what I tell you is this: Do not set yourself against the man who wrongs you. If someone slaps you on the right cheek, turn and offer him your left. If a man wants to sue you for your shirt, let him have your coat as well. If a man in authority makes you go one mile, go with him two.

A central message of the Sermon on the Mount, including the Golden Rule, is that it is unjust to do harm to others. This message is strikingly similar to Socrates' argument in the *Republic* that it can never be just to do harm to others, an argument he deploys in order to undermine the several versions of the idea of justice as reciprocity with which he is presented in the opening arguments of Plato's work. The notion that reciprocity is fundamental to justice is as alien to the Sermon on the Mount – and to the message of the Gospels as a whole – as it was to Plato in the *Republic.* Yet, as we shall see, the concept of reciprocity plays an integral and vital role in Kant's theory of justice.

In the formulation cited above, the type of object to which the categorical imperative is intended to apply is ambiguous. The most obvious type of object of the CI's commands is an action. But the CI commands that a person determine whether an action is permissible or not by reflecting on the maxim behind that action, so that, indirectly at least, the CI seems to apply to maxims (principles, rules of action, or types of action) as well. In Kant's moral theory as a whole, the CI is in fact the basis for commands – for moral laws – that apply to both types of objects. The distinction between these two types (actions on the one hand and maxims on the other) is fundamental to a division between the two major branches of his moral theory. As applied to *maxims* (and to the ends or objectives at which those maxims aim), moral laws are called *ethical* laws. Ethical laws constitute prescriptions about the range of intentions and objectives we can rightfully adopt. As applied to *actions*, moral laws are called *juridical* laws (42 [214]). Juridical laws place limits on people's conduct, not on their intentions or objectives. Kant's moral theory as a whole encompasses both types of laws. His theory of justice, however, is concerned solely with juridical laws and with the external actions that can be controlled through them.

Kant believed that it is impossible to force people to adopt intentions. (It also appears to follow from his understanding of freedom that it would be wrongful to force people to adopt intentions, even if it were possible to do so.) For this reason, duties of benevolence, which can be fulfilled only by a person who maintains intentions that are appropriate to those duties, are subject to ethical laws, not to juridical laws (i.e. laws of justice). However, it does not follow that intentions are irrelevant to Kant's theory of justice (as distinct from his ethical theory). According to that theory, public laws may *prohibit* people from acting with certain intentions, even if they may not *require* people to act with any prescribed intentions. For example, a prohibition on premeditated murder according to which that offence is distinguished from negligent homicide by the presence, in the offender, of the intent to commit the act would be consistent with Kant's theory of justice. Kant's theory of justice is designed to apply to actions and only to actions, but intentionality is integral to the description of some actions (such as premeditated murder), and the laws of justice may be directed at these kinds of actions as well as at those to which intentionality is not integral.

IV

Kant's theory of justice, then, is a theory of the moral laws or laws of freedom that place limits on people's external actions, limits that can be coercively enforced. The basis of this theory is the universal principle of right, which is derived from the categorical imperative and which Kant formulates as follows:

> Any action is *right* if it can coexist with everyone's freedom in accordance with a universal law, or if on its maxim the freedom of choice of each can coexist with everyone's freedom in accordance with a universal law. (56 [230])

As Kant quickly suggests, a major point of this principle is to justify the use of coercion to prevent people from hindering the freedom of others.

It is widely believed that Kant thought that legal coercion can be justified *only* to secure freedom. Notice, however, that this is not what his universal principle of right says. It is certainly true that, according to that principle, a coercive action (such as an action to enforce a coercive law) must be *compatible* with everyone's freedom in accordance with a universal law. Yet it does not follow that the only permissible *purpose* or objective of such a coercive action is to secure freedom. It is also important to bear in mind that Kant did not equate freedom with a lack, or even a minimization, of constraints on people's actions. In his view, a person is free if that person is subject only to laws he or she gives to him- or herself, either alone or together with others. Moreover, the relevant lawgiver in his understanding is *homo noumenon* – not *homo phaenomenon.* The person who gives laws to him- or herself is the person shorn of his or her physical attributes, including his or her individualized desires and inclinations, not the person who is laden with those attributes. A person's freedom is not curtailed if that person, as an empirical self – as *homo phaenomenon* – is subject to laws given to him by his "supersensible" self – by *homo noumenon* – nor if those laws are imposed by a decision in which others participate.

Kant draws upon the basic principle of his theory of justice – the universal principle of right – to reach conclusions about two types of subject matters. The first has to do with discrete relations among persons. His label for this subject matter as a whole is *private right,* within which he includes the now familiar subjects of property, transactions, and contracts. He also includes under this heading a discussion of rights over persons. ("Rights over persons" include the rights of a man over his wife, the rights of parents over their children, and the rights of a head of household over its servants. Although Kant believed that all human beings possess absolute worth in equal measure with all others, he also assumed that it is natural for some persons to occupy positions of superiority to others within the family.) The second subject, *public right,* has to do with the civil condition, that is, the state (or civil society, as it had been called in a usage that would soon become anachronistic).

These two subjects are inextricably intertwined. For example, Kant distinguishes between possession and property and argues that property, which is one of the principal components of private right, is possible only in a civil condition in which claims to property rights can be recognized and enforced. Even though he discusses private right before going on to the subject of public right, for Kant there can be no private right outside the civil condition, that is, outside of a state with coercive powers through which the private rights of the citizens can be enforced.

For Kant, a just society is one whose members reciprocally respect each other's rights by refraining from violations of them. Like Hume and his successors, Kant mounted a vigorous defense of the right to private property. He recognized that people acquire property because they expect it to be useful to themselves. But Kant's argument for the rightfulness of private property does not rest on the claim that the institution of private property is useful. For him, that right is based on the freedom that is inherent in human beings as *homines noumena.* The postulate that is fundamental to moral theory – without which, in Kant's view, morality makes no sense – is that human beings possess free will. To say that human beings possess free will is to say that our decisions and actions are not inexorably and exclusively caused by empirical inclinations and desires. It is to say that we are by nature capable of subjecting those actions to our wills, in accordance with laws of freedom. And, just as we are capable of subjecting our actions to our wills, we are also capable of asserting our wills over things. The right of private property is justified by the capacity of human beings to assert their wills over things.

Kant argued that the rights of human beings are rooted in the original right to freedom, which belongs to every human being by virtue of his or her humanity. He also argued that all human beings are inherently equal, in the sense that all are entitled not to be bound by others any more than others can be bound by them (63 [237]). Kant denies, however, that this inherent equality entails a right to equality in possessions. He asserts that all subjects of a state are entitled to being treated as equals by the laws, so that none should receive special privileges or be subject to unfavorable discrimination in legal matters.

He also asserts that every member of a state should be within his rights to compete for whatever positions of privileged status a society may offer, and he explicitly criticizes the institution of hereditary aristocracy. But Kant firmly defends inequality in possessions, among which he includes physical and mental advantages and skills, as well as material possessions in the more usual sense.

Despite Kant's assumption that some human beings are suited, by virtue of their "physical" attributes (their attributes as *homines phaenomena*), to occupy positions of superiority over others for the purpose of decision-making within the family, and despite his defense of inequality (even "the utmost inequality") in possessions, the concept of reciprocity is central to his theory of private right. Indeed, the most fundamental theme of that theory is that just relations among persons who are equal by nature (which, for him, means all persons) are relations of balanced reciprocity in which the relevant point of reference is *homo noumenon*, not *homo phaenomenon*. Here is one representative passage from "Theory and practice":

> Man's *freedom* as a human being, as a principle for the constitution of a commonwealth, can be expressed in the following formula. No-one can compel me to be happy in accordance with his conception of the welfare of others, for each may seek his happiness in whatever way he sees fit, so long as he does not infringe upon the freedom of others to pursue a similar end which can be reconciled with the freedom of everyone else within a workable general law – i.e. *he must accord to others the same right as he enjoys himself.*

Kant's emphasis on reciprocity among persons considered as bearers of free will is in fact evident in his formulations of the categorical imperative and of the universal principle of right. When he highlights universality in those formulations, he is at the same time highlighting reciprocity among persons considered as possessors of the capacity for freedom.

Nowhere is Kant's emphasis on reciprocity plainer than in his theory of punishment, which he discusses under the heading of public right.

Here as elsewhere Kant draws attention to the differences between utilitarian reasoning and his own approach to justice. "Punishment by a court" (here he includes judgments reached against persons for civil wrongs, as well as punishments imposed for criminal violations), he asserts, "can never be inflicted merely as a means to promote some other good for the criminal himself or for civil society. It must always be inflicted upon him only *because he has committed a crime*." The clear target of criticism here is the fact that utilitarian reasoning about justice could lead to the punishment of an innocent person for the sake of the greater good. It might be argued that this concern is directed at a possibility that is merely hypothetical, since utilitarians have not generally defended the punishment of the innocent. But Kant is equally concerned that utilitarian reasoning can lead to punishment that is insufficiently severe to constitute a balanced response to criminal wrongdoing. Indeed he aims some of the most forceful statements in his entire political philosophy at this target:

> The principle of punishment is a categorical imperative, and woe to him who crawls through the windings of eudaemonism [the view that the objective of producing happiness should be at the basis of the principles of morality] in order to discover something that releases the criminal from punishment or even reduces its amount [...]. For if justice goes, there is no longer any value in men's living on earth. (141 [331–32])

As a matter of justice, Kant believed that we should be as concerned about punishing the guilty too lightly as about inflicting undeserved punishment on an innocent person for the sake of an ostensible greater good.

What kind and quantity of punishment does justice demand? Kant's answer is unequivocal. The principle of punishment is

> [n]one other than the principle of equality (in the position of the needle on the scale of justice), to incline no more to one side than to the other. Accordingly, whatever undeserved evil you inflict upon another within

> the people, that you inflict upon yourself [...] only the *law of retribution* (*ius talionis*)[...] can specify definitely the quality and the quantity of punishment. (141 [332])

Kant places himself squarely in the camp of those who hold that the concept of reciprocity forms part of the bedrock on which the idea of justice is based. Moreover, it is clear from his arguments about punishment that he is a firm adherent to the notion of strictly balanced reciprocity. Although he does not insist that punishments inflicted on perpetrators of wrongs should always be identical in kind to the wrongs they have imposed on their victims, his theory of punishment is a very near relation to the biblical teaching of an eye for an eye, a tooth for a tooth.

Ancient writings widely endorse the notion that justice is a matter of balanced reciprocity among equals and of imbalanced reciprocity among unequals. Although Kant accepted inequalities of legitimate power as natural and was a fierce defender of inequalities in possessions (including physical and mental powers, as well as external goods), he adhered closely to the view that the relevant point of reference for thinking about justice is *homo noumenon*, not *homo phaenomenon*, the person conceived as a possessor of the capacity for freedom and as a bearer of rights rather than the individual laden with physical (including psychological) attributes. As possessors of the capacity for freedom, all human beings are equal. For Kant, then, the principle that should underpin punishment for all persons, regardless of rank, should be the principle of balanced reciprocity. Even if the punishment of people who are superior in rank cannot always be identical in kind to the punishment of those who are their inferiors, Kant argues that the punishment that is meted out to privileged persons should be equivalent in its effects to that imposed on ordinary persons (141 [332]). In his view, punishment that is too light – no matter for what reason, whether it be consideration of an ostensible greater good or regard for a person's social rank – is as serious an injustice as punishment that is too harsh (or imposed on an innocent person).

Kant reserves some of his most severe criticism for opponents of capital punishment, singling out Cesare Beccaria by name. Beccaria, he argues, was "moved by overly compassionate feelings of an affected humanity" to indulge in arguments that are nothing but "sophistry and juristic trickery" (143 [334–35]). A person suffers punishment because "he has willed a *punishable action*" (143 [335]). Beccaria's error is to fail to distinguish between *homo noumenon*, the self of pure reason who legislates in accordance with the universal principle of right, and *homo phaenomenon*, the self with physical attributes, including impulses and inclinations, which often lead to transgressions of laws and of the rights of others. Capital punishment is the penalty willed by the rational self in accordance with strict retributive justice on any person who wills and carries out the act of murder. While he wavers occasionally on points of detail, Kant never wavers in his resolution that the principle on which punishment should be based is the principle of balanced reciprocity.

V

By discussing the topic of punishment, we have already dipped into the domain Kant calls public right. Kant was emphatic that punishment can be imposed justly only by a public body, namely the state, even though most of the violations for which punishment is imposed occur in discrete relations among persons (which are the focus of private right). Here as in many other areas of his theory of justice, private right in his view is functionally dependent on public right.

Kant believed, in other words, that it is possible to maintain justice in relations among persons only by entering into the civil condition – that is, by joining with others in a commonwealth (or state). He maintained that human beings are under an absolute duty to enter into that condition:

> a union as an end in itself which they all *ought to share* and which is thus an absolute and primary duty in all external relationships whatsoever among human beings [...] is only found in a society in so far as it constitutes a civil state, i.e. a commonwealth.

So vital, in fact, is the civil condition to justice that anyone who is inclined to avoid membership in a commonwealth and remain in a "natural," pre-political state can rightly be compelled or forced to join the commonwealth.

Kant's main argument for this conclusion is that only by constituting a collective (or general) will backed by great coercive power can people be assured that others will respect their rights. Prior to the creation of such a power, each person possesses the right to do what seems right and good to that person. However, in this pre-political condition, each person is also exposed to the possibility of being constrained by the arbitrary will of others. So the first thing any set of people must do is to join with others to create a state that possesses sufficient power to enforce the rights of its citizens. The only possible kind of just society is a just state.

Kant also maintains that resistance of any kind to the legislative authority of a state, under any circumstance, is absolutely contrary to justice (130–131 [319–320]). As a matter of justice, the subjects of a state owe absolute obedience to its sovereign. His reasoning is that there can be no justice without a state, and that any rebellion, sedition, or resistance to a state constitutes a threat to its very existence, and hence a threat to justice. Writing in a period when the turmoil unleashed by the French Revolution had not yet settled, he does not seem to have considered the possibility that a political regime may be constituted in such a way that it can actually be strengthened by some forms of resistance to public laws and policies rather than being threatened by them.

These claims about the domain of public right – that people can and should justly be forced to join a state if they are reluctant to do so, and that the subjects of a state owe absolute obedience to its ruler – are striking in a political philosophy that is based on the ideas of freedom and of the absolute worth of each person. Here as elsewhere, it is important to bear in mind Kant's distinctive conception of freedom as subjection to no laws other than those that the individual gives him- or herself, either alone or along with others. Freedom is *not* "a warrant to do whatever one wishes unless it means doing injustice to others." Although Kant believed strongly that each person possesses absolute worth in equal measure with all others, his conception of freedom is far more social in character than many readers of his work have realized.

Kant asks us to think of the civil condition or state as the product of an "original contract" agreed upon by those who become members of that state. For him, this contract is an "idea of reason" rather than an empirical or historical fact – much as the idea of *homo noumenon* is an idea of reason – but one that, in his view, is of great practical import. His writings on public right show that, while a large part of the point of the civil condition is to protect the rights of individuals against each other, the terms of the agreement that underpins that condition are much more expansive than this formula might seem to convey.

Kant is firmly opposed to a paternalistic state, by which he means a state that treats its subjects as if they were children incapable of discerning what is useful and what is harmful to them. A state of this kind, however benevolent its intentions, is in his view "the greatest conceivable despotism," for it denies its citizens the fundamental human right to seek happiness in whatever ways they see fit, as long as in doing so they do not infringe on the freedom of others to do likewise. He also appears to be opposed to the redistribution of wealth for the purpose of achieving equality in possessions, since he argues that the equal treatment to which all persons are entitled under the laws of a state is entirely consistent with great inequality in possessions. These observations have led some readers to conclude that Kant was an advocate of a minimal state, one that should do little more than provide for a common defense and enforce personal rights, property rights, and contracts.

The truth is that Kant advocated a state that is much more robust than the minimal state. He did so on the basis of the idea of an original contract, which is the central idea of his theory of justice in the domain of public right. While it may be unjust for a state to redistribute wealth among its citizens for the purpose of equalizing their possessions, the state is not merely allowed, but required as a matter of justice to redistribute wealth whenever that action is necessary for the purpose of meeting needs (136 [326]). Kant is clear that the state can justly fulfill its duty to provide for those members of society who are unable to maintain themselves by transferring possessions from the wealthy to the poor. He also maintains that, as a matter of justice, the state should effect this transfer of wealth through coercively imposed taxation, explicitly ruling out the possibility that the needs of the poor can justly be met through a program of voluntary contributions. Far from supporting a minimal state, Kant argued that a just state is one that ensures that the needs of all its members, including those who are unable to provide for themselves, are met through coercively imposed measures requiring the wealthy to contribute a portion of their possessions to meet the needs of others.

Kant's reasoning is direct. The wealthy owe their very existence, and a fortiori their wealth, to the state in the sense that without it they would be unable to live, let alone prosper. They are therefore obliged, in return for these benefits, to contribute as necessary to the well-being of their fellow citizens (136 [326]). Their obligation to help support the poor is based on a principle of reciprocity.

Kant's conclusion is implicit in the idea of the original contract. If the theme of his theory of private right is that just relations among persons are relations of balanced reciprocity in which the relevant point of reference is *homo noumenon*, the theme of his theory of public right is that the idea of the original contract – a hypothetical agreement in which the members of a state assume obligations toward their fellow citizens in return for the assurance that their own rights and needs will be secured – is the principle behind all public rights, the test of whether public laws and policies are just or unjust.

For Kant, the idea of the original contract is the vehicle for determining whether or not laws and policies are just, much as the categorical imperative is the test for ascertaining whether or not individuals' maxims and discrete actions are rightful. If a law is such that a whole people could not have agreed to it in an original contract, then that law is unjust. If, on the other hand, a law is such that it could have been the object of such an agreement – an agreement to which an entire people might have given its assent – then it is at least arguably just (and Kant believes that it is the people's duty to consider such a law to be just even if they disapprove of it). A set of laws that would allow some members of a state to be deprived of the means required in order to meet their needs is a set of laws from which at least some people would have withheld their consent in an original contract. Such a set of laws would therefore be unjust. More generally, *any* law or policy that could not have commanded the assent of the entire people in an original contract is unjust. Kant did not believe that resistance to the ruler of a state could ever be just, even if that resistance is designed to oppose unjust laws. But he *did* believe that laws are sometimes unjust and that the idea of the original contract supplies an intellectually rigorous test for determining whether or not they are just.

VI

In contrast to the utilitarian writers, Kant placed the concept of reciprocity squarely at the center of his theory of justice. In the domain of private right, which is concerned with discrete relations among persons, he endorsed the notion of balanced reciprocity among equals, and, since he considered all persons, regarded as *homines noumena*, to be equal, he viewed balanced reciprocity as *the* basis of just relations among private persons. In the domain of public right, Kant's view is more difficult to categorize. It is clear that the concept of reciprocity plays a large role here as well, in the sense that all those who enjoy the benefits of the civil condition must in return assume obligations toward their fellow citizens – obligations that, under some circumstances, would compel them to give up some of their wealth to supply the needs of others. Yet it is difficult to characterize precisely the notion of reciprocity Kant deploys here. The concept of *balanced* reciprocity in a well-defined sense seems not to apply.

Kant had opened up new territory for thinking about justice. While Adam Smith had attained a vision of society as a systemic whole, with properties and products that are best accounted for by the whole rather than by its parts taken severally (this is the thrust of his conception of the division of labor and its consequences), he did not frame a distinctive conception of justice around this vision. Kant did precisely that. By reworking the already familiar notion of an original contract into a test for the legislation of a commonwealth viewed systemically, he had stepped into a new world, perhaps no more knowingly than Christopher Columbus in his first voyage to the Americas. Although the phrase "social justice" had not yet been coined, Kant had hit upon features that have remained essential to the concept of social justice for the past two centuries.

Kant bequeathed to posterity a vision of a just society that was self-consciously at odds with the vision defended by the theorists of utility. He offers a window onto that vision in this passage from the *Metaphysics of Morals*:

> By the well-being of a state must not be understood the *welfare* of its citizens and their *happiness*; for happiness can perhaps come to them more easily and as they would like it to [come] in a state of nature (as Rousseau asserts) or even under a despotic government. By the well-being of a state is understood, instead, that condition in which its constitution conforms most fully to principles of Right; it is that condition which reason, *by a categorical imperative*, makes it obligatory for us to strive after. (129 [318])

A just society, for Kant, is one whose principal aim and tendency is to maintain social relations of mutual respect and reciprocity among free and equal citizens, not to enhance their welfare, conceived in material terms. His conception of this society was flawed, to be sure. Viewing human beings in highly abstract terms, as *homines noumena,* Kant underestimated the extent to which the quality of relations among persons is necessarily a hostage to their relative circumstances. Further, his conception of private right rooted in strictly balanced reciprocity stands in some tension with his conception of public right, based as it is on the idea of an original contract, which cannot be reduced to the terms of balanced reciprocity. Yet Kant had staked out the territory, if not the terminology, of social justice, and he had done so with a vision that transcended the class struggles that were destined to turn that territory into a battlefield throughout the nineteenth century and beyond.

Chapter 7

The Idea of Social Justice

I

During the nineteenth century an enormously influential and eclectic assortment of thinkers discovered a new peak from which to survey the terrain of justice. Striking out from heights that had been conquered by writers like Smith, Bentham, and Kant, these thinkers made their way to an even more ambitious elevation. They conceived the idea of using ideal standards of justice as a basis for a thoroughgoing assessment of social institutions as a whole, one that focuses on the way in which the benefits and burdens of society are distributed and may be invoked to argue for a wholesale transformation of society. The sweeping imaginative constructs they devised from this new vantage point ultimately helped to reconfigure the very terrain they observed.

It is true that many thinkers prior to the nineteenth century had looked on their own societies with a visionary gaze. In the *Republic*, the first synoptic work of political theory, Plato drew an elaborate portrait of a *polis* which, if brought into existence, would have overturned some of the most basic assumptions of his fellow citizens, as well as many of the practices on which his native Athens was founded. Yet Plato did not expect, and probably did not intend, to see the kind of *polis* he described come into being. Similarly, Thomas More's *Utopia*,

---

A Brief History of Justice, First Edition. David Johnston.

written early in the sixteenth century, depicts an ostensibly ideal communistic society on a large island country of uncertain location. In reality, More did not intend that picture to be treated as a blueprint for a wholesale transformation of society, and he would probably have been either amused or repelled (or both) if that had happened. Writing in the seventeenth century, Thomas Hobbes proposed radical changes to the way in which his contemporaries thought about their political orders; but his proposals, though far-reaching, were almost wholly confined to a political domain, and if they had been adopted their impact on social and economic life would have been uncertain. Adam Smith proposed major changes to the conduct and regulation of economic affairs, changes that would also have had a significant impact on social relations, but he did not intend to upend the institutions of his or any other society as a whole. Of the writers we have considered so far, Bentham comes closest to conceiving the sweeping ambitions that we find in many nineteenth-century thinkers. Yet, while he claimed to have invented a new way of thinking about institutions and practices and he was a serious and committed reformer, Bentham advocated only piecemeal, albeit major, reforms. Although a tradition of thinkers, from Hobbes through to Bentham, thought of the social world as a product of human conventions that are subject to reform in the light of human design, none of these thinkers grasped the idea of using ideal standards of justice as the basis for a thoroughgoing assessment of the full range of social institutions, and none imagined the kind of wholesale transformation that became almost commonplace in the imagination of political and social thinkers in the nineteenth century.

New ways of thinking about justice emerged in the nineteenth century because perceptions of the terrain of the social world, and of the impact that human agency is capable of having on that world, had changed. Hobbes, Hume, and many others had already portrayed that terrain as a product of human actions rather than as a landscape shaped exclusively by the hand of nature. By the early nineteenth century, this portrayal had become significantly more vivid than before. Many thinkers embraced the view that major features of the social terrain – including social and institutional arrangements that condemned large portions of the population to an insecure and frequently miserable life and, often, to premature death – are the product of actions, conventions, and institutions that could be reformed or overturned and replaced by human efforts. It began to seem genuinely possible (at least to some observers), perhaps for the first time in history, to remake a polity and society from the ground up. One factor that helped to induce this change in perceptions was a steady stream of technological innovations that altered the contours of economic and social life in Britain and Europe from the early eighteenth to the early nineteenth century. The invention of precision instruments for keeping time, consequent sharp improvements in navigation (which had important consequences for intercontinental trade), the steam engine, and the power loom were among the many developments that helped to enhance productivity and to reshape the economic and social lives of most ordinary people at this time. It appeared as though the scientific discoveries that had begun to pour forth in the seventeenth century and were represented in iconic fashion by Newton's laws of mechanics had laid the groundwork for human beings to harness and command nature, much as Francis Bacon had prophesied. Without much difficulty, the thought followed that, if nature can be induced to do our bidding, why should not human society, of which we are after all the creators, be made to do the same?

A second, and perhaps decisive factor affecting assumptions about the prospects for social transformation, however, was the French Revolution, which began in 1789 and played out through the mid-1790s. Unlike the American Revolution barely more than a decade earlier, the French Revolution was seen by many of its principal promoters, as well as by its opponents, as a radical break with the past, an apocalyptic event that sought to re-found the polity and society of France on entirely new principles. The revolution had an enormous impact on the political and social imagination of innumerable observers, even if its practical consequences, as Alexis de Tocqueville suggested two or three generations afterward, were less dramatic than they seemed at the time. If the scientific and technological revolution of the seventeenth and eighteenth centuries had laid the intellectual groundwork for a new sense of possibilities for social transformation, the French Revolution completed the transition to a new set of sensibilities.

Writing in 1814 with his secretary and collaborator Augustin Thierry, Henri de Saint-Simon exhibited this sensibility in his prophetic proposal for a reorganization of the European community:

> The social order has been overturned because it no longer corresponded with the level of enlightenment; it is for you to create a better order. The body politic has been dissolved; it is for you to reconstitute it.

"Overturned" and "dissolved," "create" and "reconstitute": the terms Saint-Simon and Thierry chose to make their point suggest that a dramatic social transformation was not merely possible, but inevitable because of the collapse of the old order.

Saint-Simon's sensibility for the prospects of radical transformation was shared by many in his own and later generations, stretching well into the twentieth century. But the writer whose works represent the apotheosis of this sensibility is Karl Marx. Writing in the middle years of the century, Marx argued that human history up to that time had been made with no human awareness of the broad, systemic consequences of human actions. As a result, the major forms and patterns of social cooperation had over the course of history taken on a succession of highly consequential shapes that no human being had ever consciously designed. (Marx was especially interested in the way in which societies' productive activities and powers were organized, because he believed that the major features of all other significant institutions flow from that organization.) Marx believed, however, that humankind at his time stood at the cusp of a fundamental shift in the direction of history. A clear, accurate, and comprehensive grasp of the forces that drive human history had begun to come into view. When that enlightened understanding of the fundamental forces of history has spread to the mass of people (the proletariat), it will become possible for human beings to take command of their own destiny and to shape the future in accordance with their collective will. History will then take a new direction, one that, for the first time, will be steered consciously and deliberately by a collective human will.

In framing his conception of the unique historical juncture at which he believed he stood, Marx borrowed heavily from the ideas of Adam Smith and from later writers on the subject of political economy. Smith, you will recall, had argued that the division of labor characteristic of modern commercial societies, which he believed to be by far the major source of those societies' great productive powers, had come into being despite the fact that no person had ever consciously designed or intended it. This greatest of all sources of social wealth was the unintended product of innumerable transactions and productive activities people had undertaken over many generations for their own relatively narrow purposes, not with a view to enhancing their society's productivity or increasing its wealth. Smith and his successors worked to formulate generalizations or "laws" that could account for these activities and their overall consequences in the same way in which Newton's laws appeared to account for the motions of heavenly and terrestrial bodies.

Marx accepted many of the central ideas of Smith and of the other classical political economists. What he did not accept was the proposition that those ideas capture inescapable (or "iron") laws that must inevitably determine the future course of history as well as its past. For Marx, the past had been determined by iron laws because past history had been made by human beings who were unaware of the largest and most momentous consequences of their activities. A future driven by human beings who possess this awareness would be altogether different.

The language in which Marx reveals his sense of the possibilities for transformative change is striking. To the work he considered his crowning achievement, *Capital*, he gave the subtitle *A Critique of*

Political Economy. In the preface to the first edition of that work (1867), Marx writes of "the natural laws of capitalist production," which work "with iron necessity towards inevitable results," and of "the economic law of motion of modern society." In short, he endorses enthusiastically the claim, which he traces back to Ricardo, Malthus, and many others in the classical school of political economy in addition to Smith, that the economies of his time and of earlier eras are subject to laws that determine the direction and destination of those economies without regard to human intentions or will. But this claim is true in his view only of an epoch that he believed was about to come to an end. In an earlier work, "The German ideology" (1845–1846), which Marx wrote with Friedrich Engels but declined to publish, the authors drew a sharp distinction between two phases in human existence. In the first, man "remains in natural society," in which "a cleavage exists between the particular and the common interest." Human activity in this phase of history "is not voluntarily, but naturally, divided," so that "man's own deed becomes an alien power opposed to him," and the united power of human beings becomes

> an alien force existing outside them, of the origin and goal of which they are ignorant, which they thus cannot control, which on the contrary passes through a peculiar series of phases and stages independent of the will and the action of man [...]

Marx and Engels' mention of activity that is divided naturally rather than voluntarily appears to be an allusion to Smith's idea of a division of labor that comes into being and remains central to the coordination of human actions without being designed, intended, or foreseen by any human being. They conclude by observing:

> This fixation of social activity, this consolidation of what we ourselves produce into an objective power above us, growing out of our control, thwarting our expectations, bringing to naught our calculations, is one of the chief factors in historical development up till now.

The "fixation of social activity" that Marx and Engels here assign to a stage of history that (they believe) is about to be eclipsed refers to the same phenomena that are the subject of "natural laws" and of "the economic law of motion of modern society" in *Capital* and in the writings of earlier political economists.

In contrast to this phase of existence, Marx and Engels evoke another phase, in which human activity will be divided voluntarily, not "naturally," and in which human beings will control their deeds rather than being controlled by them. The division and the direction of labor will be subject to a united human will. The particular interests of individuals will no longer be sundered from the common interest. In short, human beings will be able collectively to seize control of their social lives as a whole and to determine, through their united will, the direction that human history will take.

Although Marx and Engels' faith in the potential capacity of human beings to remake their societies was extreme, their broad view that humanity, or at least European humanity, was on the cusp of an escape from subjection to ostensibly natural relations was shared by thinkers spanning a wide ideological spectrum. John Stuart Mill, for example, was a frequent critic of the tendency to regard social relations as natural relations, and he extended his campaign against this tendency into areas that were left untouched by most of his communist and socialist contemporaries, for example in his polemic against the subjection of women. Of course, many thinkers in the nineteenth century adopted more modest assumptions about the possibilities for reform than either Marx or Mill, and conservative thinkers from Edmund Burke onward defended the illusion of naturalness as a salutary attribute of the way human beings tend to view their social world. The stance of these thinkers was worlds apart from that of Marx and diametrically opposed to the views of Mill. But the chroniclers and interpreters of the scientific revolution, of the industrial revolution, and of the French Revolution had opened the floodgates to a new way of thinking about the social world, which could be ignored by no one who wished to play a meaningful role in the conversations that shaped the ways in which writers and others in the nineteenth century thought about justice. The deluge that followed would ultimately carve the territory of justice into a new shape.

Henry Sidgwick, a leader of the utilitarian tradition in the generation that followed John Stuart Mill, offered the most perspicuous statement of the question to which the new way of thinking led. If human beings are capable, at least in principle, of remaking their political and social (and economic) institutions from the ground up, then it makes no sense to fall back on "natural" forms of human life, as thinkers as diverse as Hume and Kant had done in the eighteenth century, to answer central questions about justice. After a brief critical discussion of the notion of the natural in relation to justice in his *Methods of Ethics*, Sidgwick posed the following question: "Are there any clear principles from which we may work out an ideally just distribution of rights and privileges, burdens and pains, among human beings as such?"

The idea of a set of principles from which we may work out an ideally just distribution of rights and privileges, burdens and pains, which can be deployed to assess a society's institutions as a whole and to argue for a transformation of those institutions if they are found wanting, is the idea of social justice. The preparatory work that made possible the articulation of this idea had been performed by Adam Smith, and Immanuel Kant stumbled upon the territory out of which it grew. Only after the departure of these thinkers, however, were the concepts and terminology that gave shape to this idea invented, at first in rudimentary manner and later in a more developed and sharpened form. In the domain of ideas about justice, Sidgwick had posed *the* question of the nineteenth century.

II

Philosophers and critics offered two principal answers to this question, two main candidates for the title of ideal standard of social justice. One of these is intimated in a number of Saint-Simon's writings in the first quarter of the century. Consider, for example, a contribution he published in 1819, in a periodical entitled the "Organizer." Saint-Simon asks his readers to entertain two hypothetical scenarios. In one of these, France loses in one day thirty thousand of its leading citizens, including the king's brother and several additional highest-ranking members of the aristocracy, all the leading officers of the royal household, all the ministers in government, all the counselors of state, and, in short, virtually all its leading public officials, along with all the leading figures in the Catholic church and ten thousand of its wealthiest landowners. France would have suffered a great loss. But Saint-Simon argues that this loss would result in no "political evil" for the state and that, although many people would grieve the loss of so many eminent persons, the reasons for their grief would be purely sentimental.

In the alternative scenario, France loses just three thousand, not thirty thousand, of its citizens. But in this scenario those three thousand include the country's leading scientists, artists, and artisans, from poets, painters, and musicians to physicists, chemists, doctors, and clockmakers and from farmers, tanners, linen-makers, and hardware manufacturers to masons, carpenters, smelters, and businessmen. These men, Saint-Simon argues, are its most essential producers, the people most useful to their fellow-citizens and those who contribute the most to France's civilization and prosperity. If these three thousand were to be lost at once, France would, he argues, instantly become a "lifeless corpse."

In posing these alternative hypothetical scenarios, Saint-Simon draws a razor-sharp contrast between those who contribute to national eminence and to the well-being of their compatriots and those whose existence is essentially parasitic on the efforts and contributions of others, who in his estimation are not merely useless, but positively harmful to the nation, because they consume resources that could otherwise be channeled into useful pursuits and because they wield whatever power they can muster to preserve a defective status quo.

The prominence of this latter group shows that "society is a world which is upside down." The nation operates on the principles that the poor should deprive themselves of necessities on a daily basis in order to supply the rich with luxuries; that the most guilty men – those who rob their fellow-citizens on a grand scale – should hold responsibility for punishing minor offences by their social inferiors; and that the ignorant and idle should rule those who are able and industrious.

One of the axes of contrast in Saint-Simon's critique is that between the rich and the poor, and it is clear that he objects adamantly to the former's accumulation of wealth at the expense of the latter, which he believes to be no better than robbery. But the primary contrast he draws is between those who contribute and are useful to society and those who consume without contributing, who are useless at best and harmful as a rule. He attacks the rich not because they are rich, but because they are parasites who contribute nothing to the common good or the good of their countrymen, and he aligns himself with the talented and the poor because they fail to reap the rewards they deserve on the basis of the contributions they make. The foundation of Saint-Simon's ideas about a rightful and just social order is a principle of desert according to which what people deserve to receive is based on what they contribute to society.

Saint-Simon's principle of justice (if we can call it that, since he wrote as a polemicist and reformer rather than as a systematic philosopher) is close in spirit to the theme that underlies Kant's theory of private right. Recall that that theme is the idea that just relations among persons are relations of balanced reciprocity. Balanced reciprocity implies, roughly, that justice is realized when people receive the equivalent in value of what they have given (or when they give the equivalent in value of what they have received). Saint-Simon's version of this principle is far more prosaic than Kant's. For Kant, the relevant point of reference for ascertaining whether relations among persons meet the standard of balanced reciprocity is *homo noumenon*, not *homo phaenomenon* – the person as a postulated agent of perfectly free will rather than the person laden with particular inclinations, emotions, abilities and other empirical attributes. Saint-Simon had little patience for these metaphysical conceits. For him, people – ordinary, flesh-and-blood people – deserve to reap what they (actually) sow. And what (or how much) they sow is a matter of how much they actually contribute, of how useful their activities and products are.

Like Marx some two generations later, Saint-Simon regarded the principle of desert as a socialist principle. He assumed that the best way to assure that the rewards people receive are proportional to the contributions they make to society is for the social product (roughly speaking, the wealth generated by the combined efforts of all the members of society) to be subject to allocation by unbiased authorities, who should also bear ultimate responsibility for directing the productive efforts of the citizenry as a whole. In short, Saint-Simon was an early prophet of technocracy. But the principle of desert was not championed exclusively by socialists and technocrats. Many people in fact believed that market demand is an accurate measure of desert, at least insofar as markets can be perfected. And enthusiasm about the perfectibility (and the alleged self-sustaining capabilities) of market systems attained, and remained at, a high point in the nineteenth century among a large and influential body of intellectuals and reformers. Socialists and technocrats like Saint-Simon were united with defenders of free markets and of laissez-faire in their opposition to, and in many cases contempt for, the regime of privileges and special protections for the few that came to be known as the *ancien régime* (through association with the hierarchical political and social order that had prevailed in France up to the time of the revolution). Moreover, many of those who fell into these two camps were united by their support for the idea that social justice is achieved when contributions are rewarded in accordance with the principle of desert. However, these camps parted ways over questions about the manner in which the notion of a "contribution" should be conceived, and a fortiori over the institutional means for achieving social justice.

Recall that Saint-Simon included poets, painters, and musicians among the major contributors to France's achievements and to the well-being of its citizens. In his time poets, painters, and musicians were notoriously unable to command substantial incomes by offering their services and products on the open market. These artists typically were dependent on the good will of wealthy patrons for their economic survival, and even some of the most renowned and artistically successful among them spent much of their lives in poverty. For Saint-Simon, the fact that artists and others of their kind are poorly rewarded by a system in which compensation is distributed via free markets is evidence of the defects of that system of distribution, not a sign that artists fail to contribute or lack desert. For him, the remedy was to adopt a system of distributing rewards in proportion to desert that departs from free market principles. Needless to say, the advocates of free market systems and laissez-faire saw things differently.

Despite being an idiosyncratic thinker in many respects, Herbert Spencer offered arguably the clearest explication of a line of reasoning that most advocates of the principle of desert as determined by the institution of a free market grasped only dimly. Spencer argued that the idea of justice contains two elements. One of these is an element of equality. If each person were to pursue his objectives without paying heed to the claims of others, the result would be continual conflict. Awareness of this fact leads people to realize that they need to set bounds on the freedom of action of each, and experience suggests that these bounds should be the same for all. One element of justice, then, is the idea that each person is entitled to freedom of action within a sphere that is bounded by the equal spheres to which all others are entitled.

In addition to this element of equality, Spencer argues that the idea of justice contains a second and more primordial element of inequality. That element can be expressed in the statement that "each shall receive the benefits and evils due to his own nature and consequent conduct." This statement is a version of the principle of desert. Since human beings differ from one another in their nature (their capabilities and inclinations) and conduct, this principle entails that different individuals will receive unequal benefits and evils and will enjoy unequal results. If this principle of justice were effective, then those who contribute a great deal to society would receive a great deal in return. Those who contribute only a little would receive only a little, and those who cause harm would be requited with harm.

The true conception of justice, for Spencer, contains both these elements in balance with one another. A society is just if (1) its members are equal insofar as each is guaranteed freedom within a sphere of action limited by like spheres for others; and (2) the good and evil consequences that flow to its members are equivalent in value to the good and/or harmful consequences they cause.

Spencer believed that this balanced, reciprocal result is best achieved in a society in which each person enjoys broad freedom to engage in, or to decline, transactions with any other person, with few limitations apart from those imposed by the parties involved. He believed, in other words, that justice as defined by the principle of desert is best achieved in a market society.

Spencer's notion of the range of freedoms individuals should enjoy in a market society was quite sweeping, but his ideas about the proper extent of individual freedom were not exceptional for his era. In effect, the nineteenth-century enthusiasts of market society appropriated Adam Smith's conception of a system of natural liberty, which Smith had conceived of as a pattern for the organization of productive forces, and they turned it into a model for social relations as a whole. Many of the ideas that are distinctive of the century flowed from this extension. The idea of freedom of contract is a prime example. This idea, which arguably reached its crest as a practical matter in the 1860s (though it continued to have enormous legal consequences far into the twentieth century), is based on the repudiation of limits on the freedom of private parties to enter into binding agreements with one another, whatever the reasons for those limits. The fact that private parties are often vastly unequal to each other in point of bargaining power or of command of information, as was often the case with factory owners and manual laborers, did not deter the advocates of freedom of contract from maintaining that the removal of restrictions on individuals' freedom of this kind would lead to a just allocation of rewards for contributions based on the principle of desert.

At the ideological core of this new conception was the notion that social relations should be the product of the wills of private individuals rather than being constrained by rules and conventions that might be contrary to those individuals' wishes. Like Marx, the champions of market society wished to throw off the constraints of "alien powers." But, whereas Marx believed that those powers can be overcome only in a society that is directed by the collective will of its members (and he assumed that such a collective will would emerge in a post-capitalist society), the advocates of market society maintained that they can be vanquished only when individuals are free to act on their particular wills, with virtually no restrictions except those imposed by the need to allow all other individuals sufficient freedom to do the same. For these thinkers, individuals ideally should be burdened only with whatever obligations they have consented to assume through voluntary agreements.

Of course, even the most enthusiastic supporters of market society did not extend this ideal to every kind of social relation without exception. Virtually all advocates of market society assumed that some areas of human life should be exempt from the pattern of highly individualistic social relations they saw as the defining feature of a just society. Spencer himself drew a sharp distinction between a sphere of the state and a sphere of the family. In the state, social relations should be based on voluntary agreements among free individuals. The idea of a justice based on the principle of desert applies to this sphere and to this sphere only. The family, however, should be regulated by different norms, which affirm the value of responsiveness to individual needs. The ethics of the family, as Spencer saw it, entails unequal treatment of family members in the interest of striving for equal outcomes, whereas the ethics of the larger society or state entails equal treatment that leads inevitably to unequal outcomes on the basis of inequalities of desert.

Spencer's primary interest, however, like that of nearly all the other champions of market society, was in social relations outside the family. Like many other prominent thinkers in his era, he believed that he was living at a time when the moral basis of society had shifted decisively. In all these thinkers' view, social relations in the past had been dominated by conventions that were transmitted from generation to generation. The convention-dictated patterns that shaped those relations were resistant to deliberate alteration and were generally subject to change only through gradual and usually imperceptible intergenerational processes. To Spencer and many of his contemporaries, it seemed as though this ponderous domination of the past over the present had been overthrown in their own era. They believed that social relations in the future would be shaped primarily by agreements among private individuals in accordance with those individuals' wills. It seemed that the basis of social relations had undergone a momentous and perhaps permanent shift, from status to contract.

The principle of desert, then, could be understood either as a socialist principle, which is realized when competent and unbiased authorities allocate rewards according to some collectively defined conception of desert, or as a liberal principle, which is realized when individuals are as free as possible to enter into transactions with others and to reap the returns those others, taken individually, are willing to bestow. Interpreted either way, the principle of desert seemed – despite its affinities with ideas that had previously been articulated by Aristotle, Kant, and others – to represent a radical break from the practices of the *ancien régime*, and indeed from practices that had prevailed in all or virtually all known societies in the past.

III

The main alternative to the principle of desert for the title of ideal standard of social justice in the nineteenth century was the principle of need. The formula that was to become famous during that century, "from each according to his ability, to each according to his needs," is credited to the nineteenth-century thinker and activist Louis Blanc, though it has been suggested that the central idea behind that formula can be found at least as early as the mid-eighteenth century. In any case the idea that wealth should be distributed on the basis of need had begun to circulate by the 1790s. In the mid-1790s, François-Noël Babeuf (who took the pen name "Gracchus" Babeuf, from the name of a branch of *gens Sempronia* in the ancient republic of Rome – a branch made famous by the social reformer Tiberius Gracchus and his brother Gaius) helped to found a political society after the Constitution of the Year III (1795) revoked the radical democratic principles of an earlier phase of the revolutionary period. One of the principal aims of the society was to seek economic as well as political equality for all citizens of France. In the spring of 1796, the society produced a manifesto calling for a "Republic of Equals" that would abolish individual ownership of land and establish an educational system providing access to the same kind of education for all, among other measures. Arrested and tried for plotting to overthrow the government in 1797, Babeuf gave a lengthy and memorable prepared speech in his defense, before he was convicted and subsequently led away to his execution. Babeuf's ideas were not original. Egalitarian, and even communistic ideas were very much in the air in France in the 1790s, and in some cases even earlier. But his eloquence and martyrdom gave rise to a legend that played a significant role in the development of an idea of social justice based on need.

Around the time of Babeuf's execution, the German philosopher Johann Gottlieb Fichte, one of Kant's most eminent followers, reached conclusions that were similar to Babeuf's, and were based on more rigorous philosophical arguments. Using the idea of an original contract in much the same way as Kant had done, Fichte argued that everyone in a state is entitled to having the state guarantee that he will be able to make a living from his labor. If the state fails to make good on this promise, then the subject "has not been given what is absolutely his" and "the contract is completely cancelled with respect to him." Fichte reaffirmed and arguably strengthened this view in a later piece of writing, by claiming that a "rational" state would ensure that goods are distributed to all its citizens, with the aim of enabling each to have an agreeable life, and that each citizen is entitled "by right" to an adequate share of goods.

The principle of need drew strength from several ideas that had been developed during the eighteenth century. As we have seen, Thomas Hobbes, David Hume, and Adam Smith had all argued that nearly all human beings are roughly equal in capabilities and that the differences in skills and accomplishments we find among them are almost entirely the product of education and socialization rather than of innate talents. Neither Hobbes nor Hume believed that this equality of talents should, as a matter of justice, entail that all persons enjoy equal material possessions or be entitled to have their needs met equally, and Smith, who seems to have been more disturbed by vast inequalities than either of these earlier thinkers, did not believe that equality of possessions or of need satisfaction is reconcilable with the system of natural liberty, which he prized. To many thinkers in the nineteenth century, however, the connection between equality of talents and equality of need satisfaction seemed obvious. If in general no person is more capable than any other by nature, why should the benefits of society accrue to some in greater share than to others? On this line of reasoning, the principle of need has sometimes been considered to be compatible with the principle of desert rather than to be an antagonistic alternative to that principle.

An alternative line of reasoning draws upon the premise that all human beings are strictly equal in worth, regardless of how equal or unequal their natural capacities and talents might be. We have seen that this premise is fundamental to Kant's theory of justice. Indeed, the idea of justice as equal satisfaction of needs is a near relation to, and in some of its guises a direct descendant of, Kant's theory of public right. The main element in that theory is the idea of the original contract, which tells us that, if a law is such that an entire people would not have agreed to it in an original contract, then that law is unjust.

While Kant was a vigorous opponent of the opinion that justice requires equality of possessions (largely in reaction to a cluster of radical ideas that cast a long shadow over much of Europe in the aftermath of the French Revolution), he was an equally vigorous proponent of the view that a state that allows some of its members to be deprived of the means necessary to meet their needs is in that respect unjust, since the terms on which such a state is founded could never have been the object of a universal agreement in an original contract. Over time, the Kantian premise of equal worth attained a more prominent position in the constellation of ideas about social justice than Hume's and Smith's postulate of the equality of talents.

Karl Marx, who was a close reader of Smith and who, as we have seen, borrowed some of his most important ideas from his predecessor, repudiated the very idea of justice as a potentially constructive notion and did this throughout his life, from his early published essay "On the Jewish question" (1843) to his "Critique of the Gotha program" (1875). So it might seem misleading to portray him as a proponent of the idea of social justice based on the principle of need. It is important, however, to consider the basis on which Marx rejected the idea of justice. Marx consistently associated justice with the concept of rights, and he associated the concept of rights with (what he called) bourgeois society, that is, with a form of society whose members see each other as separated and independent from one another, as "isolated monad[s]" rather than mutually interdependent members of a whole. He closely associated the concept of rights with private property and argued that rights are by nature destined to serve as bulwarks of inequality. Marx was not a proponent of social justice *if* social justice is to be achieved in the way Fichte imagined, that is, through entitlements enforced by a state. Marx considered the state itself to be a part of the large social problem he hoped would be resolved through a revolutionary transformation of society.

Nevertheless, Marx was a vigorous advocate for the formula given above: "From each according to his ability, to each according to his needs." In a well-known programmatic letter he composed in 1875,

Marx considered and rejected the principle of desert as the basis for an ideal distribution of goods. Considering the transition he hoped would take place from a capitalist society to a communist one, he asserts:

> What we have to deal with here is a communist society, not as it has *developed* on its own foundations, but, on the contrary, just as it *emerges* from capitalist society; which is thus in every respect, economically, morally and intellectually, still stamped with the birth marks of the old society from whose womb it emerges. Accordingly, the individual producer receives back from society – after the deductions have been made – exactly what he gives to it [...] The same amount of labour which he has given to society in one form he receives back in another.

Marx regarded the principle of desert (the contribution principle) as a socialist principle, and he considered socialism a necessary stage on the way toward the emergence of communism. But socialism for him is *only* a stage on the way to an ideal society, and the distributive principle on which it is based is, accordingly, flawed:

> But one man is superior to another physically or mentally and so supplies more labour in the same time, or can labour for a longer time [...] [the contribution principle] tacitly recognizes unequal individual endowment and thus productive capacity as natural privileges. *It is, therefore, a right of inequality, in its content, like every right.*

Marx's alternative to the contribution principle is the principle of need: "From each according to his ability..." It is true that he did not consider this formula to be a principle of social *justice*, because he did not endorse the idea that the result the formula prescribes should be achieved by way of entitlements enforced by a state. He believed, on the contrary, that, in a sufficiently humane society, human beings would treat each other in accordance with the principle of need, without being forced to do so by a coercive state. Yet, in spite of all the distance he sought to put between himself and talk about justice, Marx was (in our terms, though not in his own) the most influential nineteenth-century proponent of the idea of social justice based on the principle of need.

It cannot be emphasized strongly enough that the formula "from each according to his ability, to each according to his needs" has two parts, as does the principle of desert. The principle of desert says, in essence, that the benefits people enjoy (or the harms they suffer) should be equivalent in value to the contributions they make (or to the harms they inflict). The principle of need (as I have called it for the sake of economy of expression) likewise offers a prescription for the contributions that people should make as well as for the benefits they should receive. However, the principle of need breaks the connection between contributions and benefits that is maintained by the principle of desert.

It would be possible to construct a line of reasoning that connects the principle of need with the concept of reciprocity. As we have seen, the idea of justice as equal satisfaction of needs can be viewed as a descendant of Kant's theory of public right. For Kant, the idea of the original contract – a hypothetical agreement in which the members of a state assume obligations toward their fellow citizens in return for the assurance that their own rights and needs will be secured – is the principle behind all public rights. So it is plausible, at least *prima facie*, to think of the principle of need as the product of a relationship of reciprocity among the members of a society.

Yet it is important to bear in mind that, because the agreement that enters into this line of reasoning is hypothetical, its terms are subject to a wide range of interpretations. When one is considering a hypothetical contract that two or more people would or might have made with one another, the terms one supposes those parties would have reached will depend heavily on a set of assumptions that are not contained in the idea of the agreement itself. When reciprocity is hypothetical, the implications of reciprocity are uncertain. If there is a connection between the concept of reciprocity and the principle of need, it is a tenuous one.

It is more plausible to think of the principle of need as a teleological principle than as a principle based on reciprocity. The contribution side of this principle, "from each according to his ability," is specified independently of the benefit side, "to each according to his needs." Each part of this principle suggests its own (partial) *telos*, and, while it is obvious that there can be no benefits without contributions, either part of the principle of need could be altered without affecting the principle underpinning the other part. (For example, we might propose the principle "from each according to his ability, to each according to his bargaining power.") In this structural sense, the principle of need, as a principle of social justice, resembles a Platonic or a utilitarian conception of justice more nearly than it resembles any of the ideas of justice based on the concept of reciprocity that have dominated most people's thoughts about justice, from the ancient Babylonians through to Aristotle and onward.

IV

The two major principles of social justice that rose to prominence in the nineteenth century – the principle of desert and the principle of need – are fundamentally at odds with each other. Even if the claim that nearly all human beings are roughly equal in capabilities were correct, it is not true that nearly all make roughly equal contributions to their fellow citizens. In addition, needs are unequally distributed across persons. It is evident that those who contribute most to a society's social product are not, in general, those whose needs are greatest. If the principle of desert is interpreted in the way its nineteenth-century proponents intended, that principle entails an ideally just distribution of rights and privileges, burdens and pains – a distribution that would be wholly incompatible with the distribution entailed by the principle of need. Moreover, while the principle of desert is based squarely on the concept of reciprocity, the principle of need clearly is not.

The contrast between these two principles of social justice is at the nub of the great social conflict that ruptured the seeming calm that settled over Europe in the immediate aftermath of the Napoleonic wars. Regardless of whether it is interpreted in a socialist or in a liberal fashion, the principle of desert favors the upwardly mobile middle class of achievers that was unleashed by the collapse of the *ancien régime*. Many of these people shared Saint-Simon's intuition that a world whose benefits accrue mainly to a class of people who retain their status through inherited and jealously guarded privileges is "a world which is upside down." To those thinkers it seemed self-evident that those who contribute most to the social product should receive the greatest share of that product and that any other distributive principle must be an impediment to progress.

In contrast, the principle of need favors the less well endowed members of society, those whose lack of talents – or (more often) lack of opportunities to cultivate their talents or lack of bargaining power to reap the full benefits of their talents even when they have cultivated those talents into productive skills – leaves them well behind their better-off fellow citizens. Both principles are antithetical to the regime of hereditary privilege that was characteristic of the *ancien régime*, but they are also antithetical to each other.

Each of these principles is subject to major objections. As a criterion of social justice, the principle of desert on the basis of contribution faces several difficulties.

First, in the context of the kind of commercial society within and for which it was conceived, the implications of the principle of desert are somewhat opaque. One of the key features of a commercial society is a complex division of labor, which in Adam Smith's perspicacious view is by far the most important source of productivity in such societies. If the division of labor itself is the source of nearly all the goods a society produces – in the sense that this unintended collective invention is responsible for drawing out various productive talents of individuals that would otherwise remain latent, and for weaving the efforts of those individuals into what is effectively an immensely productive machine – then the wealth of that society is essentially a social product, and not merely an aggregation of the products of a mass of independent producers. But if the wealth of society is a social product in this sense, it is not evident that the just apportionment of that product is the one prescribed by the principle of individual desert. People's productive abilities and performances are what they are only because of the complementary and supporting abilities and performances of others. Without these others, the talents and efforts of any one individual would come to nought.

A second, related difficulty is that the principle of desert suffers from a kind of circularity. This objection can be illustrated by an analogy between desert in the context of social justice and desert in the context of games.

A highly productive striker in football (soccer) generally contributes more to the team's prospects for success than an average team player does. For this reason we are likely to conclude that the productive striker deserves greater praise (and perhaps a greater share in other rewards) than the average player. However, the striker's contributions count as contributions only in light of the stipulated objective of the game (to win) and of the rules and conditions that prescribe the ways in which that objective can be pursued (by scoring more goals than one's opponent within a complex set of rules). If we were to adopt a different understanding of the objective of the game (for example, we might suppose that the principal objective of a social game is to promote comity among the members of both teams), then we would reach a different view of what counts as a contribution and therefore of the basis on which praise is deserved. And if the rules or other conditions of the game were to change markedly, then the capabilities and skills that bring success and recognition to the outstanding striker in football (as we know it) would give way to another set of capabilities and skills, which are better suited to the redefined game. Assessments of desert in games are feasible only within a framework defined by these parameters.

The same points hold for the ideas of contribution and desert in the context of social justice. An activity counts as a contribution only in light of a stipulated objective or set of objectives, whether these are defined collectively or severally by the individual members of a society. And the specific sets of capabilities and skills that enable individuals to make contributions depend upon the rules and conditions that shape social activity in that society. Although it is sometimes argued that desert is a natural (or "pre-political") notion, meaning that we ascribe desert to persons independently of specific rules or institutional settings, this claim is not persuasive for the kind of desert that is earned, or otherwise acquired, through actions whose meanings are shaped by conventions or social institutions. Most of the desert claims that are relevant to social justice are of this kind.

An appeal to ideal standards to assess the institutions and social arrangements of a society as a whole is part and parcel of the idea of social justice. Yet the principle of desert appeals to standards that are contingent on the objectives, institutions, and social arrangements of the very society to which those standards are to be applied. Different societies value different objectives, whether these are defined collectively or individually, by each member. For example, some are more interested in glory, while others are more interested in luxury, and these two objectives are far from exhausting the universe of available alternatives. Even when different societies value roughly the same objectives, the conditions within which they pursue those objectives vary in ways that affect the sets of capabilities and skills through which individuals can best contribute. For example, the attributes that have enabled warriors to command widespread respect in societies whose security is under constant threat differ from those which enabled Albert Einstein to attain heroic status in the twentieth century. The principle of desert cannot serve as an independent, ideal, and sufficient criterion for assessing the justice of a society's institutions and practices, because the kind of desert it invokes is not in fact independent of those institutions at all.

Although these objections seem decisive insofar as that principle is conceived as the exclusive basis for an ideally just distribution of rights and privileges, burdens and pains, they are not fatal to the concept of desert itself, nor do they prove that desert should be ruled out as an important element in a sound conception of social justice. Some forms of desert are relatively independent of both complex divisions of labor and social conventions. If two people are relative equals and one of them does a great and welcome service for the other, then it is just for the beneficiary to return the favor if and when he or she is in a position to do so without violating other important obligations. In this kind of case, there is a sense, relatively independent of convention, in which the first person deserves to be rewarded for the service he or she has done. So, while the principle of desert is unsound as *the* principle of social justice, the concept of desert retains some persuasive force, which a sound conception of social justice should not ignore.

The principle of desert also suffers from a third, most serious difficulty, which is that, in a hypothetical society whose benefits and burdens are distributed strictly in accordance with the principle of desert, many people would reap little or no benefit, because many would be able to contribute little or nothing at all. Many people would suffer severe deprivation; some of them would die prematurely as a consequence.

This implication did not perturb Malthus or Spencer, two of the more prominent champions of the principle of desert in the early years of the nineteenth century and in its latter half, respectively. Some might argue that, although this implication shows that the principle of desert may be *inhumane*, it raises no problem of *justice* at all. But if all human beings possess at least *some* worth – even if not all possess equal worth – and if a conception of justice is intended to be useful for the purpose of assessing human activities and social arrangements, this implication of the principle of desert may be counted as a powerful objection to it.

If the principle of desert seems inadequate to serve as the fundamental principle of social justice, the principle of need is subject to significant objections as well.

One difficulty with the principle of need is that the concept of need does not take us very far. The things a person needs in order to survive are highly consequential, of course – they include access to breathable air, potable water, and adequate nutrition – but fairly minimal. The things one needs to live a healthful and long life are more extensive. Finally, the set of things a person requires to live a life without shame is larger still and subject to considerable variation across cultures. Adam Smith observed that in England in his time even a person from the lowest order of society would be unable to go about in public without shame unless he owned a linen shirt and leather shoes. Yet, even if we define need in a relatively expansive way, so as to include access to the things a person needs to live a life of dignity and self-respect, only a small portion of the social product in the more productive societies would be required in order to meet nearly everyone's needs. The principle of need understood in this way can be only a partial principle of social justice.

We must therefore turn to some other criterion to supplement the bare principle of need. The criterion that is explicit in the writings of many advocates of the principle of need, from Babeuf to Louis Blanc to Marx and beyond, is equality. The thought is that, after all persons' needs in the sense sketched above have been met, the remainder of the social product should be distributed to every member of society in equal shares (perhaps in the form of private goods, but perhaps in large part through the provision of public goods accessible to all, such as parks and numerous other amenities of a common social life).

A major difficulty with the criterion of equality is that distribution of the social product, in equal shares, to the members of a society (after basic needs have been met) would require a great deal of self-abnegation on the part of those members who contributed the most to that product. People generally perceive their relations with others to be just when those relations are at least broadly reciprocal. They reasonably expect to reap the rewards of their labors. The principle of need supplemented by the criterion of equality would deny them that reward. For that principle decrees that the social product should be distributed without regard for the contributions people make to their society and its members. As the sole principle of social justice, the principle of need supplemented by the criterion of equality would deprive people of the fruits of their labors, would break all connection between what people contribute to the common social product and the share of that product that accrues to their benefit, and would expel the notion of reciprocity from the domain of justice.

In expelling the notion of reciprocity from the domain of justice, the principle of need, unlike the principle of desert, would also sever any connection between social justice and corrective justice. Recall that Spencer's account of the principle of desert is that "each shall receive the benefits and evils due to his own nature and consequent conduct." This statement suggests a prescription for corrective justice within a larger principle of social justice. If those who contribute to the social product are to receive benefits as a reward for their positive desert, those who impose harms on their fellow citizens can expect to receive harm in requital for their negative desert. Under the principle of desert, a principle of corrective justice is a component or corollary of the larger principle of social justice.

The principle of need includes no component of this kind. Many of its advocates in the long nineteenth century, from Babeuf just before the turn of the century to Marx in mid-century and to Kropotkin, whose career as a writer extended into the early twentieth century, thought of wrongdoing as a facet of a seriously defective form of social life, a facet that would disappear or at least diminish sharply when that form had vanished. These thinkers do not seem to have considered it important to devote serious thought to justice in relation to wrongdoing.

The principle of desert extends the concept of balanced reciprocity, in which every benefit provided to others is ultimately returned to the provider in the form of an equivalent benefit and every harm imposed on others is requited with an equivalent harm, to all aspects of justice, indiscriminately. But the concept of balanced reciprocity cannot bear the weight that the idea of social justice imposes. Like a hand shovel, the concept of balanced reciprocity is a timeless tool that has been and likely will remain useful for thinking about justice for as long as we can imagine. For the purpose of reconstructing the terrain of justice as a whole, however, heavier equipment is required. The concept of balanced reciprocity has a vital role to play in shaping just relations among persons; but, at least in its simple form, it is inadequate for assessing the terrain of social justice as a whole.

The principle of need dispenses with the concept of reciprocity altogether. While this principle embodies a premise that is fundamental to any credible conception of justice – the premise that every human being possesses worth – it does so at the expense of undermining justice in relations among persons.

One way of responding to the difficulties raised by these two principles would be to retreat from the idea of social justice altogether. One might argue that the concept of justice is tailored for discrete transactions among persons and cannot meaningfully be applied to a society's institutions and social arrangements as a whole. Or one might argue that, while we can indeed assess the justice or injustice of a society's institutions and social arrangements, this kind of assessment makes sense only if it is based on standards that are already immanent in those arrangements, so that the idea of an ideal and independent standard of social justice makes no sense.

The first of these responses would have us abdicate our responsibility for shaping our social world, when the fact of the matter is that we do so consciously and deliberately, even if by fits and starts, through trial and error, and with failures as well as successes. The second response, while endorsing the notion that we are responsible for shaping the social world we pass down to the future, insists that our cognitive limitations are so severe that we can do so only within the imaginative confines of the present. This insistence is belied by the record of human creativity and inventiveness.

An alternative way of responding to these difficulties would be to conclude that it may be a mistake to apply a single principle of justice to all subjects. The emergence of the idea of social justice in the nineteenth century changed the landscape of justice dramatically. It is plausible to suppose that, while that landscape cannot be comprehended (or reshaped) adequately with tools that were invented for less monumental tasks, it is within the range of human capability to invent new tools to assist us with the challenges that have been brought into view by the new vantage point of social justice. In order to adopt new tools for new tasks, we need not allow those which have long seemed adequate for more modest purposes to fall into disuse.

In a few broad strokes, this suggestion describes the route the twentieth-century philosopher John Rawls attempted to navigate through the recently discovered terrain of social justice. Let us now retrace some of the major turns he took and make a survey of the destination he reached.

Chapter 8

The Theory of Justice as Fairness

I

In the mid-twentieth century, John Rawls began work on a set of questions that quickly led him to formulate the central ideas of a new theory of social justice. Working steadily through the 1950s and 1960s, his labors led to the publication of *A Theory of Justice* in 1971. This long and intricately argued work, parts of which Rawls had circulated among scholars in the years leading up to its completion, had an immediate and major impact on academic political philosophy and beyond, stimulating a range of questions and inquiries that was far more extensive than that generated by any other theory of social justice in the twentieth century. Rawls called his theory "justice as fairness." The development and later elaboration of this theory occupied him for his entire professional life, from his first published essay in 1951 to his final efforts in 2000, just two years before his death. As one might expect, Rawls's thinking evolved over the nearly half a century he devoted to this work, with a particularly significant break in his conception of the theory occurring in the 1980s. In the short space I have available I shall for the most part ignore these developments, to focus on central features that remained relatively constant in the various statements of the theory.

A Brief History of Justice, First Edition. David Johnston.

Although Rawls was aware of the constellation of ideas about social justice that focused on the concepts of desert and need, the principal target of his criticism was utilitarianism, which in his view had come to dominate discussion of social institutions and policies so thoroughly as to exclude from serious consideration any alternative ways of thinking about them. Rawls offered several complaints about utilitarian theories. First, he argued that utilitarianism offers inadequate protection for liberty. Under some circumstances, it might be the case that happiness for a majority can best be attained by depriving a minority of persons of their liberty. If the aggregate gains in happiness to the majority are greater than the loss of happiness suffered by the minority, then the greatest happiness principle would justify the minority's loss of liberty. For Rawls, this possibility is sufficient by itself to demonstrate the inadequacy of the greatest happiness principle.

Just how likely this scenario is, is a question worthy of some debate. But it is at least a plausible scenario, and in rejecting utilitarianism Rawls had in mind momentous historical facts, as well as theories. Throughout his adult life, Rawls was profoundly conscious of the deep injustice that had been perpetrated by Americans of European origin through the enslavement of Africans and their descendants over multiple generations. Whenever he visited Washington, DC, he made a point of visiting the Lincoln Memorial, in recognition of the depravity of this practice and of the importance of its abolition. For him, any idea of justice that provides inadequate protection for liberty is necessarily flawed.

Rawls also argued that utilitarianism is based on a monistic conception of the good. What he had in mind here is that, by treating happiness as the sole ultimate measure of human well-being, utilitarian theory fails to accord due recognition to the fact that human beings have diverse interests and pursue diverse ends, of which happiness may be only one. On this point Rawls's view is a near relation of Kant's claim that human freedom rather than happiness should be at the focus of our ideas about justice. For

Rawls, it is an important, indeed fundamental fact that human beings embrace a variety of (what he called) conceptions of the good. Some people may believe that a life of happiness is the best kind of life a human being can have and that, ultimately, all other ends or objectives of life should be subordinated to the objective of attaining happiness. Others may consider a life of integrity in accordance with some particular conception of that virtue to be the best possible kind of human life, even if it must be purchased at the cost of happiness. Still others may hold still different ideas about the proper ends or objectives of human life. Rawls believed that utilitarianism does not take into account the full variety of human ends (or conceptions of the good), thereby failing to accord due recognition to the distinctive human capacity freely to formulate and to embrace a "plurality" (as Rawls and many other recent writers have called it) of legitimate conceptions of the good.

This criticism of utilitarianism may not be fully justified. Rawls himself seems to recognize that it may not apply to all the forms of utilitarian theory, and he accordingly defines the central object of his criticism as "classical" utilitarian theory, to which he believes Bentham, Mill, and Sidgwick subscribed. It is reasonable, however, to question Rawls's claim, even considering it to be directed only at these theorists. As we have seen, Bentham recognized and attempted to accommodate within the scope of utilitarian theory the fact that human beings hold "idiosyncratical" values; John Stuart Mill did the same. At least some of the utilitarian writers may be less vulnerable to this criticism than Rawls believed.

More generally, Rawls was dissatisfied with utilitarianism because that body of theory does not treat distributive questions as the central questions that must be asked about justice. In fact, generally speaking, utilitarian theories focus on aggregate human well-being, not on justice. Any claims these theories make about justice generally are derivative from and subordinate to claims about aggregate utility. In contrast, Rawls argued that questions about justice are the most important questions we can ask about social institutions. He declares, on the opening page of *A Theory of Justice*, that "[j]ustice is the first virtue of social institutions [. . .] laws and institutions no matter how efficient and well-arranged must be reformed or abolished if they are unjust" (3/3). The terms "efficient" and "well-arranged" allude to the utilitarian values whose primacy Rawls was attempting to challenge. He often expressed the difference between his theory and its principal rival by asserting that, whereas the central concept in utilitarian theories is the concept of the good, from which the idea of the right must be derived, in the theory of justice as fairness the right is prior to the good (31/28).

In view of the status of utilitarianism as the prime target of his criticism, it is noteworthy that in one of his earliest essays, "Two concepts of rules" (1955), Rawls actually mounts a limited defense of utilitarianism. As we have seen, one familiar objection to utilitarianism is that the arguments utilitarians use to justify the punishment of wrongdoers could also be used to justify the "punishment" of innocent persons, if that practice would contribute to the good of society. Rawls argues that this criticism is misplaced.

Although Rawls offers a limited defense of utilitarianism against some criticisms in this essay, its main objects, as the title suggests, are to distinguish between two levels of argument about rules and to show that failure to observe this distinction has contributed to confusion in moral argument. He argues that there is a crucial difference between the justification of a *practice* and the justification of *actions within* that practice – and in this case, specifically, between justifying the practice of punishment and justifying actions within that practice. The practice of punishment can be justified (perhaps) by appealing to the greatest happiness principle. Actions within that practice, however, can be justified only by appealing to the rules by which that practice is constituted, not by appealing to the greatest happiness principle directly. The rules by which the practice of punishment is constituted are retributive rules, not (directly) utilitarian ones. So, according to Rawls in this essay, utilitarianism is not vulnerable to the criticism that it might justify the punishment of innocent persons. This misplaced criticism (he argues) inappropriately applies utilitarian standards, which should be applied to the practice of punishment, to specific acts of punishment, which should be judged by retributivist standards, not by utilitarian ones.

Although Rawls's defense of utilitarianism against this criticism is not wholly persuasive, his essay is still of considerable interest for two main reasons. First, it reveals substantive inclinations that are confirmed throughout Rawls's writings from this point forward. Rawls took utilitarianism with the utmost seriousness. He considered it to be the pre-eminent theory for assessing social institutions and policies in his time and regarded it, consistently, as the most serious contender for this role – with the exception of his own theory of justice as fairness. He did not accord the same respect to retributivism. In the essay, he discusses utilitarianism and retributivism as *prima facie* rivals. Rawls suggests – with little argument – that retributivism cannot justify the practice of punishment. He argues for a division of labor between the utilitarian and retributivist views: the utilitarian argument, he suggests, provides a basis on which it might be possible to justify the practice of punishment, while the retributivist argument justifies actions within that practice. According to this conception of the field of argument, we can think of utilitarianism as a description of the point of view that a legislator should take up in considering whether to adopt the rules that constitute the practice of punishment, while the judge who is charged with applying those rules appeals to the retributivist point of view. It follows that "the utilitarian view is more fundamental." Even within its apparently "natural" domain, then, Rawls dismisses retributivism – a view of justice in relation to wrongdoing that is based on the concept of reciprocity – as a derivative and secondary view, one that has its proper place, but only in subordination to (what he believed to be) a more comprehensive and more fundamental theory. Rawls never seriously defended the assumptions that led to this dismissal.

A second interesting point about Rawls's essay is that it exemplifies a strategy he would deploy consistently throughout his career. He does not simply reject retributivism. Instead, he subordinates it to an allegedly broader view, in this case the utilitarian view. For Rawls, retributivism is a valid approach to punishment, but only from within a point of view that is highly constrained, as the point of view of the judge is supposed to be constrained by the legislation he or she is charged with enforcing. This strategy of argument, which is strikingly reminiscent of the method that Hegel had deployed in his major philosophical works, from his *Phenomemology of Spirit* (1806) onward, contributed significantly to the magisterial impression created by Rawls's work and served as a kind of template, to which he would return repeatedly in contending with views that appeared to be at odds with his own.

II

Rawls describes the subject of his theory as the "basic structure" of society. A society's basic structure comprises its major social institutions, including its political constitution, its fundamental economic structures, and its principal social arrangements. For example, the institutions of private property in the means of production and of competitive markets are central components in the economic structures of some societies, whereas others have been based on collective ownership of the means of production and on command economies. Some countries' political constitutions provide strong legal protections for freedom of thought and for liberty of conscience; others do not. The monogamous family is a bedrock social institution in many societies, while in others the polygamous family in one form or another has stood for centuries as one of society's principal social arrangements.

What does the basic structure of a society *not* include? In various passages, Rawls takes special note of two categories of things that can be said to be just or unjust, yet are not the subject of his theory. One of these consists of the kinds of rules that regulate interactions and transactions among private persons, such as those which regulate contractual agreements and those which apply to the practices of private associations (8/7). The other category is made up of individual actions and transactions. These things can certainly be said to be just or unjust, but they are not the subject of Rawls's theory. His topic is social justice, and in his view the appropriate subject of a theory of social justice is a society's basic structure.

Why focus on the basic structure of society? Rawls's main argument is that the institutions and practices that comprise a society's basic structure determine how well the members of that society are able to do in life, both in absolute terms and in comparison with others. In fact, in the most precise sense, it is the division of advantages that results from a society's basic structure rather than the basic structure itself that is the real subject of the theory (7/6). In identifying the basic structure as the primary subject of his theory of justice, Rawls was in effect adopting the view that justice is an attribute first and foremost of the terrain of society. For Rawls, the idea of justice applies principally to the landscape that determines the loci of privilege and deprivation in a society rather than to the character of relations among persons.

We can glean some additional features of Rawls's argument for focusing on the basic structure if we look at the following passage:

> The basic structure is the primary subject of justice because its effects are so profound and present from the start [...] men born into different positions have different expectations of life [...] the institutions of society favor certain starting places over others. These [...] inequalities [...] affect men's initial chances in life; yet they cannot possibly be justified by an appeal to the notions of merit or desert. (7/7)

This passage reveals two significant points. First, when Rawls argued for the basic structure as the appropriate subject of a theory of social justice, it is evident that his concerns about inequalities were concentrated on inequalities in people's life chances – on the (differential) opportunities available to people – and not on ultimate outcomes. He writes here of the different positions men are "born into," of their "starting places" and "initial chances." Second, the passage hints at the fact (made clearer in later discussions) that Rawls was concerned about the ways in which major social institutions shape individuals' aspirations and expectations, as well as about the ways in which those institutions determine the division of advantages. Even if they have similar objective opportunities, some people do less well than others in life because they have lower aspirations or expectations. These aspirations and expectations are themselves shaped by the basic structure of society, and these subjective disparities among people were as worrisome to Rawls as objective differences in opportunities.

Rawls's argument for focusing on the basic structure also alludes to the inadequacy of the notions of merit and desert. Although his primary target of criticism is classical utilitarianism, he also takes aim at the idea that goods should be distributed in accordance with moral desert (310–315/273–277). It would take us too far afield to explore the intricacies of his discussion of this point, but it is worth noting here that Rawls dismisses desert as something fundamental to social justice in much the same way as he once dismissed attempts to justify the practice of punishment on retributivist grounds. He essentially replaces the concept of desert with that of legitimate expectations, a concept that separates the goods to which the members of a society are entitled from the contributions they make to that society in roughly the same way in which the principle "from each according to his ability, to each according to his needs" severs any connection between contributions and benefits (310–311/273–274).

For Rawls, the basic structure is not merely one among several possible subjects of a theory of justice, and social justice is not merely one among several possible types of justice. Social justice is instead justice in the most comprehensive and fundamental sense. Rawls envisages a division of labor between the principles of justice that apply to the basic structure and the rules or criteria of justice that apply to all other subjects. This division of intellectual labor is similar to the division he once conceived between a utilitarian justification of the practice of punishment and a retributivist set of rules designed to constitute that practice. The principles of social justice are distinct from the rules and criteria that apply to other subjects. This is why he says that the "way in which we think about fairness in everyday life ill prepares us for the great shift in perspective required for considering the justice of the basic structure itself." At the same time, those principles are also intellectually prior to these other rules and criteria and serve as a foundation for defensible ideas about justice with regard to other subjects. As he observes in *A Theory of Justice*, once we have a sound theory of social justice, "the remaining problems of justice [including those which have to do with transactions, with criminal actions and punishments, and with compensatory justice, among other subjects] will prove more tractable in the light of it" (8/7).

The distinction Rawls draws between the principles of justice that apply to the basic structure and the rules and criteria of justice that apply to other subjects serves an important substantive purpose for his theory of justice as a whole. Recall that one of Rawls's principal objections to utilitarianism is that it is based on a monistic conception of the good – in other words, that it fails to accord due recognition to the fact that human beings legitimately hold a plurality of conceptions of the good. In his view, classical utilitarianism is a "comprehensive" theory, that is, a moral theory that offers prescriptions for the design of human institutions as well as for the decisions individuals should make, and indeed for all subjects to which any moral theory can be applied. The strong distinction he draws between principles of justice that apply to the basic structure – in effect, to the terrain of the social world itself – and criteria of justice for other subjects enables him to leave room for a plurality of moral views about those other subjects, which he believes should be accommodated by a theory of social justice.

Rawls characterizes his theory of justice as an "ideal" theory. By an ideal theory of social justice he means a theory that depicts a perfectly just society (8–9/7–8). Another phrase he uses for ideal theory is "strict compliance theory," which he contrasts with "partial compliance theory." Rawls does not intend to diminish partial compliance theory, which deals with such topics as punishment; justice in the initiation, conduct, and aftermath of war; the justification of civil disobedience, militant resistance, and revolution; and compensation for wrongdoing, among many others. These matters are, he observes, pressing and urgent. Rawls's claim is that only by understanding the characteristics of a perfectly just society (he typically uses the phrase "well-ordered society," although for him that phrase has a broader meaning, encompassing societies that are not perfectly just) can we obtain a systematic grasp of the basis on which we should approach questions about justice in the real world. He regards ideal theory as more fundamental than non-ideal theory because he believes that we can best devise solutions to problems of justice that arise in the non-ideal world if we have first developed a sound conception of the principles of justice that would apply under ideal circumstances.

III

Rawls begins to lay out the most basic ideas of his theory with the following words:

> Let us assume [. . .] that a society is a more or less self-sufficient association of persons who [. . .] recognize certain rules of conduct as binding [. . .]. Suppose further that these rules specify a system of cooperation designed to advance the good of those taking part in it. Then [. . .] a society [. . .] is typically marked by a conflict as well as by an identity of interests. There is an identity of interests since social cooperation makes possible a better life for all than any would have if each were to live solely by his own efforts. There is a conflict of interests since [. . .] they each prefer a larger to a lesser share. A set of principles is required for choosing among the various social arrangements which determine this division of advantages [. . .]. These principles are the principles of social justice. (4/4)

With this passage as a touchstone, let's now look briefly at the theory's central ideas.

The most rudimentary of all the ideas underlying Rawls's theory is the idea of society as a fair system of social cooperation among free and equal persons over time, from one generation to the next. He sometimes calls this the "most fundamental intuitive idea" of the theory. Rawls offers no argument to defend this idea. Instead, he assumes that his readers will accept it as a plausible and appealing point of departure and concentrates his creative energies on the construction of an argument on the basis of this idea rather than on its defense.

This idea, then, plays a role in his theory of justice as fairness that is similar to the role played by the fundamental intuitive ideas of geometry in geometric reasoning. Although he did not believe it possible to construct a robust and persuasive theory of justice through pure deduction, Rawls aspired to make the argument of his theory as much like moral geometry as possible. The fundamental ideas on which theories of this kind are based are neither true nor false, and it makes little sense to attempt to prove or disprove them. Ultimately, those ideas stand or fall because of their usefulness or lack thereof. If the propositions and theories that are based on those ideas yield plausible or compelling accounts of the subjects to which they are addressed, then the usefulness of those ideas has been demonstrated. If not, then the ideas in question may be discarded in favor of alternatives.

Rawls believed that the idea of society as a fair system of social cooperation would be appealing to his readers. For most of his career (into the early 1980s) he appeared to believe that this appeal would be universal, at least to readers who had grappled sufficiently with the arguments of his theory to grasp its main points correctly. In his later years he seemed to retreat from this assumption by suggesting that his theory is designed to appeal distinctively to people who inhabit cultures that have been shaped by democratic and liberal ideals.

It is worth noting in any case that there is nothing bland or anodyne about the proposition that society should be conceived as a fair system of social cooperation among free and equal persons. Rawls's theory is built on a proposition that is in fact highly controversial, both in an historical and in a geographical sense. Aristotle, for one, would have been aghast at this claim. Insofar as he conceived of persons as bearers of worth, he believed that they are of radically unequal worth because they are categorically unequal in capabilities, so that the notion that we should think of society as a system of cooperation among equal persons would have made no sense to him. Nor would he have had much sympathy or appreciation for the emphasis this proposition places on freedom. For him, human beings are endowed with functions that are prescribed by nature. Excellence is exhibited through outstanding performance of those prescribed functions, much as excellence in acting is displayed through outstanding performance in a scripted role. Many pre-modern thinkers would have found the fundamental intuitive idea of society as a fair system of social cooperation among free and equal persons incomprehensible, and some would have found it reprehensible. The same can be said of many people today who have escaped the influence of, or rejected, modern European ideas (it can also be said of some people who embrace modern anti-liberal European ideas). On an historical and worldwide scale, the foundation on which Rawls constructed his theory is by itself a radical proposition.

For Rawls, the idea of society as a fair system of social cooperation is a basis for reasoning about societies in what he, following David Hume, calls the circumstances of justice (126–130/109–112). The circumstances of justice are circumstances of moderate scarcity, in which the hand of nature is neither so generous as to give human beings all they want, with no need for labor or social cooperation, nor so harsh as to force people into a struggle for survival so elemental as to preclude social cooperation. The circumstances of justice are those in which we neither enjoy unlimited abundance nor suffer extreme deprivation.

If the fundamental idea of Rawls's theory is that of society as a fair system of social cooperation among free and equal persons, the key question of that theory is: on what terms should this cooperation proceed? For the purposes of his theory of social justice, Rawls thinks of society as a collaborative enterprise of a sort that is akin to a business partnership, a "cooperative venture for mutual advantage." (He did not, however, think of society as a voluntary association, because for the most part membership in societies is thrust upon individuals who have little or no chance either to grant or to withhold their consent.) This conception of society is rooted in Adam Smith's contention that a complex division of labor is the principal source of the great wealth of modern societies. For Rawls, questions about social justice arise as a result of the productivity, broadly construed, that is made possible by the division of labor. As he says, "social cooperation makes possible a better life for all than any would have if each were to live solely by his own efforts." Society is a sort of partnership that is undertaken for the mutual benefit of those who enter into – or in this case, typically find that they are already in – that partnership. The key question of social justice is a question about the terms of this partnership, and in particular about the way in which its benefits will be distributed among the participants.

From this conception it follows that, for Rawls, the distributive questions to which the idea of social justice points focus distinctively on the social product, that is, on the "goods" (in a broad sense) that are generated by the joint efforts of the partners. These goods may not all be "material" or "economic" goods of the sort Smith had in mind. For example, they may include enjoyments of a non-economic kind that can be achieved only through collaboration with others, such as the enjoyments we derive from participating in a game that requires a number of participants, or from friendship. It is for these goods – the diverse class of goods that are generated by the joint efforts of the partners – and for these goods alone, however, that we require a set of principles to determine the proper distributive shares.

Rawls's key question is a variation of the question of social justice Sidgwick had raised roughly a century earlier, namely whether any clear principles may be found on the basis of which we can discover an ideally just distribution of rights, privileges, burdens, and pains. Notice, however, that, whereas Sidgwick had raised this question about a distribution of these things "among human beings as such," Rawls narrows the question to one about the distribution of advantages among the members of a given society conceived as a cooperative venture for mutual advantage. Rawls appears to have believed that we can find a compelling set of principles of social justice only by restricting the scope of our inquiry to a particular (even if hypothetical) society rather than by extending it to all humankind.

Notice also that, while Sidgwick had written with equal emphasis about the distribution of burdens and pains as well as that of rights and privileges, Rawls's emphasis is decidedly on the division of advantages. One reason for this emphasis may lie in his conception of society as a mutually advantageous undertaking. While some members benefit far more than others, Rawls supposes that normally all are made better off by participating in a scheme of social cooperation than they would be if "each were to live solely by his own efforts." So the significant thing that is generated by a scheme of social cooperation is benefits, not burdens; and it is the things generated by social cooperation that are subject to principles of social justice.

A second and more interesting reason, however, may lie in his assumption that all the members of such an enterprise will be active participants not only in the narrow sense of adhering to its rules of conduct, but also in the wider sense of contributing to it by being normal cooperating members. The principal conceptions of social justice that were developed during the long nineteenth century either offered a prescription for the contributions members should make to society and for the benefits they should receive (*from* each according to his ability/*to* each according to his needs) or linked the benefits individuals should receive to their contributions (the principle of desert). In contrast, Rawls's theory focuses on benefits while bracketing questions about contributions. Rawls appears simply to assume that the members of a just society will contribute to that society's social product in accordance with their diverse talents. This assumption seems to be part of what he intends when he suggests that the members of a society that is based on a fair system of cooperation among free and equal persons over time, from one generation to the next, would be "normal cooperating members of society over a complete life."

To find an answer to his central question, Rawls adopts a method that is borrowed in part from Kant and some of his predecessors in early modern political thought, including Thomas Hobbes, John Locke, and Jean-Jacques Rousseau. The method is to imagine that a society has been founded by an agreement among its members that determines the terms of their association. Kant had employed this method in his theory of public right by invoking the idea of the original contract to test the justice of public laws and policies. If it is plausible to suppose that the law or policy in question would have received the approval of all the members of a society in an original contract, then according to Kant we must assume that that law or policy is just. If this supposition is implausible, then we may conclude that the law or policy is unjust.

Kant limited his use of the idea of a hypothetical original contract to the task of testing the justice or injustice of laws and policies. In contrast, Rawls uses the idea of a hypothetical contract to identify a set of principles of social justice. Rawls's use of this device is more ambitious and more elaborate than Kant's.

Rawls asks his readers to imagine that each member of society is represented by an agent in a condition he calls the "original position," a hypothetical state of affairs in which the agents come together to reach an agreement that will shape the terms on which the society operates. The object of the agents' agreement (adopting legalistic language, Rawls typically calls these agents the "parties" in the original position) will be a set of principles of social justice focused on the distribution of advantages in society. Once these principles have been adopted, they can be used in a second stage of deliberation, which he called the stage of the constitutional convention, to make a choice among the various alternative basic structures that are available to the society. The basic structure they select will in turn provide the framework within which laws will be adopted, policies developed, and specific decisions reached. Since his entire theory of social justice is an ideal theory, these principles of justice will of course be framed for a perfectly just society.

Because he wants his readers to imagine a hypothetical contract that will be far more ambitious (in the sense of doing more intellectual work) than Kant's idea of the original contract, Rawls provides a significantly more detailed description of the original position than Kant does of the original contract. He emphasizes that the parties in the original position are rational in the sense that they prefer for the members of society whom they represent to obtain a greater rather than a lesser share of the benefits of social cooperation. The fact that the parties are rational does not entail that they or the members of society whom they represent are egoistic. Those members may, for example, wish to use a portion of their shares to promote causes that benefit others. He also emphasizes that the parties are reasonable. They understand that they must be willing to reach agreement with their counterparts on fair terms. In order to help guarantee their reasonableness, Rawls asks us to imagine that the parties in the original position have been placed behind (what he calls) a "veil of ignorance" that prevents them from knowing the abilities, social positions, or indeed the very identities of the members they represent. This kind of knowledge might sway them to bargain for unfair advantages. For example, if a representative were to know that the member he represents is intellectually exceptional, he or she might demand principles of justice that would tend to favor the intellectually gifted. Finally, Rawls suggests that the parties in the original position would adopt a distinctive measure to determine how well-off the members they represent are in comparison with others. The measures that are most commonly used for this purpose are income and wealth. Classical utilitarians used happiness (though they usually supposed that people with greater income or wealth are happier than others). Rawls argues that the appropriate measure would be made up of several diverse elements, including certain rights and liberties, income and wealth, and the social bases of self-respect, elements that he called "social primary goods."

Rawls's proposal, then, is that we can discover the best set of principles of social justice by imagining a number of representatives, in the hypothetical scenario he calls the original position, who want to reach an agreement with one another that will best serve their clients' interests, where their "clients" are the members of the perfectly just society that will be brought into being on the basis of those principles. As we have seen, it is a premise of Rawls's theory that some members of such a society – not merely of any actual society, but of a perfectly just society – will be better off than others. And not only that: some will be born into different positions, develop different expectations, and be endowed with different chances in life from others. Just as he borrowed from Adam Smith the idea that the division of labor is by far the most important source of productivity and ultimately of wealth, so did he also inherit from some of the classical political economists the assumption that the same division of labor leads ineluctably to disparities in the opportunities available to the different members of a society. Rawls assumed that human beings are equal to one another in worth. That assumption is one of the points conveyed by his beginning with the fundamental intuitive idea of society as a fair system of social cooperation among free and equal persons. But he also assumed that all members of a society can benefit from advantages obtainable only through a complex division of labor and that inequalities are an inevitable by-product of such a division of labor. Rawls's premises are egalitarian, but the principles of social justice at which he arrives are designed to justify those inequalities which (he believed) work to the advantage of all.

IV

The principal conclusion of the theory of justice as fairness is that the terms of social cooperation that would constitute the basic principles of social justice in a perfectly just society – the terms to which the parties in the original position would agree – can be summarized as follows:

1 Each person has an equal right to a fully adequate scheme of equal basic liberties which is compatible with a similar scheme of liberties for all.
2 Social and economic inequalities are to satisfy two conditions. First, they must be attached to offices and positions open to all under conditions of fair equality of opportunity; and second, they must be to the greatest benefit of the least advantaged members of society.

The first of these principles has (what Rawls calls) lexical priority over the second, and the first part of the second principle has lexical priority over its second part. In other words, the first principle must be fully satisfied before the second comes into play, just as all the words that begin with the letter "a" are listed in a dictionary before the words that begin with the letter "b." The way in which a society's social and economic inequalities are distributed is relevant for an evaluation of the justice of that society's basic structure only when all its members enjoy a fully adequate scheme of liberties. Let us call the first of these requirements the *basic liberties principle.* Since the second principle has two parts, let's call its first part the *equal opportunity principle* and the second (following Rawls's own consistent usage) the *difference principle.*

Rawls also reaches a second major conclusion, to which he believes the parties in the original position would agree. He argues that, in addition to a set of principles that can be invoked to choose among alternative basic structures (the two principles of justice specified just above), those parties would agree that the members of a just society should possess certain attributes. First, they would want the members (citizens) of such a society to possess an effective sense of justice. By this he means that they would want those members to be able to understand, to apply, and to act on the basis of a set of public principles of justice (namely the two principles of justice as fairness). Integral to his conceptions of social justice and of a well-ordered society is the conviction that, for a society truly to be just, its members must understand and consent to the terms of social cooperation by which they are governed. This first point underscores this conviction. Second, they would want the members to possess and to develop their capacities for a conception of the good. In other words, each member of society would want all the others to develop the capacity to form, to revise, and rationally to pursue a conception of the good, a conception that would form the basis of a member's plan of life. Rawls calls these attributes the two "highest-order" moral powers because they are the attributes he believes the parties in the original position would most want the citizens of a perfectly just society to develop. He labels the theory that describes these powers "the theory of moral personality." So for Rawls the theory of justice as fairness specifies both a set of principles of social justice (the two principles of justice as fairness) to which we should turn in choosing among alternative basic structures of society, and a set of attributes (the attributes of moral personality) that a just society should cultivate in its members.

These two major conclusions are intertwined. For example, the liberties that are to be protected by the basic liberties principle are, according to Rawls, just those liberties which are essential to the development and exercise of the two highest-order powers of moral persons. Rawls does not attempt to supply a complete list of these liberties, but he mentions, among others, freedom of thought, liberty of conscience, and freedom of association; personal liberties such as freedom from arbitrary arrest, the rights to due process of law and to a fair trial; and political liberties such as the right to vote and freedom of the press. He lays special emphasis on political liberties, and insists that the members of a just society must enjoy the "fair value" of these liberties, by which he means that each member should be in a position to exercise as much influence over common decisions as any other member.

The equal opportunity principle entails that the positions or roles in society to which unequal rewards are attached must be open to fair competition on a basis of equal opportunity. This principle should be underwritten by education for all, among other measures.

The difference principle prescribes that social and economic inequalities are justified only insofar as they work to the benefit of the least advantaged members of society. At first glance, the notion that such inequalities might be beneficial to the least advantaged – to the members of society who enjoy the most restricted opportunities and the fewest resources – seems paradoxical. Remember, however, that Rawls inherited from earlier political economists the assumption that the same division of labor that accounts for the unprecedented productivity and wealth of modern societies also leads inevitably to disparities in the opportunities available to different members of society. If the increase in goods (wealth and other goods, as measured by an index of social primary goods) made possible by a complex division of labor is sufficiently great, then even the least advantaged members of a society might be better off in a basic structure in which that complex division of labor prevails than they would be in an alternative basic structure without it. The difference principle takes this possibility into account.

The difference principle is the most distinctive of all the conclusions of the theory of justice as fairness. Here as elsewhere, Rawls's principal target is the theory he considers the most serious rival to the theory of justice as fairness, namely classical utilitarian theory. To see why, consider an illustration. Suppose you are a member of a society of one hundred members. Assume that the well-being of each of those members, as measured by an index of social primary goods, can be expressed on a cardinal scale of 1 to 10, with 10 representing the highest possible standard of well-being (as measured by one's share of primary goods) and 1 representing the lowest possible share. (In a cardinal scale, a share of 4 has twice the value of a share of 2 and a share of 8 has twice the value of a share of 4, while a share of 8 is more valuable than one of 7 by just the same amount as a share of 5 is more valuable than a share of 4. Having a single share is like having a single orange, or a single unit of any other good, while having three shares is like having three oranges.) Now imagine that your society is faced with a choice between two alternative basic structures whose distributive consequences can be represented as follows:

Shares of Primary Goods	Basic Structure A	Basic Structure B
10		
9	25 persons	
8		
7		25 persons
6	50 persons	
5		50 persons
4		25 persons
3	25 persons	
2		
1		

In Basic Structure A, then, 25 of the society's 100 members enjoy 9 shares of primary goods each, while 50 enjoy 6 shares each, and 25 must make do with 3 shares each.

If we think of shares of primary goods as units of well-being, then it is easy to see that the aggregate well-being that would be enjoyed by the members if they were to adopt Basic Structure A can be represented by the figure 600 $[(25 \times 9) + (50 \times 6) + 25 \times 3)]$, while a similar calculation will show that Basic Structure B would yield an aggregate well-being of 525. If we suppose, for the sake of the argument, that well-being as measured by shares of primary goods is equivalent to well-being as measured by utility, then it is clear that the greatest happiness principle would direct us to adopt Basic Structure A. Yet the difference principle would prescribe the adoption of Basic Structure B, since under that structure the least advantaged members of society are better off (at 4 on the scale of primary goods) than they would be under Basic Structure A (which would leave them at 3 on the scale). Basic Structure B leads to inegalitarian consequences, but those consequences are more advantageous to the least advantaged members of society than the consequences of the alternative.

This illustration assumes that Basic Structures A and B are the only available alternatives. If any additional option were available that would leave the least advantaged members of society even better off than they would be under Basic Structure B, then the difference principle would prescribe that, as a matter of social justice, we should adopt that third basic structure. For example, if the range of possible basic structures included a Basic Structure C under which all the members of society would command identical shares of primary goods rated at 5 on our scale of 1 to 10, then the difference principle would direct us to adopt that structure, even though aggregate well-being under it would be lower than under either of the alternatives [$100 \times 5 = 500$], because the least advantaged members of society would be better off under Basic Structure C than under either A or B. Because of his assumptions about productivity and the division of labor, Rawls did not seem to believe that such an alternative would be possible, but the principles of justice as fairness do not rule it out.

Rawls's standard statement of the difference principle seems slightly discrepant with his defense of the basic structure as the appropriate subject of the theory of social justice. The difference principle, which states that "social and economic inequalities [. . .] must be to the greatest benefit of the least advantaged members of society," suggests a focus on ultimate outcomes, that is, on how well off (as measured by shares of primary goods) the members of a society turn out to be. Yet Rawls's defense of the basic structure as the primary subject of his theory of justice focuses on opportunities ("starting places"), not on ultimate outcomes. In fuller statements of the difference principle, he sometimes speaks of the "greatest *expected* benefit"; and it is evident, in various places in his work, that Rawls understood the important difference between initial chances and ultimate outcomes. In his discussions of the principles of justice as fairness, however, Rawls frequently elides this distinction.

V

The theory of justice as fairness is an extraordinary accomplishment. As a vision of social justice for a society whose members are presumed to be free and equal citizens, it has no peer. Nevertheless, the theory is not flawless. I shall focus my comments on the way in which Rawls construes the subject of his theory.

Rawls's assertion that the basic structure of society is the appropriate subject of a theory of social justice is widely understood to be one of the most distinctive claims of his theory. As we have seen, the claim is not merely that the basic structure happens to be the appropriate subject of a theory of social justice in the same way in which (say) law violations are the appropriate subject of a theory of penal justice. It is rather that the basic structure has a kind of priority over all other kinds of subjects pertaining to justice, so that social justice is justice in the most comprehensive and fundamental sense. For Rawls, a sound theory of social justice provides the necessary foundation on which we can construct solutions to other, less comprehensive problems of justice. (In the latter years of his career, Rawls took up a set of questions about justice beyond national borders, questions that are arguably as comprehensive as, or more so than, questions about social justice within borders.)

If we examine Rawls's arguments closely, we can see that his claim consists of three distinct parts. The first is a causal claim that the institutions and practices that comprise a society's basic structure determine how well the members of a society are able to do in life. The second is the conceptual claim that the principles of justice that apply to the basic structure may be quite different in character from the rules and criteria that apply to other problems of justice. The third is a claim of intellectual priority. The claim is that we can best address the wide range of questions that arise about justice by first developing a sound theory of social justice. This theory can then constitute the foundation for defensible ideas about justice with regard to other subjects.

The first of these claims, in a general form, is incontrovertible. How completely a society's basic structure determines how well its members are able to do may be controversial, but there can be little doubt that a society's major institutions have profound effects on its members and on the division of advantages among them.

It is not difficult to see the force of Rawls's second claim as well. Consider the example of labor contracts. In a society made up of employers who are small business owners with limited resources and employees who are independent proprietors with a significant range of employment opportunities from which to choose, we can expect that justice will be served if all parties are free to enter into labor contracts on whatever terms are mutually agreeable. Since all parties possess roughly equal bargaining power, the bargains they reach typically can be expected to be fair. Matters will be different in a society dominated by giant corporate employers with vast resources at their command and by employees who have few alternatives (or, in the limiting case of some company towns, only one serious employment opportunity). Because of the great disparities in bargaining power in the latter scenario, freedom of contract is likely to lead to labor agreements that are unfair to employees. In that case collective bargaining arrangements, which reduce disparities in bargaining power between employees and employers, may restore some balance and justice to the labor contracts to which the parties agree. (In some cases, of course, collective bargaining arrangements may confer excessive power on those who bargain on behalf of employees.) A significant shift in perspective is required to grasp the fact that, in situations of great disparity in bargaining power, fairness is best secured by arrangements that differ sharply from those which typically lead to fair bargains in situations of relatively equal bargaining power. It is not surprising that a similar or greater shift in perspective may be required to grasp the fact that fair principles of justice for the basic structure of a society may differ markedly from the rules or criteria of justice that apply to ordinary interactions among individuals.

The claim that the principles of social justice are intellectually prior to, and serve as a foundation for, defensible ideas about justice with regard to other subjects is more problematic. Consider for another brief moment the example of labor contracts. If agreements reached by employers and employees who possess roughly equal bargaining power under conditions of freedom of contract are likely to be fair, the reason for this fact is that those agreements will typically embody the norm of balanced reciprocity. If collective bargaining arrangements help to restore fairness under conditions of highly unequal bargaining power, the reason is that those arrangements bring labor agreements more nearly into line with the norm of balanced reciprocity.

Nothing is more central to the way in which human beings think about fairness among relative equals than the norm of balanced reciprocity. In a chapter in *A Theory of Justice* on "The sense of justice," Rawls observes:

> reciprocity, a tendency to answer in kind [. . .] is a deep psychological fact [. . .]. A capacity for a sense of justice built up by responses in kind would appear to be a condition of human sociability. (494–495/433)

The kind of reciprocity Rawls has in mind here is balanced reciprocity, "a tendency to answer in kind." Although the justice of collective bargaining arrangements is not intuitively obvious to most people, the argument for the justice of those arrangements rests on intuitions that are highly accessible as well as widely, perhaps even universally, shared. The same thing can be said of the principles of social justice, as Rawls seems to acknowledge when he observes that the "most stable conceptions of justice are presumably those for which the corresponding sense of justice is most firmly based on these tendencies" (495/433).

In short, while it seems sensible to claim both that a society's basic structure plays a large causal role in determining how well its members are able to do and that the principles of social justice may be distinct from those which apply to other subjects, it is misleading to suppose that the principles of social justice are intellectually prior to and constitute the foundation for ideas about justice in relation to all other subjects. The kind of justice that applies directly to relations among persons is not trumped by the principles of social justice. Instead, the principles of social justice are rooted in the idea of justice in direct relations among persons. This idea – that justice among relative equals is based on the norm of balanced reciprocity – possesses an integrity that is not overshadowed by, and in fact provides the intellectual foundation for, sound ideas about social justice. Principles of social justice are distinct from the principles that apply to direct relations among relative equals, because the complexity of social institutions and practices requires adjustments to those principles. Ultimately, however, sound principles of social justice will be based on the norm of balanced reciprocity among relative equals.

If sound ideas about social justice are rooted in the norm of balanced reciprocity, then the concept of desert, which Rawls dismisses perfunctorily, may have a role to play in the way we think about justice, including social justice, after all. If two persons, A and B, are relative equals, and A confers a benefit on B, then there is a sense in which A deserves to be requited with a benefit similar in value to the benefit she has conferred, and B has an obligation of justice to bestow a benefit on A in return for the benefit he has received. Similarly, if Q inflicts a harm on R, then there is a sense, independent of any particular conception of social justice, in which Q deserves to suffer some harm in return.

Of course, the norm of balanced reciprocity in its simplest form – the form that applies to bilateral relations between relative equals – is not adequate as a guide to justice in relations among persons in complex circumstances. In situations that are multilateral or in which people are unequally placed, the social arrangements that would lead to justice in relations among persons may be dramatically different from those which apply to simple bilateral relations between equals. To accommodate these situations, major adjustments are needed, in much the same way as adjustments are required in bargaining between employees and employers when the disparities in bargaining power between them are large.

We can therefore see how the *concept* of desert might play a significant role in the way we think about justice, without leading us to endorse either the *principle* of desert (the contribution principle) or retributivist reasoning in its classic form (the form that is based on strict balanced reciprocity between putative equals). Rawls was right to see that the principles of justice that apply to the basic structure of a society are conceptually distinct from the rules of justice that apply to simple bilateral relations between persons. In fact his insight is generalizable to many subjects in addition to the basic structure of society. Yet, regardless of the particular subject for which the principles of justice are designed, if they are to be recognizable and acceptable to human beings, they must be rooted in the sense of justice – a sense that is best expressed through the concepts of reciprocity and desert.

Epilogue

From Social Justice to Global Justice?

The most significant innovation in the history of ideas about justice, at least in modern times and perhaps in the entirety of that history, has been the development of the idea of social justice. This idea is an outgrowth of the notion that human beings are capable of reshaping the terrain of their social world to conform to an intentional design – a notion that first appeared in ancient Athens, but gained widespread acceptance only in the eighteenth century. Rooted in the postulate that all human beings are equal in worth, the modern idea of social justice has spawned a series of perceptions of and theories about justice that are intertwined closely with recent and contemporary institutions and practices. Whether we conceive of these theories and perceptions as causes or as consequences of the institutional innovations that have accompanied them, it is impossible to understand the modern world without them.

Most theories of social justice have incorporated the insight that virtually all the wealth generated in modern societies, as well as the highly developed skills that enable human beings to produce that wealth, are social products made possible only by a complex division of labor rather than merely the sum of the products of individuals taken singly. The major exception is the earliest conception of social

A Brief History of Justice, First Edition. David Johnston.

justice to take on a definite shape, namely the conception embodied in the principle of desert. The principle of desert is vitiated by its failure to come to grips with this insight and its implications. The fact that virtually all our skills and all our wealth are social products need not compel us to discard the *concept* of desert from the repertoire of ideas to which we can turn to understand problems of justice, but it does give us good reasons to reject the *principle* of desert as the fundamental principle of social justice.

The other major conception of social justice that emerged in the nineteenth century, embodied in the principle of need, does not suffer from this weakness. The principle of need expresses some of the loftiest and most magnanimous aspirations human beings have ever conceived. Yet the principle of need is flawed, because it would sever all connections between the contributions individuals make to others and the benefits they are entitled to receive. The principle of need takes no account of the sense of justice, to which a sensibility for reciprocity in relations among human beings is integral.

The theory of justice as fairness, which articulates a third major conception of social justice – one that has dominated discussions of social justice, especially in the English-speaking world, for forty years – was developed with a great appreciation for the implications of the fact that both the wealth and the most valued skills we find in highly developed societies are social products. Like the principle of need, the theory of justice as fairness expresses a noble and generous vision of human society. Yet, for all its trimmings and despite the best intentions of its creator, the theory of justice as fairness, too, neglects the sense of justice and the understanding that justice cannot be severed from some kind of reciprocity among human beings, which is central to that sense. Recent theories of social justice, for all their nobility, have lost touch with the roots of the idea of justice, which are intertwined with the concept of reciprocity.

If justice were something that existed in the world in complete independence from human thought, as stars and trees do, it would, at least arguably, be unimportant for a theory of justice to maintain a palpable connection with the intuitions and sensibilities that constitute the sense of justice. For in that case the point of such a theory would be to account for a set of things in the world that may be knowable to human beings, but are in no sense products of human activity. While the interests of human beings might determine whether those things were treated as objects of knowledge at all, the intuitions and sensibilities of human beings would have no appropriate bearing on the content of such a theory. A theory of justice in this case would be like the theory of quantum mechanics, or like theories in astrophysics, or biology, or many other fields in which we assume that an object of knowledge exists independently of human beings and we hope to discover the attributes and features of that object. Although many people, from at least Plato onward, have thought about justice (and about many other abstract ideas) in roughly this way, it is not credible to assume that justice is an objective feature of the world in this sense.

If, on the other hand, justice were a strictly subjective construct that can be formulated in any way one pleases, then it is evident that the failure of a theory of justice to remain tied in some manifest way to the sense of justice would constitute no objection to that theory. This view, or some close variant, has been upheld by many skeptical thinkers, from Thrasymachus (at least as Plato represents him) to Nietzsche and beyond. It became a popular view in the twentieth century, when difficulties with objectivist theories of value drove many, intellectuals as well as others, to endorse the claim that all values are strictly subjective, as matters of taste are often believed to be. The upshot of this view, however, is that no theory of justice can be defended by reasons, since many different and contradictory theories of justice would all be equally sound and equally vacuous.

In reality, neither of these views is correct. Justice is a concept. Like all concepts, it is a tool invented and refined by human beings – by many human beings, for most of whom any contribution toward shaping or transmitting the concept of justice is an unintended byproduct of thoughts and actions that aim at other purposes.

Although the concept of justice is subject to refinement, revision, and even (potentially) transformation, it is not infinitely plastic, and we are not free to reinvent it in any form we like – at least not if we want it to do work for us, as we generally want tools to do. If we want ideas about justice to be recognized and accepted as ideas about *justice*, rather than as arbitrary fabrications, we must respect the intuitions that are fundamental to the sense of justice.

A sensibility for reciprocity in relations among human beings is integral to that sense. It is commonplace for people who have received significant benefits from others to feel that they ought to requite those benefits in some fashion, if they are able to do so. Perhaps even more strikingly, people will often go to great lengths to retaliate against others who have inflicted harm, if they are able to do so. It is not unusual for people to retaliate against perpetrators of harm even if they are not the victims and the act of retaliation is costly to themselves. It is true that people's willingness to incur costs in order to act fairly or to punish others for acting unfairly varies considerably from one individual to the next. It is also true that perceptions of what constitutes fair reciprocity vary significantly across cultures. Nevertheless, both monocultural and cross-cultural studies of behavior related to fairness have found that people generally are motivated by considerations of reciprocity and are willing to make personal sacrifices in order to satisfy the demands of reciprocity. The authors of one of the most impressive cross-cultural studies of this kind of behavior suggest that long-run evolutionary processes may have given human beings predispositions to forego benefits to themselves in order to requite benefits or injuries received.

Any attempt to predict the future of the idea of justice would be even more speculative than the effort to reconstruct the prehistory of that idea. But we can say with some confidence that a sensibility for reciprocity in relations among persons would be a central feature of any persuasive future theory of justice.

The concept of reciprocity was central to ancient, pre-philosophical ideas about justice. In the writings of the Babylonians, the ancient

Israelites, and the early Greek poets, we can perceive a pattern in which justice is associated with balanced reciprocity among those equal in status and with imbalanced reciprocity between those unequal in status. Among unequals, it was considered just (according to the written records that have been passed down to us) for individuals of low status to be punished more severely than individuals of higher status who had committed equivalent offences and, in general, for persons of low status to receive less and to give more than persons of high status. Among unequals, reciprocity was imbalanced in a way that favored those of higher standing or status and was disadvantageous to people of lower status.

This ancient pattern is incompatible with the postulate that all human beings are equal in worth. On the basis of that postulate, one might conclude that justice, at least in transactions between individuals, is best conceived as strictly balanced reciprocity. This is roughly the conclusion reached by Kant. Yet this conclusion is blind to the fact that human beings who are considered equal in *worth* commonly are not also equal in *capabilities.*

We should consider revising the notion of justice as reciprocity so as to make it accommodate inequalities in human beings' capabilities in a way that inverts the priorities evident in ancient ideas about justice. Among individuals who are relative equals, we might think of justice in transactions as a matter of equality in exchanges, or of essentially balanced reciprocity. Among persons who are unequal in capabilities – whether the inequality arises from differences in their talents or in their other resources – it seems sensible to suggest that justice is done when less is required or expected of those with lesser capabilities and more is expected of those with greater capabilities. Suppose I have an acquaintance who is confined to a nursing home, requires a great deal of personal care, and has little or no capacity to do favors for others. Imagine, further, that I do a great deal to benefit this acquaintance, perhaps by visiting with her frequently, by bringing her interesting and flavorful foods to supplement the drab nursing home fare, and by supplying her with a stream of good reading matter and musical recordings. It would seem perverse to suggest that my acquaintance does me an injustice by failing to repay me for these benefits with goods or favors of equivalent value. On the contrary, it seems reasonable to say that she does justice by thanking me occasionally. In her circumstances, this kind of requital is proportional to her capabilities.

In maintaining that a strong sensibility for reciprocity in relations among persons would be a central feature in any persuasive theory of justice, I do not mean to suggest that we should abandon the idea of social justice or the problem of distributing the social product in a just manner. On the contrary, the distributions to which a society's institutions and practices lead have a major impact on the character and quality of the relations among its members. My point is that the priority, especially the intellectual priority, Rawls and many other theorists of social justice have accorded to this topic is misplaced. A revision in our thinking of the kind I suggest would remove the idea of social justice, as it has usually been conceived, from the role of a master conception to which all other topics and ideas about justice should be subordinated. The idea of social justice should be re-invented as part of a larger conception of justice, at the center of which lies the concept of social relations of mutual respect and reciprocity among citizens.

This re-inventing might seem to entail an ineluctable turn toward small-scale issues and away from questions about justice of the largest kind. In fact, while such a revision would remove the idea of social justice from the pedestal it has occupied for many years, that removal would also open a pathway that could lead toward newly invigorated ways of thinking about the most urgent problem of justice in the world today, namely the problem of global justice and injustice.

The idea of social justice, at least in the form it has taken over the past two centuries or so, has tended consistently to reinforce a parochialism that has plagued views on justice since ancient times. Since the beginning of recorded history, most thinkers who have written about justice have applied that concept only to relations among persons who share a common political or cultural identity. Some of the ancient Stoic thinkers (including Cicero, who was not "officially" a Stoic but a Platonist), count as important exceptions to this general truth, and the universalistic ideas of these thinkers were transmitted to later centuries by compilers and commentators on Roman law and by the apostles and organizers of the Christian movement. However, this impulse toward universalism has consistently encountered powerful forces of resistance, especially in the modern era of the national state.

Thomas Hobbes's thinking about the subject is typical. Following Grotius and other writers in the tradition of natural rights theories, Hobbes developed an account of the law of nature that could in principle serve as a basis for relations of peace and cooperation among all human beings. Yet Hobbes argued that most of the laws of nature apply to human actions only among people who are united in a political association that is subject to a sovereign power. In the absence of a sovereign who is capable of enforcing these and other laws, the laws of nature apply only *in foro interno* (in the internal forum of conscience). Hobbes reasoned that only within a political association with the power to enforce laws do people enjoy the guarantee that others will engage with them in relations that are fair and reciprocal. In their relations with all persons who are not subject to their sovereign's power, people are at liberty to set aside considerations of justice to seek their own security and advantage through whatever means they see fit. In Hobbes's view, the laws of nature, which are the laws of natural justice, impose no meaningful constraints on people's behavior toward outsiders.

Despite considerable lip service to universalistic ideals, most advocates of social justice over the past two centuries have either expressly endorsed or tacitly accepted parochial conclusions of the same broad type as those to which Hobbes's argument leads. The primary source of this acceptance has been these advocates' focus on the social product as the central concern of social justice. If the social product is the consequence of a complex division of labor, in which producers achieve a high level of productivity by acquiring specialized skills and by attaining great efficiency – and if the principal question of social justice is how the social product should be divided among the members of the society that produces it – then it seems to follow that only those who contribute to that product, or at least who are members of the society that produces it, should be given consideration as potential beneficiaries of a scheme of social justice. Those who are essentially outsiders and are not participants in the division of labor have no claim on this product. The logic of a conception of social justice that is focused on the division of the social product, or more generally on the division of advantages and disadvantages within a complex division of labor, is a logic that points toward a rigorous distinction between insiders, who are the appropriate human subjects of a scheme of social justice, and outsiders, who are not.

Lines of reasoning that resemble this one can be observed as they play out in the writings of both the earliest and some of the more recent major advocates of social justice. Johann Gottlieb Fichte was one of the earliest proponents of the modern idea of social justice. The central thought of his work on the *Closed Commercial State* is that a state can provide for the well-being of its members in the way that is required by justice only if it maintains a robust commercial society within its borders while preserving its self-sufficiency in relation to other states. Later advocates of social justice as diverse as John Maynard Keynes, Gunnar Myrdal, and William Beveridge, who is credited with being the intellectual founder of the modern British welfare state, flirted with similar lines of argument. More recently, in one of his last works, *The Law of Peoples*, John Rawls makes it clear that, in his view, principles of social justice of the kind he envisaged in his theory apply only to relations among persons who constitute a "people," defined by a collective identity based on cultural or historical affinities. Those principles do not, according to Rawls, apply universally or across all peoples.

Collectivities of the kind on which Fichte, Rawls and many others have focused have important consequences for justice. The individuals who constitute them are bound together by special ties of obligation and trust. It follows that these individuals are likely to have duties toward one another that differ from the obligations of justice they owe to outsiders. Just as a person can owe special duties to specific others (such as a spouse or a child), so can the bonds that unite a people or the members of a political association partially define the relations of justice among them. Yet special bonds and relationships do not render inapplicable the duties of justice that human beings owe to one another as such. These duties are rooted in the notions of mutual respect and reciprocity.

The principal actors in international relations today, both "public" and "private," are, as always, driven overwhelmingly by the pursuit of their own advantage, with little regard for justice and only as much regard for reciprocity as is dictated by considerations of prudence. This largely unregulated pursuit of advantage has resulted in, and continues to lead to, a great deal of injustice across the globe. Many "transactions" across borders are imposed by stronger powers on weaker ones. Even when international transactions appear to be voluntary, it is commonplace for those transactions to result from bargaining between parties who possess highly unequal bargaining power. Within state borders, inequalities in bargaining power are sometimes subject to regulations or institutional arrangements (including, as we noted above, collective bargaining arrangements) to reduce the injustices that flow from them. Beyond state borders, however, regulations rarely work to the benefit of weaker parties.

This longstanding and systematic injustice in global relations bears a substantial share of responsibility for the immiseration of a large portion of the world's population. The central problem of global injustice – the most pressing problem of injustice in the world today – is caused primarily by the more powerful parties' lack of willingness to engage with weaker parties on terms of mutual respect and reciprocity and by the absence of any systematic means for correcting the accumulated injustices of many unfair international transactions – and not by the wealthier countries' refusal to share their social product with poorer nations. The problem of global injustice has less to do with an unfair division of the wealthier societies' social products and more to do with an absence of mutual respect and reciprocity across borders than is widely supposed.

Recall that, in the fourth century BCE, Aristotle observed:

> It cannot, perhaps, but appear very strange, to a mind which is ready to reflect, that a statesman should be expected to be able to lay his plans for ruling and dominating border states without any regard for their feelings [. . .] men are not ashamed of behaving to others in ways which they would refuse to acknowledge as just, or even expedient, among themselves. For their own affairs, and among themselves, they want an authority based on justice; but when other men are in question, their interest in justice stops.

It is likely that Aristotle intended his observations to apply only to relations among Greeks. Yet over 2,300 years later, in a world that has grown in population by orders of magnitude, in which states and empires have arisen and collapsed, and in which humans' knowledge and understanding of the world have expanded tremendously, his words seem eerily prescient.

Glossary of Names

Aristotle (384–322 BCE): Greek philosopher, student of Plato and teacher of Alexander the Great.

François-Noël Babeuf (1760–1797): French journalist and political activist during the period of the French Revolution. After his execution in 1797, he came to be widely thought of as a committed republican and a harbinger of communism.

Babylonia: Ancient kingdom located mainly in territories that presently comprise Iraq.

Francis Bacon (1561–1626): English philosopher, scientist, and political figure; he served as Lord Chancellor of England and was a major advocate of early modern scientific methods of inquiry.

Cesare Beccaria (1738–1794): Italian political figure, and philosopher whose *On Crimes and Punishments* is considered a founding work in modern penology.

Jeremy Bentham (1748–1832): English jurist, philosopher, and legal and social reformer. A leading theorist in Anglo-American philosophy of law, Bentham is usually considered the founder of the rigorous utilitarian tradition in philosophy.

A Brief History of Justice, First Edition. David Johnston.

Louis Blanc (1811–1882): French historian and political figure, who became well known as a socialist and champion of the urban poor.

Anicius Manlius Severinus Boethius (c. 480–524/5): early Christian philosopher, author of the *Consolation of Philosophy*. He has long been recognized as an important student of ancient philosophy and a conduit for its transmission to the medieval west.

Edmund Burke (1729–1797): Irish politician, orator, and philosopher who served for many years in the House of Commons of Great Britain and is well known both for his support of the American Revolution and for his opposition to the French Revolution. Burke is widely considered a major spokesperson for modern conservatism.

Marcus Tullius Cicero (106–43 BCE): great Roman philosopher, politician, lawyer, orator, and political thinker. He also translated Greek philosophical works into Latin, thus contributing to the formation of a technical philosophical vocabulary in this language.

Dio Chrysostom (40–120 CE): Greek orator, philosopher, and historian of the Roman Empire.

Friedrich Engels (1820–1895): German historian, political theorist, and economic and social scientist who collaborated with Karl Marx in *The Communist Manifesto* and other works and helped toward supporting him and his work financially.

Johann Gottlieb Fichte (1762–1814): German philosopher in the tradition of German idealism, placed chronologically between Immanuel Kant (1724–1804) and Georg Wilhelm Friedrich Hegel (1770–1831).

Hammurabi (died c. 1750 BCE): King of Babylonia, who extended his kingdom's reach through a series of wars. He is best known to modern scholars for the *Code of Hammurabi*, one of the earliest extensive codifications of law in recorded history.

Georg Wilhelm Friedrich Hegel (1770–1831): German philosopher in the tradition of German idealism, which sprang mainly from the thinking of Immanuel Kant. He is best known for his first major book, the *Phenomenology of Spirit*, and for his last book, the *Philosophy of Right*. As a young man Karl Marx studied and eventually criticized Hegel's philosophy intensely.

Hesiod (fl. c. 700 BCE): early Greek epic poet. Unlike Homer, with whom he is often contrasted, he describes the life of hardworking Boeotian farmers like himself.

Thomas Hobbes (1588–1679): English philosopher and scholar who translated works by Thucydides and Homer from Greek into English and developed a systematic philosophy, sometimes known as mechanical materialism. He is best known for his 1651 book *Leviathan*, one of the foundational works of modern political philosophy.

Homer: Traditional author of the first great Greek epic poems, the *Iliad* and the *Odyssey*, which probably took shape between the eighth and the seventh century BCE. Since late antiquity, no scholarly consensus has existed about whether the poems were the creation of one historical individual or of a guild of oral poets (the Homeridae), but it is certain that the Homeric poems were transmitted through oral recitation and improvisation for centuries before being committed to writing. Most scholars today regard the *Iliad* and the *Odyssey* as poems composed by two distinct authors.

David Hume (1711–1776): Scottish philosopher and historian; he is considered a major figure in the modern history of philosophical empiricism.

Justinian (483–565): Emperor of the Eastern Roman Empire (with the capital at Byzantium), renowned for ordering the codification of Roman law.

Immanuel Kant (1724–1804): German philosopher whose work had a towering influence on modern ethics and metaphysics. His *Critique of Pure Reason* is one of the central works of modern philosophy.

Peter Kropotkin (1842–1921): Zoologist and evolutionary theorist who advocated anarchism (i.e. a society free of any central government) and a communism based on voluntary associations of workers.

Thomas Robert Malthus (1766–1834): English economist and demographer who, in contrast to some thinkers of his era, warned that population growth would limit the possibilities for progress in human societies.

Karl Marx (1818–1883): German economist, philosopher, political thinker, and revolutionary activist, widely known for his magnum opus, *Capital: A Critique of Political Economy.*

Matthew the Evangelist (1st century BCE–1st century CE): Traditionally identified as author of one of the Gospels, according to which he was a tax collector when he was called by Jesus of Nazareth to be one of his disciples.

John Stuart Mill (1806–1873): British economist, philosopher, political thinker, and administrator. He is known as a defender of empiricism in philosophy, of utilitarianism, and of the liberal tradition of political thought.

Thomas More (1478–1535): English lawyer and statesman; also a major figure in the Catholic church who resisted the English Reformation. More coined the word "utopia" from Greek, by placing the negative particle *ou* ("no") in front of the noun *topos* ("place"), and used it as the title for his most famous work, *Utopia.*

Isaac Newton (1642–1727): English mathematician, scientist, philosopher, alchemist, and theologian, best known for his formulation of a theory of universal gravity and for developing the calculus in mathematics.

Plato (429–347 BCE): ancient Greek philosopher and founder of the Academy in Athens, which is regarded as the first formal "school" of philosophy. Plato's numerous writings had a massive influence on the entire subsequent development of philosophy. They are all in dialogue form, portraying Socrates in conversation with various interlocutors; no single view in the dialogues is reported in Plato's own name.

John Rawls (1921–2002): American philosopher whose book *A Theory of Justice* (1971) is credited with initiating a major revival of political philosophy.

Jean-Jacques Rousseau (1712–1778): Swiss-born writer who was raised in Geneva and lived much of his life in France. Rousseau is best known for his major work of political philosophy, *On the Social Contract*, which is considered a seminal work in democratic theory, and for *Emile*, his treatise on education in the form of an account of the education of a young man.

Henri de Saint-Simon (1760–1825): French writer and prominent public character. He had a technocratic vision of a socialist society, which he advocated, and he is thought of as a significant figure in the history of sociology.

Henry Sidgwick (1838–1900): English moral philosopher; his *Methods of Ethics* is often regarded as the culminating work of the classical utilitarian tradition of moral and political philosophy.

Adam Smith (1723–1790): Scottish moral philosopher, whose *Wealth of Nations* is considered the founding work of modern economic theory.

Socrates (469–399 BCE): Greek philosopher and teacher of Plato. He left no writings, but he initiated the dialectical method (the method of arguing systematically through dialogue), and, with it, the practice of philosophy as a way of life. All the disciples in his circle wrote Socratic dialogues, the most famous of which were Plato's.

Sophists: A label applied to itinerant intellectual–lecturers in the Greek world of the late fifth century BCE (about the time of Socrates). They offered instruction in all possible subjects, but their overarching principle was the skilful use of oratory, directed at persuading others.

Herbert Spencer (1820–1903): English philosopher, sociologist, and evolutionary theorist.

Stoics/Stoicism: One of the four leading Hellenistic schools of philosophy in Athens. Stoicism was founded by Zeno of Citium in the last quarter of the third century BCE and developed a wide following among later Greek and Roman intellectuals.

Theognis (seventh or sixth century BCE): a poet or group of poets associated with the beginnings of ancient Greek elegy. "Cyrnus" is the name of a youth to whom Theognis' poems are addressed.

Alexis de Tocqueville (1805–1859): French political figure, sociologist, political theorist and historian; he is best known for his two-volume work *Democracy in America*, composed in the 1830s after a wide-ranging visit to the United States, and for *The Old Regime and the Revolution*. Tocqueville is considered a major contributor to the development of democratic theory.

Edward Westermarck (1862–1939): Finnish philosopher and sociologist, best known for his works on ethics and on the incest taboo.

Source Notes

Short Titles Used in Notes

Aristotle, *Ethics*	*The Fifth Book of the Nicomachean Ethics of Aristotle*, edited and translated by Henry Jackson. Cambridge: Cambridge University Press, 1879.
Aristotle, *Politics*	Aristotle. *The Politics of Aristotle.* For this work I have used two translations. Most references are to *The Politics of Aristotle*, translated by J. E. C. Welldon. London: Macmillan, 1901. For some passages that appear in Chapter 4, I have adopted the version in *The Politics of Arisototle*, translated with notes by Ernest Barker. Oxford: Clarendon Press, 1960. Where I have used Barker's translation, I have noted this fact.
Beccaria, *Crimes*	Cesare Beccaria, *On Crimes and Punishments and Other Writings*, edited by Richard Bellamy, translated by Richard Davies. Cambridge: Cambridge University Press, 1995.

A Brief History of Justice, First Edition. David Johnston.

Bentham, *Principles*	Jeremy Bentham, *An Introduction to the Principles of Morals and Legislation*. New York: Hafner, 1965.
Cicero, *De legibus*	Cicero, *On the Laws*, in *On the Commonwealth and On the Laws*, edited and translated by James E. G. Zetzel. Cambridge: Cambridge University Press, 1999.
Code of Hammurabi	*The Babylonian Laws*, edited and translated by G. R. Driver and John C. Miles, vol. 2. Oxford: Clarendon Press, 1955.
Hobbes, *Leviathan*	*Leviathan, or the Matter, Forme, and Power of a Commonwealth Ecclesiastical and Civil*, in Thomas Hobbes, *Leviathan: A Norton Critical Edition*, edited by Richard E. Flathman and David Johnston. New York: W. W. Norton, 1997.
Homer, *Iliad*	Homer, *Iliad*, translated by Richmond Lattimore. Chicago and London: University of Chicago Press, 1951.
Hume, *Enquiry*	*An Enquiry Concerning the Principles of Morals*, in David Hume, *Hume's Moral and Political Philosophy*, edited by Henry D. Aiken. New York: Macmillan, 1948.
Kant, *Critique*	Immanuel Kant, *Critique of Pure Reason*, translated by Norman Kemp Smith. London: Macmillan, 1973.
Kant, "Perpetual peace"	"Perpetual peace: A philosophical sketch," in Immanuel Kant, *Political Writings*, edited by Hans Reiss, translated by H. B. Nisbet, 2nd ed. Cambridge: Cambridge University Press, 1991.
Kant, *Rechtslehre*	Immanuel Kant, *The Metaphysics of Morals*, translated by Mary Gregor. Cambridge: Cambridge University Press, 1991.

Kant, "Theory and practice"	"On the common saying, 'This may be true in theory, but it does not apply in practice,'" in Immanuel Kant, *Political Writings*, edited by Hans Reiss, translated by H. B. Nisbet, 2nd ed. Cambridge: Cambridge University Press, 1991.
Marx, "Gotha"	Karl Marx, "Critique of the Gotha program," in *The Marx–Engels Reader*, 2nd ed., edited by Robert C. Tucker. New York: Norton, 1978.
Marx, *Ideology*	Karl Marx, *The German Ideology: Part I*, in *The Marx-Engels Reader*, 2nd ed., edited by Robert C. Tucker. New York: Norton, 1978.
New Testament	*New English Bible: New Testament.* Cambridge: Oxford University Press and Cambridge University Press, 1961.
Old Testament	*New English Bible: The Old Testament.* Cambridge: Oxford University Press and Cambridge University Press, 1970.
Plato, *Republic*	Plato, *Republic*, translated by Alexander Kerr. Chicago: C. H. Kerr & Co., 1918.
Rawls, *Collected Papers*	John Rawls, *Collected Papers*, edited by Samuel Freeman. Cambridge, MA: Harvard University Press, 1999.
Rawls, *Restatement*	John Rawls, *Justice as Fairness: A Restatement*, edited by Erin Kelly. Cambridge, MA: Harvard University Press, 2001.
Rawls, *Theory*	John Rawls, *A Theory of Justice* [1971], rev. ed. Cambridge, MA: Harvard University Press, 1999.
Saint-Simon, "Organizer"	"First extract from 'The organizer,'" in Henri de Saint-Simon, *Social Organization, the Science of Man, and Other Writings*, edited and translated by Felix Markham. New York: Harper & Row, 1964.

Smith, *Sentiments*	Adam Smith, *The Theory of Moral Sentiments*, edited by D. D. Raphael and A. L. Macfie. Oxford: Clarendon Press, 2001.
Smith, *Wealth*	Adam Smith, *An Inquiry into the Nature and Causes of the Wealth of Nations.* New York: Modern Library, n.d.
Spencer, *Principles*	Herbert Spencer, *The Principles of Ethics*, 2 vols. New York: D. Appleton, 1898.

Prologue: From the Standard Model to the Sense of Justice

7 "*some Good to himselfe*": Hobbes, *Leviathan*, ch. 14, p. 74.

8 "*but of their advantages*": Smith, *Wealth* I.2, p. 14.

8 "*their own self-interests*": Richard Alexander, *The Biology of Moral Systems.* Hawthorne, NY: A. de Gruyter, 1987, p. 3.

8 "*we are born selfish*": Richard Dawkins, *The Selfish Gene*, new ed. Oxford: Oxford University Press, 1989, p. 3. Dawkins' intent was to describe the tendency of genes to propagate themselves, but his statement was widely understood to apply to individual human beings rather than to their genes.

8 *whatever those objectives may be*: For a fuller and more precise discussion, see Jon Elster, "Introduction," in Jon Elster (ed.), Rational Choice, New York: New York University Press, 1986, pp. 1–33.

10 *beneficiaries of the unfairness*: Austin, G. and Walster, E., "Participants' reaction to 'equity with the world,'" *Journal of Experimental Social Psychology* 10 (1974): 528–548. This experiment and others are discussed in Melvin J. Lerner, "The justice motive in human relations and the economic model of man: A radical analysis of facts and fictions," in Valerian J. Derlega and Janusz Grzelak (eds.), *Cooperation and Helping Behavior: Theories and Research.* New York: Academic Press, 1982, pp. 249–278.

10 *leaving (or withholding) a tip*: Daniel Kahneman, Jack L. Knetsch, and Richard Thaler, "Fairness as a constraint on profit seeking: Entitlements

in the market," *American Economic Review* 76:4 (September 1986): 728–741.

11 *punish others for acting unfairly*: See Ernst Fehr and Simon Gächter, "Altruistic punishment in humans," *Nature 415* (10 January 2002): 137–140 and Ernst Fehr and Urs Fischbacher, "The nature of human altruism," *Nature* 425 (23 October 2003): 785–791.

11 *victims of injustice*: See Kristen R. Monroe, *The Heart of Altruism: Perceptions of a Common Humanity.* Princeton: Princeton University Press, 1996.

11 *from one person to the next*: See Ernst Fehr and Urs Fischbacher, "The nature of human altruism," *Nature* 425 (23 October 2003): 785–791.

11 *vary significantly across cultures*: See Joseph Henrich, Robert Boyd, Samuel Bowles, Colin Camerer, Ernst Fehr, Herbert Gintis, and Richard McElreath, "In search of homo economicus: Behavioral experiments in 15 small-scale societies," *Economics and Social Behavior* 91: 2 (May 2001): 73–78.

11 *not unique to humans*: See Frans de Waal, *Good Natured: The Origins of Right and Wrong in Humans and Other Animals.* Cambridge, MA: Harvard University Press, 1996; and Claudia Rutte and Michael Taborsky, "Generalized Reciprocity in Rats," *PLoS Biology* 5:7 (July 2007): e196.

13 "*justice and injustice and the like*": Aristotle, *Politics* I.ii, 1253[a] (Welldon's translation).

13 "*offended with their fellows [. . .]*": Hobbes, *Leviathan*, ch. 17, pp. 94–95.

14 *matters of a similar kind*: This hypothesis is suggested by Richard Joyce in *The Evolution of Morality.* Cambridge and London: MIT Books, 2006, p. 89.

Chapter 1: The Terrain of Justice

16 "*to give light to the land*": *Code of Hammurabi*, p. 7.

17 "*one mina of silver*": *Code of Hammurabi*, p. 77.

17 "*he shall be put to death*": *Code of Hammurabi*, p. 17.

18 "*from his hand shall be put to death*": *Code of Hammurabi*, p. 15.

18 "*the orphan [and] the widow [. . .]*": *Code of Hammurabi*, p. 97.

20 "*when I am weary with fighting*": Homer, *Iliad* I, 161–168.

20 "*wrenched out the ash spear*": Homer, *Iliad* VI, 55–65.

22 "*Whoever reviles his father or mother shall be put to death*": Exodus 21: 12–17 (in the Old Testament).

23 "*retribution on his enemies*": Isaiah 59: 15–18 (in the Old Testament).

23 "*on such a people?*": Jeremiah 5: 20, 27–29 (in the Old Testament).

24 "*plead the widow's cause*": Isaiah 1: 17.

24 "*says the Lord of Hosts*": Malachi 3: 5 (in the Old Testament).

25 *profits handsomely from the arrangement*: Genesis 13: 2 (in the Old Testament).

26 "*compensation for the tooth*": Exodus 21: 2, 7, 8, 10, 11, 26, 27 (in the Old Testament).

27 "*bruise for bruise, wound for wound*": Exodus 21: 23–25.

27 "*he shall repay two*": Exodus 22: 1–3.

28 "*which the Lord your God is giving you*": Exodus 20: 12.

29 *values pertaining to reciprocity*: See Jonathan Haidt and Craig Joseph, "Intuitive ethics: How innately prepared intuitions generate culturally variable virtues," in *Daedalus* (Fall 2004): 55–66.

30 "*forgetful of a benefit*": Quoted by Alvin W. Gouldner in "The norm of reciprocity: A preliminary statement," *American Sociological Review* 25:2 (April 1960): 161.

30 "*regarded as a duty*": Edward Westermarck, *The Origin and Development of the Moral Ideas*. London: Macmillan, 1908, vol. 2, p. 155.

30 *for a benefit it has received*: For a useful discussion of this range, see Marshall D. Sahlins, "On the sociology of primitive exchange," in Michael Banton (ed.), *The Relevance of Models for Social Anthropology*. London: Tavistock Publications, 1965, pp. 139–236.

34 *values pertaining to reciprocity and fairness*: See again Jonathan Haidt and Craig Joseph, "Intuitive ethics: How innately prepared intuitions generate culturally variable virtues," in *Daedalus* (Fall 2004): 55–66.

Chapter 2: Teleology and Tutelage in Plato's *Republic*

All references to Plato's *Republic* are given in the main text in brackets, in Stephanus numbers: this notation reproduces the page and column number of the text as it appeared in the editio princeps of Plato's dialogues, prepared by Henricus Stephanus (Henri Estienne) in

Geneva in 1578, and it is the standard way of referring to Plato; as such, it is reproduced in all modern editions and translations. Thus the passages I cite may be found in most modern translations (or in editions of the original text) by referring to the Stephanus numbers. As noted in the list of short titles above, I have adopted Alexander Kerr's translation, to which I made modest revisions.

39 "*if he is just* [*dikaios*] ": These lines are attributed to the poet Theognis, lines 147–148. The Greek text is reprinted in Arthur W. H. Adkins, *Merit and Responsibility: A Study in Greek Values.* Chicago: University of Chicago Press, 1960, p. 78n. Scholars disagree about the proper translation of these lines, especially the crucial second line. Adkins' translation is: "every man, Cyrnus, is *agathos* [good] if he is *dikaios* [just]. " Michael Gagarin and Paul Woodruff, however, have "every good man, Cyrnus, is just" (*Early Greek Political Thought from Homer to the Sophists.* Cambridge: Cambridge University Press, 1995, p. 32). For Adkins, the line suggests that, if a man is just, then he is necessarily good; Gagarin and Woodruff read the line as suggesting that, if a man is good, then he is necessarily just. Although I have not accepted Adkins' translation in its entirety, on balance his seems more accurate than Gagarin and Woodruff's. However, it is important to bear in mind that poetry by its nature draws on ambiguity of meaning, and this point is certainly true of Greek archaic poetry, so both readings may be warranted. The remarkable thing about the passage is that the stronger role for justice suggested by Adkins' reading could be contemplated in this era at all.

60 *relations among equals* : A well-known formulation of this idea appears in the "Melian Dialogue" in Thucydides' *History of the Peloponnesian War,* translated by Rex Warner. Harmondsworth, Middlesex: Penguin, 1972, Book V, Chs 84–114 (pp. 400–407).

Chapter 3: Aristotle's Theory of Justice

All references to Aristotle's *Nicomachean Ethics* and *Politics* are noted in the main text in parentheses. I have referred to Aristotle by the traditional page numbers and column letters that derive from

Immanuel Bekker's massive edition of the Corpus Aristotelicum (Berlin, 1831–1870) and are universally followed in modern editions and translations (except for the few works not known to Bekker and not included in his edition). For quotations from the *Politics* I have also added book and chapter numbers, which are common enough in references to Aristotelian works. As noted in the list of short titles above, for the *Nicomachean Ethics* I have used the partial translation by Henry Jackson, to which I have made small revisions. For the *Politics* passages given in this chapter, I have used the translation by J. E. C. Welldon (in the list of short titles above), to which I have made minor revisions.

76 *1926 edition of the Nicomachean Ethics*: Aristotle, *Nicomachean Ethics*, translated by H. Rackham. New York and London: G. P. Putnam's Sons, 1926.

Chapter 4: From Nature to Artifice: Aristotle to Hobbes

91 "*he brings justice to all who have been wronged*": Psalm 103: 6 (in the Old Testament).

91 "*and try the cause of the peoples fairly*": Psalm 9: 7–8.

91 "*all memory of them is lost*": Psalm 9: 5–6.

92 "*pay the highest honours to military prowess*": Aristotle, *Politics* 1324^b (Barker's translation).

92 "*their interest in justice stops*": Aristotle, *Politics* 1324^b (Barker's translation).

93 *Zeno's thinking in subsequent writings*: For this reconstruction of Zeno's and later Stoic thinking, I rely heavily on Malcolm Schofield, *The Stoic Idea of the City*. Cambridge: Cambridge University Press, 1991.

94 "*the whole subject of universal justice and law*": Cicero, *De legibus* I.17, p. 111.

94 "*before any state was established*": Cicero, *De legibus* I.19, p. 112.

94 "*no dissimilarity within the species*": Cicero, *De legibus* I.30, p. 116.

95 "*reach virtue with the aid of a guide*": Cicero, *De legibus* I.30, 116.

96 *36th ("Borysthenitic") discourse*: Dio Chrysostom, with English translation by J. W. Cohoon and H. Lamar Crosby, in five vols. Cambridge, MA: Harvard University Press, 1961, vol. 3, pp. 417–475.

96 "*how he will know himself*": Cicero, *De legibus* I.61, p. 127.

97 *the Digest compiled under the Byzantine Emperor Justinian*: *The Digest of Justinian*, translated and edited by Alan Watson, rev. ed., 2 vols. Philadelphia: University of Pennsylvania Press, 1998.

97 "*armed with the power of the Spirit*": *Luke* 4: 14 (in the New Testament).

100 "*which constitutes a household or a polis*": Aristotle, *Politics* I.ii, 1253^{a} (Welldon's translation).

100 "*without himself possessing it*": Aristotle, *Politics* I.v, 1254^{b} (Welldon's translation).

100 "*body to be ruled by the soul*": Aristotle, *Politics* I.v, 1254^{b} (Welldon's translation).

100 "*slavish subjection is advantageous*": Aristotle, *Politics* I.v, 1254^{b} (Welldon's translation).

101 "*the condition of slavery is alike expedient and just*": Aristotle, *Politics* I. vi, 1255^{a} (Welldon's translation).

101 *era had not yet appeared on the horizon:* For a thorough discussion of the history of the iconography of justice, see Judith Resnick and Dennis Curtis, *Representing Justice: Invention, Controversy, and Rights in City-States and Democratic Courtrooms.* New Haven and London: Yale University Press, 2011.

102 "*identical in ideas*": Cicero, *De legibus* I.30, p. 116.

102 "*the other flawed portions of the mind?*": Cicero, fragment quoted by St. Augustine in *The City of God*; as translated in Cicero, *On the Commonwealth and On the Laws*, edited James E. G. Zetzel. Cambridge: Cambridge University Press, 1999, p. 73.

103 "*made subject to the ownership of another*": *The Digest of Justinian*, translated and edited by Alan Watson, rev. ed., 2 vols. Philadelphia: University of Pennsylvania Press, 1998, I, 5 (emphasis added).

103 "*to enter the kingdom of God*": Matthew 19: 24 (in the New Testament). The traditional text of this verse is very likely a corruption of the original, which probably read: "it is easier for a rope to pass through the eye of a needle [. . .]." The words for "rope" and "camel" in the Greek language, in which the Gospel was written, were very similar (*kamilos* and *kamelos*).

105 "*the aptest means thereunto*": Hobbes, *Leviathan*, ch. 14, p. 72.

105 "*than be governed by others [. . .]*": Hobbes, *Leviathan*, ch. 15, p. 85.

106 "*as from habit, custom, and education*": Smith, *Wealth* I.2, p. 15.

108 *the sophist Protagoras (490–420 BCE) sketches a myth*: As recounted by Plato at *Protagoras* 320c–322d, translated by W. K. C. Guthrie in *The Collected Dialogues of Plato*, edited by Edith Hamilton and Huntington Cairns (Princeton: Princeton University Press, 1973).

108 "*as a plague to the city*": Plato, *Protagoras* 322d.

109 *monarchy, oligarchy, and democracy*: Herodotus, *Histories*, translated by Robin Waterfield. Oxford: Oxford University Press, 1998: Book III, Chs 80–82.

110 "*man is naturally a political animal*": Aristotle, *Politics* I. ii, 1253[a] (Welldon's translation).

111 "*justice of which I speak is natural*": Cicero, *De legibus* I.33, p. 117.

111 "*justice is established not by opinion but by nature*": Cicero, *De legibus* I.28, p. 115.

111 *in the capacities of humans to understand and to bring order to their world*: R. W. Southern offers a now classic discussion of this process in *The Making of the Middle Ages*. New Haven and London: Yale University Press, 1953.

113 *Sir Thomas More's Utopia*: Thomas More, *Utopia*, edited by George M. Logan and Robert M. Adams. Cambridge: Cambridge University Press, 2002.

114 "*they never yet saw any so well built*": Hobbes, *Leviathan*, ch. 30, pp. 170–171.

114 "*such are those which I have in this discourse set forth*": Hobbes, *Leviathan*, ch. 30, p. 171.

Chapter 5: The Emergence of Utility

118 "*the instinct of generation and the institution of property*": Hume, *Enquiry* III, pt. 2, p. 200.

120 "*Newton's chief rule of philosophizing*": Hume, *Enquiry* III, pt. 2, p. 201.

120 *divine justice, natural justice, and political justice*: Beccaria, *Crimes*: "To the reader," pp. 4–5.

120 "*rewards of the after-life*": Beccaria, *Crimes*, ch. 2, p. 11.

120 "*influences beyond measure the happiness of all*": Beccaria, *Crimes*, ch. 2, p. 11.

121 "*the association of mankind [. . .]*": Smith, *Sentiments* II. ii, p. 86.

121 "*that general opulence to which it gives occasion*": Smith, *Wealth* I. 2, p. 13.

121 "*nonsense upon stilts*": Jeremy Bentham, *Anarchical Fallacies*, in *The Works of Jeremy Bentham, Published under the Superintendence of his Executor, John Bowring*, 11 vols. Edinburgh: 1838–1843, vol. 2, p. 501.

122 "*subject them to any authority*": "Of the original contract," in David Hume, *Hume's Moral and Political Philosophy*, edited by Henry D. Aiken. New York: Macmillan, 1948, p. 357.

122 *of command and obedience, not of justice*: Hume, *Enquiry* III, pt. 1, pp. 190–191.

122 *subjecting women to what amounts in practice to slavery*: Hume, *Enquiry* III, pt. 1, p. 191.

123 *should be accepted as a witness*: Beccaria, *Crimes*, ch. 13, pp. 32–33.

123 *having every accused person tried by peers*: Beccaria, *Crimes*, ch. 14, pp. 34–36.

123 "*from habit, custom, and education*": Smith, *Wealth* I. 2, p. 15.

123 "*to a few very simple operations*": Smith, *Wealth* V. 1, p. 734.

124 "*as is the happiness of the other*": Jeremy Bentham, as quoted in Paul J. Kelly, *Utilitarianism and Distributive Justice: Jeremy Bentham and the Civil Law*. Oxford: Oxford University Press, 1990, p. 179.

124 "*nobody for more than one*": John Stuart Mill, *Utilitarianism*, in *John Stuart Mill On Liberty and Other Essays*, edited by John Gray. Oxford: Oxford University Press, 1998, p. 199.

125 "*the sole foundation of its merit*": Hume, *Enquiry* III, pt. 1, p. 185.

125 "*its merit and moral obligation*": Hume, *Enquiry* III, pt. 1, p. 189.

126 "*to procure happiness and security*": Hume, *Enquiry* III, pt. 1, p. 187.

127 "*the propagation of the species*": Smith, *Sentiments* II. ii, p. 87.

127 "*the purposes of circulation or digestion*": Smith, *Sentiments* II. ii, p. 87.

128 "*which in reality is the wisdom of God*": Smith, *Sentiments* II. ii, p. 87.

128 "*to chastise the guilty*": Smith, *Sentiments* II. ii, p. 86.

129 *a murderer to escape punishment*: Smith, *Sentiments* II. ii, pp. 90–91.

129 "*no other race of animals*": Smith, *Wealth* I. 2, p. 13.

129 "*which was not part of his intention*": Smith, *Wealth* IV. 2, p. 423.
130 "*obscure academic interpreters*": Beccaria, *Crimes*: "To the reader," p. 3.
131 "*a fleeting and haphazard necessity*": Beccaria, *Crimes*: "Introduction," p. 7.
131 *in his view they rarely do*: Beccaria, *Crimes,* ch. 3, pp. 12–13.
131 "*can derive from the crime*": Beccaria, *Crimes,* ch. 27, p. 64.
132 "*turn back the clock?*": Beccaria, *Crimes,* ch. 12, p. 31.
132 "*shared among the greater number*": Beccaria, *Crimes*: "Introduction," p. 7.
132 "*to their greatest happiness*": Beccaria, *Crimes,* ch. 41, p. 103.
132 "*that is uniformly censorial*": Bentham, *Principles,* ch. 17, p. 329, note 1.
133 "*the measure of right and wrong*": Jeremy Bentham, quotation from *A Fragment on Government,* in *A Comment on the Commentaries and A Fragment on Government,* edited by J. H. Burns and H. L. A. Hart. Oxford: Clarendon Press, 2010), p. 393.
133 *the "greatest happiness principle"*: Paul Kelly discusses this change in Bentham's formulation in *Utilitarianism and Distributive Justice: Jeremy Bentham and the Civil Law.* Oxford: Oxford University Press, 1990, p. 75.
133 "*fastened to their throne*": Bentham, *Principles,* ch. 1, p. 1.
135 "*security-providing principle*": Paul Kelly offers an extensive discussion of this principle in Bentham's later writings in ch. 6 of *Utilitarianism and Distributive Justice* (above).
135 "*the profit of the offence*": Bentham, *Principles,* ch. 14, p. 179.
137 "*a regular administration of justice*": Smith, *Wealth* V. 3, p. 862.
137 "*the division of labor*": Smith, *Wealth* I. 1, p. 3.
137 "*many an African king [...]*": Smith, *Wealth* I. 1, p. 12.
138 *determining the severity of punishments*: Adam Smith, *Lectures on Jurisprudence,* edited by R. L. Meek, D. D. Raphael, and P. G. Stein. Oxford: Clarendon Press, 1978. See the notes on Smith's lecture of February 3, 1763, 158–160 (pp. 132–133 in Meek et. al.) and the report of his lectures dated 1766, 197–198 (p. 483 in Meek et. al.).
138 "*undoing a crime already committed [...]*": Beccaria, *Crimes,* ch. 12, p. 31.
139 *Some writers have argued*: See below, ch. 8, I.

Chapter 6: Kant's Theory of Justice

All references to Kant's *Rechtslehre* (Part I of his *Metaphysics of Morals*) are noted in the main text in parentheses by page number. The first number refers to the pagination in the translation by Mary Gregor (see the list of short titles above). The second number, in square brackets, refers to the pagination in the Royal Prussian Academy of Sciences edition (commonly called the Academy edition), which provides a standardized basis for referring to Kant's works. References to Kant's *Grounding for the Metaphysics of Morals* in the notes below also include pages numbers from the Academy edition, in brackets. The references to Kant's *Critique of Pure Reason* in the notes below include both the page number from Norman Kemp Smith's translation (see the list of short titles) and the page number from the first and second German editions of the *Critique*, with Smith's denotation of the first edition by the letter "A" and the second by the letter "B."

142 *An example Kant offers*: "Theory and practice," pp. 70–71.

144 *how to act in accordance with duty*: "Theory and practice," p. 70,

144 *how best to pursue his or her happiness*: see also "Theory and practice," p. 74.

144 *any particular conception of happiness*: "Theory and practice," p. 74.

145 *to keep from drowning*: "Theory and practice," p. 81n.

147 *capable of knowing*: Kant, *Critique* (generally).

148 *the existence of God*: Kant, *Critique*, p. 631 [A798/B826].

149 *does happen in the world*: Kant, *Critique*, p. 634 [A802/B830]; see also the similar discussion in Kant, *Rechtslehre* p. 42 [213–214].

149 "*as affected by physical attributes, man* (*homo phaenomenon*)": *homo noumenon* and *homo phaenomenon* (passim in this chapter) are not phrases of the type *Homo sapiens* (noun + agreeing adjective), but identity formulae between the Latin masculine noun *homo* and a Greek neuter participle (*noumenon, phainomenon*), treated as a noun: in its

nominal use, *to noumenon* regularly designates in Kant *das Ding an sich*, "the thing in itself." This term belongs in the same family as *nous* and *noesis* discussed above.

150 *arbitrary wills of others*: See also Immanuel Kant, "Perpetual peace," p. 99n.

151 "*become a universal law*": Immanuel Kant, *Grounding for the Metaphysics of Morals*, translated by James W. Ellington, 3rd ed. Indianapolis and Cambridge: Hackett, 1993, p. 30 [421]. Kant offers similar formulations in his *Rechtslehre* p. 51 [224] and in "Perpetual peace," p. 122.

151 "*do unto you*": Matthew 7: 12.

152 "*go with him two*": Matthew 5: 38–42.

156 *a right to equality in possessions*: Kant, "Theory and practice," p. 75.

157 *material possessions in the more usual sense*: Kant, "Theory and practice," p. 75.

157 "*the utmost inequality*": Kant, "Theory and practice," p. 75.

157 "*the same right as he enjoys himself*": Kant, "Theory and practice," p. 74 (emphasis added).

161 "*a civil state, i.e. a commonwealth*": Kant, "Theory and practice," p. 73.

161 *contrary to justice*: In addition to Kant's *Rechtslehre*, see his "Theory and practice," p. 81 and his "Perpetual peace," pp. 118n and 126.

162 "*doing injustice to others*": "Perpetual peace," p. 99n.

162 *of great practical import*: "Theory and practice," p. 79.

162 *what is harmful to them*: "Theory and practice," p. 74.

162 "*the greatest conceivable despotism*": "Theory and practice," p. 74.

162 *with great inequality in possessions*: "Theory and practice," p. 75.

164 *law is unjust*: "Theory and practice," p. 79 and "Perpetual peace," p. 99n.

165 *for the past two centuries*: Kant's distinctive conception of (what would later come to be called) social justice is *not* contained in or conveyed by his usage of the phrase "distributive justice." For him that phrase refers to allocations of goods and responsibilities that are determined – or "distributed" – by a public court of justice. See his *Rechtslehre*, pp. 113 [297] and 118 [302].

Chapter 7: The Idea of Social Justice

167 *come into being*: Plato, *Republic* 592b.

168 *if that had happened*: Thomas More, *Utopia*, edited by George M. Logan and Robert M. Adams. Cambridge: Cambridge University Press, 2002.

169 *much as Francis Bacon had prophesied*: Francis Bacon, *The New Organon*, edited by Fulton H. Anderson. Indianapolis: Bobbs-Merrill, 1960.

170 *less dramatic than they seemed at the time*: Alexis de Tocqueville develops this argument in *The Old Regime and the Revolution*, edited by François Furet and Françoise Mélonio, translated by Alan S. Kahan. Chicago: University of Chicago Press, 1998.

170 "*it is for you to reconstitute it*": Saint-Simon, "The Reorganization of the European Community," in *Social Organization, the Science of Man, and Other Writings*, edited and translated by Felix Markham. New York: Harper & Row, 1964, p. 29.

172 "*towards inevitable results*"; "*of modern society*": Marx, *Capital: A Critique of Political Economy*, edited by Frederick Engels, translated by Samuel Moore and Edward Aveling. New York: International Publishers, 1967, pp. 8, 10.

172 "*an alien power opposed to him*": Marx, *Ideology*, p. 160.

172 "*the action of man [. . .]*": Marx, *Ideology*, p. 161.

172 "*historical development up till now*": Marx, *Ideology*, p. 160.

173 *against the subjection of women*: John Stuart Mill, *The Subjection of Women*, in his *On Liberty and Other Essays*, edited by John Gray. Oxford: Oxford University Press, 1998.

174 "*among human beings as such?*": Henry Sidgwick, *The Methods of Ethics*, 7th ed. Indianapolis and Cambridge: Hackett, 1981, p. 274.

175 *in a periodical entitled the "Organizer"*: Saint-Simon, "Organizer," pp. 72–75.

175 "*lifeless corpse*": Saint-Simon, "Organizer," p. 72.

176 "*society is a world which is upside down*": Saint-Simon, "Organizer," p. 74.

177 *some two generations later*: Marx, "Gotha," pp. 529–530.

178 *to which all others are entitled*: Spencer, *Principles*, vol. 2, p. 37.

178 *"his own nature and consequent conduct"*: Spencer, *Principles*, vol. 2, p. 37.

179 *as a practical matter in the 1860s*: For an extensive discussion, see P. S. Atiyah, *The Rise and Fall of Freedom of Contract.* Oxford: Clarendon Press, 1979.

180 *a sphere of the family*: Spencer, *Principles*, vol. 2, p. 42.

181 *from status to contract*: Henry Sumner Maine's *Ancient Law* (first published 1861, reprinted by Dorset Press, 1986) is one of the more prominent of several major works that suggested this shift.

182 *as early as the mid-eighteenth century*: See David Thompson, *The Babeuf Plot: The Making of a Republican Legend.* London: Kegan Paul, 1947, p. 7

183 *"cancelled with respect to him"*: Johann Gottlieb Fichte, *Foundations of Natural Right*, edited by Frederick Neuhouser, translated by Michael Baur. Cambridge: Cambridge University Press, 2000, p. 185.

183 *an adequate share of goods*: Johann Gottlieb Fichte, "*The Closed Commercial State,*" translated by Abraham Hayward, revised by H. S. Reiss and P. Brown, in *The Political Thought of the German Romantics, 1793–1815*, edited by H. S. Reiss. Oxford: Blackwell, 1955, p. 90.

184 *"isolated monad[s]"*: Karl Marx, "On the Jewish question," in *The Marx–Engels Reader*, 2nd ed., edited by Richard C. Tucker. New York: Norton, 1978, p. 42.

184 *associated the concept of rights with private property*: Karl Marx, "On the Jewish question" (above), p. 42.

184 *bulwarks of inequality*: Marx, "Gotha," p. 530.

184 *"to each according to his needs"*: Marx, "Gotha," p. 531.

185 *"he receives back in another"*: Marx, "Gotha," pp. 529–530.

185 *"like every right"*: Marx, "Gotha," p. 530.

190 *specific rules or institutional settings*: For example, see Joel Feinberg, "Justice and personal desert," in his *Doing and Deserving: Essays in the Theory of Responsibility.* Princeton: Princeton University Press, 1970.

192 *a linen shirt and leather shoes*: Smith, *Wealth* V. 2, p. 822.

193 *"his own nature and consequent conduct"*: Spencer, *Principles*, vol. 2, p. 37.

194 *a society's institutions and social arrangements as a whole*: This is a key theme in Friedrich A. Hayek's later writings, especially *Law, Legislation and Liberty*, vol. 2: *The Mirage of Social Justice.* Chicago and London: University of Chicago Press, 1976.

194 *independent standard of social justice makes no sense*: This view has been defended by Michael Walzer in *Spheres of Justice: A Defense of Pluralism and Equality*. New York: Basic Books, 1983, and in a more nuanced form in *Thick and Thin: Moral Argument at Home and Abroad*. Notre Dame and London: University of Notre Dame Press, 1994.

Chapter 8: The Theory of Justice as Fairness

All references to Rawls's *Theory* are noted in the main text in parentheses; the first page number refers to the first edition of this book (1971), and the second number refers to the revised edition (1999), as in "the right is prior to the good (31/27–28)."

197 *the importance of its abolition*: Rawls mentioned this custom during a conversation with the author in Washington, DC in September 1991.

197 *a monistic conception of the good*: The clearest discussion of this facet of his theory is in John Rawls, "Social unity and primary goods," in Amartya Sen and Bernard Williams (eds.), *Utilitarianism and Beyond*. Cambridge: Cambridge University Press, 1982, pp. 159-85 (reprinted in Rawls, *Collected Papers*, pp. 359–387).

199 *the right is prior to the good*: This view is distinctively Kantian. For a brief discussion, see above, Ch. 6, I.

199 *one familiar objection to utilitarianism*: See above, Ch. 5, III.

200 "*the utilitarian view is more fundamental*": John Rawls, "Two concepts of rules," *Philosophical Review* 64:1 (January 1955): 3–32 (reprinted in Rawls, *Collected Papers*, pp. 20–46, at p. 23).

204 "*the justice of the basic structure itself*": John Rawls, "Kantian constructivism in moral theory," *Journal of Philosophy* 77 (September 1980): 515–572 (reprinted in Rawls, *Collected Papers*, pp. 303–358, at p. 337).

206 *from one generation to the next*: See Rawls, *Restatement*, pp. 4–8 for a fuller statement of this idea.

206 "*most fundamental intuitive idea*" *of the theory*: Rawls, *Restatement*, p. 5.

206 *as much like moral geometry as possible*: "Justice as fairness: Political not metaphysical," *Philosophy and Public Affairs* 14 (1985): 223–251 (reprinted in Rawls, *Collected Papers*, pp. 388–414, at p. 403n).

208 *to withhold their consent*: Rawls, *Restatement* p. 4.

210 "*over a complete life*": Rawls, *Restatement* p. 4

213 "*the least advantaged members of society*": John Rawls, *Political Liberalism*. New York: Columbia University Press, 1993, p. 291.

214 "*the theory of moral personality*": John Rawls, "Kantian constructivism in moral theory" (above) and Rawls, *Restatement*, pp. 18–19.

217 *the members of a society turn out to be*: In his *Restatement*, Rawls observes: "To say that inequalities in income and wealth are to be arranged for the greatest benefit of the least advantaged simply means that we are to compare schemes of cooperation by seeing *how well off the least advantaged are under each scheme*" (p. 59, emphasis added).

Epilogue: From Social Justice to Global Justice?

226 *to satisfy the demands of reciprocity*: Joseph Henrich, Robert Boyd, Samuel Bowles, Colin Camerer, Ernst Fehr, Herbert Gintis, and Richard McElreath, "In search of homo economicus: Behavioral experiments in 15 small-scale societies," *Economics and Social Behavior* 91: 2 (May 2001): 73–78.

230 *The Law of Peoples*: John Rawls, *The Law of Peoples*. Cambridge, MA: Harvard University Press, 1999.

232 "*their interest in justice stops*": Aristotle, *Politics* 1324^{b} (Barker's translation).

Index

A Brief History of Justice, First Edition. David Johnston.

Printed and bound by CPI Group (UK) Ltd, Croydon, CR0 4YY

09/06/2025

14685977-0001